PIECES *of* EIGHT

PIECES *of* EIGHT

STILL BEST FRIENDS
AFTER ALL THESE YEARS

ROSALIE MAGGIO, FRANK MAGGIO,
PATRICK MAGGIO, KEVIN MAGGIO,
MARY MAGGIO, PAUL MAGGIO,
MARK MAGGIO, MATTHEW MAGGIO

Library of Congress Control Number:		2010901031
ISBN:	Hardcover	978-1-4500-3349-7
	Softcover	978-1-4500-3348-0
	Ebook	978-1-4500-3350-3

This book was printed in the United States of America.

To order additional copies of this book, contact:
Xlibris Corporation
1-888-795-4274
www.Xlibris.com
Orders@Xlibris.com
71041

CONTENTS

Chapter 9: *A Kind of Hodgepodge Chapter in Which We Come to Some Conclusions About Growing Up Together, Including Discussions of the Birth Disorder Factor*...286

Addenda..325

To Irene Nash Maggio and Paul J. Maggio
With all our love

ACKNOWLEDGMENTS

We are indebted to our families and friends for the love, support, and good humor that extend back over our lifetimes and, we feel sure, forward into the future.

INTRODUCTION

We were born in 1943, 1945, 1947, 1949, 1951, 1953, 1957, and 1959. The gap is probably obvious. By 1955, we realized that we owed our lives to the rhythm method—and that it wasn't always reliable. That was one of our earliest if most rickety truths.

We lived on an acreage three miles outside Fort Dodge, Iowa. Dad was a dentist (two of the boys turned out to be dentists too, if you find that interesting, which we do). Mother felt the one thing we didn't need at our house was more children. When we asked to invite friends out, she guilelessly told us, "Go play with yourselves."

We deduced another, stronger truth: we were all we had.

Today we are progressives, conservatives, Catholics, Unitarians, AA, New Agers, chiefs, and Indians. We are unmarried, divorced, and married. We are ectomorphs, mesomorphs, and endomorphs. We parent four adopted children and eleven biological children. We are renters, homeowners, and land barons. We are a tribe of many truths.

And we're crazy about each other.

People ask us why we are still each other's best friends. And they ask, "How did you turn out like this?" (Never mind what they mean by that.)

After a fruitless discussion of these issues (although one of us kept referring to a study about the robust ties among the survivors of the *Titanic*), we decided to tell stories until the truth emerged. We should have remembered that we are a tribe of many truths.

Note: We call each other names. Frank is known to us as Ciccio (Sicilian nickname for Francesco), even sometimes Cheeto, if we are standing far enough away from him. To avoid confusion with Dad who was also Paul, within the family Paul Thomas goes by P.T. or, when we want him to know how much we love him, by Peeeeeteeeey. He refers to himself as El Mismo. Just to make him happy, we sometimes call him that. Rosalie is, inexplicably, Punky, despite years of moving around the country trying to leave it behind. In his other life, Kevin officially uses his middle name, Michael, although to his many friends he is simply Maggio. We like to call him The Brother Formerly Known as Kevin, Kev, Kedin, or Ken. For no good reason. Because we can.

CHAPTER 1

A Fair Chapter in Which Everyone Takes a Turn Telling a Story (Although Some People Took More Space Than Other People)

The Former Baby of the Family
Rosalie

I was robbed. Oh, not from the beginning. At first, it was cushy. I was born in Victoria, Texas (Dad was in the Air Force), to a witty, intelligent, good-looking-in-a-Sicilian-way father and to a movie-star-gorgeous, youthful, intelligent mother.

They had no idea that the lumpy, placid baby they brought home from the military hospital was your run-of-the-mill, at-least-they-didn't-drop-it-on-its-head sort of infant. They attributed to me all the superlatives favored by parents of firstborns. They took thousands of photographs to prove to faraway relatives that they had won the baby sweepstakes.

Today, were you to see a photo of my infant self (which you would not, as I have had them all destroyed), you would be astonished at the unprepossessing appearance of this particular former baby of the family.

But love was blind. And Mother had never had a baby before, so when I asked for seconds, I got them. By the time my godmother Juanita pointed out that giving me twelve ounces of milk every time I opened my eyes was not normal, I had thighs bigger than most Easter hams. And did I mention placid? I was drunk, stoned on lashings of milk and, soon after, unlimited ice cream that I was given while still toothless and speechless.

I had only to look pathetic and someone rushed to cuddle and soothe me. Life was good.

And then one day—rudely, abruptly, and without consulting me—Mother and Dad made another trip to the military hospital and came home with Ciccio.

This . . . this misunderstanding, this blunder happened less than fifteen months after my arrival. No one in our family enjoyed less time as the baby of the family than I did. I brood on this.

Dad always laughed when he described the transformation of our peaceful little home when Ciccio came to live there. Dad loved the new baby's energy and determination. Mother gave him lots of milk, maybe even milk she had originally bought for me. I wasn't laughing. I didn't think the little roly-poly in *my* bassinet was anything I would have brought home.

No one was more surprised than I when the other short person in the house turned out to be a fun little buddy.

Marguerite Kelly and Elia Parsons say that "each child has one extra line to your heart, which no other child can replace." I feel this way about Ciccio and Pat and Kevin and Mary and P.T. and Mark and Matt. Each one has a line to my heart that no one else has; each does something for me that no one else can. So yes, I learned to like that good-natured, if exceedingly loud, little intruder. And he was fine practice for what came later.

....

A sibling is the lens through which you see your childhood.—Ann Hood

....

At Least Two Idiots in the Family
Frank

I did a lot of hard living in our kitchen while growing up, and I shared most of my near-death experiences with Pat. There was, for example, the dustup when, as second—and fourth-graders, we were caught by Mom washing dishes (good) and chanting, "Art let a fart and blew himself apart" (not good). In retrospect, I see that little doggerel was the foundation of all our subsequent taste in humor. At the time, it was the death of our experiments in picturesque language—at least in the house.

One winter, when I was about eleven years old, we had one heck of a snowstorm. About 8:00 p.m., Pat and I were looking out the basement door window, marveling at the storm and the enormous snowdrifts piling up on the road between the house and the pasture gate. Two lights on twenty-foot poles illuminated the three-hundred-foot area from the house to the gate. Pat asked if I would give him a quarter to run out to the gate and back. I said, "Nice try."

"No," he said. "I mean I'll do it dressed just like this." We were wearing T-shirts and briefs as we were on our way to bed. What could I do? I accepted his offer.

Without further discussion, he opened the door and started running. I couldn't believe him! As he approached the gate, I could hardly see him because of the heavy snow. But then he reemerged from the end of the visible world, approached the basement door at high speed, and was soon back in the warmth of the house. His whole attitude was "piece of cake!"

Rather than pay him the quarter, I asked him to cancel the bet if I also made the trip. He said okay, and I took off. After my fifteenth or sixteenth step, I had no feeling below the knee. The drifts were waist deep in spots. I couldn't breathe. I planned to kill Pat if I got back to the house. How did he make it look so painless?

I made it back, but I was too worried about being a lifelong cripple to kill him.

Moments later, we heard the all-too-familiar voice travel down the stairs and through the length of the house right into our frozen ears. Dad.

"Pat, Ciccio, would you come up here right now?"

We scrambled into our pajamas and headed upstairs to the kitchen. Our overworked dad stood at the sink, gazing out the picture window. He asked us to come closer. As the yard lights were still on, a winter wonderland was spread before us.

Dad said, "The strangest thing just happened to me. I was standing here thinking about the awesome beauty of nature when all of a sudden, I thought I saw an idiot running on my gravel road out to the barn, turn around, and run back to this house."

Pause.

"I thought at first that I was imagining it. I blinked my eyes and looked again. And there was another idiot doing the same thing."

Pause.

"Would you boys know anything about that?"

He was so cool about it, I wanted to laugh. But I knew neither laughing nor lying could have a good outcome. We told the truth about our bet and listened for some time to a lecture about being more careful in planning our physical activities. On our way back downstairs, we decided that if we ever did that again, we'd turn off the yard lights first.

··

> I am convinced that most people do not grow up. We
> find parking spaces and honor our credit cards. We
> marry and dare to have children and call that growing
> up. I think what we do is mostly grow old. We carry
> accumulation of years in our bodies and on our faces,
> but generally our real selves, the children inside, are still
> innocent and shy as magnolias.—Maya Angelou

··

Camp Foster
Pat

In May of 1959, we were winding down a very active school year. In this case, "active school year" is a euphemism for "Pat being in hot water for nine or ten months."

I'm a great believer in luck and timing, so if I had to explain the unfortunate events of those nine or ten months, I'd have to say luck and timing played big roles, uniformly negative.

Let's see: Despite being grounded, I dressed up, cleverly, as a dwarf and went trick-or-treating on my knees. When I came home with my bag of sugar,

Mom opened the door—and my disguise was not sufficient unto the day. The following week I got caught throwing snowballs at passing cars by the chief of police.

Given all that, imagine my delight when Mom asked if I'd like to go to Camp Foster for a couple of weeks that summer. Camp Foster! Was I lucky, or what? Camp Foster was located at the famous and—to us—glamorous and exciting Iowa resort of Okoboji.

At this point, I am saying to myself, "What is she thinking? I have been a virtual storm of trouble all school year, and she is rewarding me with Camp Foster? Go figure."

I suspected, even then, that it wasn't a good idea to try to out-think Mom, so I just smiled and accepted. As an added incentive—an act of kindness that spiced the offer with an inexplicable bit of additional sweetener—Mom told me that a newfound friend of mine, Mike Von Bank, was going to be there too.

And so, somewhat bewildered yet enthused at the great experiences awaiting me, I sprang out of bed on my first morning at camp and grabbed the day by the tail.

Mike invited me to "play" with a small but wise group of fellow campers. The game consisted of placing me in a ropeless body lock on a light pole, which caused my legs to be wrapped around the pole and my body weight to descend onto my locked legs. The challenge for me was to try to extricate myself from this tried-and-true five-hundred-year-old Cherokee Indian ropeless body lock situation. The details are a bit murky now—somewhat as I imagine the memory of childbirth is for some women—but I recollect a sensation much like that of one's tongue being frozen to a car hood ornament on a cold Iowa day.

With the exception of hourly visits from my camp mates, I was left alone for over four hours. Well, not quite alone.

I soon began to understand that the mosquito leader had met with the chigger king and reached a consensus about how they were going to divide me up. The chigger king agreed to postpone the activation of the chigger itch until a day after the mosquitoes had ravished me. There was, had I been of a mind to appreciate it, a pleasing symbiotic symmetry to their feast.

I've had plenty of time to think since then, and what I think is that "chiggers" may be a polite term for "the devil." Although I've never seen one, I feel certain I have gained the right to describe what I think they look like. They are smaller than the baby toenail of a gnat with teeth larger than that common implement of husbandry, the farmer's alfalfa rake.

Mike's dad drove a street sweeper. I should have suspected he was sadistic. I found out later that summer that Mike had been suspended from school for handing a mutual acquaintance of ours his shorts one day after school.

At the time I was aware only of the mosquito bites, which left no part of me untouched. But all in all, after being released from the Indian lock, I felt confident that Mike and the guys hadn't really gotten the best of me. I had suffered through the mosquito bites and the indignity of it all; but now, thanks to baking soda, I was on the mend.

As I say, I had never seen a chigger, so who could have predicted the unspeakable agonies that appeared twenty-four hours later?

The following days are hazy, although I remember "swimming lessons" (Mike Von Bank holding my head underwater), "dinner" (Mike and his friends trading me my hamburger for their green beans), and "craft time" (has anyone in the entire history of the world actually used a lanyard?).

Several days after the locked-body game, I was limping toward the infirmary (leeches, a broken-glass cut, and infected mosquito bites), wearing my largest shirt and pants to accommodate the work of both mosquitoes and chiggers, when I heard the roar of a Chris-Craft motorboat buzzing the Camp Foster dock.

I was able to open my eyes wide enough to see Mom and several of my brothers and sisters, waving and laughing from the sparkling boat, cans of soda in their hands, feet up on the side of the boat. I felt I was hallucinating. Yet I saw the smiling faces and heard the happy voices: "Hey, Pat, heh heh, how ya doin', ha ha!"

Well, hey, I got it. Little did I know that the plan was for the black sheep to attend Camp Foster with the toughest bully in school while my brothers and sisters lived it up on a fabulous vacation.

The irony of it all? Many of my siblings believe that I was the lucky one, that I enjoyed favored-son status, that I was the guy who got a week at Camp Foster.

I don't think so.

Christmas in April
Kevin

In Iowa, snow stays on the ground all winter. The late October and November snows lie underneath newer layers of snow, which in turn lie underneath . . . Well, anyway, in late March or early April, the many layers of snow, in various shades of gray, begin to melt. Dad used to call this time of year Christmas.

Dad loved his tools—a made-in-heaven marriage between a pair of hands that were never idle and the means to keep them that way. I'll never forget looking down at Dad as he lay in his coffin at the funeral home while next to me Ciccio muttered fondly, "He was a busy little bugger."

Dad had a clearly identified place for each tool in his spacious toolroom. Pegboards looked like art installations, hung with pliers and screwdrivers and staple guns and hammers. Shelves held jars and coffee cans organized by size for nails, screws, bolts, washers, cotter pins, hooks, and anything else a good carpenter might need. His extension cords were coiled and shelved together. His power tools were clean and sat neatly in their own space. Because keeping up the house and property involved nonstop construction, repair, and replacement, Dad had a tool for every purpose. After use, each tool was fastidiously returned to its proper home in the toolroom.

But we had our needs too. We were often involved in important projects requiring tools—repairing a sled in the backyard, fixing a tree house stair in the woods, fortifying a barn door out in the pasture. In our case, however, when we finished using a tool, we left it where it was convenient to us; and this was rarely the same place. We knew no seasons, toiling summer and winter. Dad had some hope of recovering the summer tools, but the winter tools gradually disappeared under new layers of snow, requiring us, of course, to fetch others from Dad's well-supplied toolroom.

And so, as the snow melted in the spring, Dad salvaged his tools, not all at once but layer by layer, week by week—a hammer here, a screwdriver there. One spring he hit the mother lode, reporting to us that he found four hammers in a two-week period.

Every day or two there was news from the tool front. It might be a demonstration of two or three saws of different shapes and sizes covered with—he was careful to indicate this—rust from having spent the winter in the snow. Another day, he might be musing on some newly rescued specialty tools, wondering to what purpose they had been put. Who—he looked at us one by one—who would ever need such a tool? And why, he used to wonder aloud, why in winter? We were silent. Nobody ever had to explain to us what a rhetorical question was.

After a few years, finally grasping our pure incorrigibility, Dad surrendered to the inevitable. His annual scoldings became tempered with comments about how happy he was that his Christmas had finally arrived. He called us together less to chide us than to display his discoveries and share his joy with us by listing all the tools he had found *so far*. We too were happy that Dad's Christmas was finally here because the longer the winter went on, the harder it became for us to find a hammer. Dad's April Christmas meant that we were now equipped for our spring and summer projects.

....

By now we know and anticipate one another so easily, so deeply, we unthinkingly finish each other's sentences, and often speak in code. No one else knows what I mean so exquisitely, painfully well; no one else knows so exactly what to say, to fix me.—Joan Frank

....

How to Make a Rhubarb Pie
Mary

Ingredients:

ten old bricks
machete
used pot pie tin
fresh rhubarb
contraband sugar and flour
precious matches
stuff that will burn
a barn
friends

The machete could be used for anything, and we always carried one with us. You could pound nails, repel wild dogs, scare a sibling, and make way for a new tree house. It could also be used for chopping up rhubarb. Why we had a machete as children I'll never know. We may even have had our own personal machetes. I know I always had access to one if I needed it.

Back to the rhubarb pie. This took the logistics and coordination skills of an awards banquet planner. It was not for the faint of heart: there was stealing involved and therefore potential retribution. Your group had to be fearless.

You first decided who would steal the sugar and flour. With that important task assigned, others picked the rhubarb, washed it at the outdoor pump, and macheted it into small pieces. That group also got the pie tins from their hidden stash and gathered the bricks and charcoal. Finally, the most important person of the group, next to the stealer, produced real matches. (That's probably why they were invited to share in the pie in the first place. They were the only ones with matches.)

Meanwhile, the chosen one, who would get kudos in many ways for stealing sugar and flour, prepared a run for the dry goods. This involved reconnaissance to determine Mom's exact location. Never never never enter the kitchen on a summer day if Mom is in there. You will be put to work. You may get spanked. You may have to rat out someone.

I figured, counting certain windows, we had about twelve ways to get in or out of the house. When you finally determined that Mom was in the basement washing clothes, you got into the kitchen as quiet as a mouse, careful not to step on squeaky spots. Up you went onto the counter. Carefully, slowly you eased open the cupboard door. All this time, your ears were stretched to their limit while they listened for the slightest note of danger. Man, I can hardly breathe just writing this.

You had to be still as death so you could hear all the way down to the basement and way back to the laundry room.

You got the sugar and flour sacks. The procedure was the same. You had to get out as much as you could fit into the plastic bread sack you saved from becoming garbage. You might not have needed it all, but you took as much as you could safely get away with. Who knew, maybe you'd get enough for two pies.

Then you did everything in reverse, careful not to kneel or step on any squeaky spots. You inspected the cupboard door. Was it closed exactly as it was when you came in? Inspected the counter. Any traces of sugar or flour? This was important because Mom was a good housekeeper. I remember her washing the blue linoleum kitchen floor ("Half a dozen of you, get out of here!") and then laying down newspapers so she could walk on it.

She had such fine-tuned eyes in the back of her head; she could see what we did even when we didn't do it. She saw stuff a week after we thought we were in the clear. I wonder how much she saw and didn't mention. She had to pick her battles since there was only one of her and eight of us.

Back to the pie. The others had been gathering and chopping and oven-building in the barn. We swept the dirt floor, so it was flattish. We then placed the bricks in a square, filled the square with charcoal, and lit it. Sometimes, by the time we had all the ingredients, we didn't have a fire, having started the fire part of the pie too soon. It's hard to resist a fire when you're a kid. If you have matches and you have coal, you must have fire. Now.

One of us mixed water from the pump with the flour and carefully patted out a dough in the pie tin. Another mixed the rhubarb and sugar. This was often done by making a "bowl" out of the front of your T-shirt. You poured this mixture into the pie tin. Then you cooked it. For a while. Eventually, after much fighting and arguing over other things, it was time to eat. Mmmm, raw dough and uncooked rhubarb. The best pie in the world.

Clowns and Wild Dogs
Paul

Clowns and wild dogs top my list of things to avoid. I'm not sure why I have an aversion to people dressed like big hobos with ghastly grins and demonic eyes, but my fear of wild dogs is rooted in my childhood.

One of Jack Handey's "Deep Thoughts" holds high meaning for our family: "It's sad that a family can be torn apart by something as simple as a pack of wild dogs."

Growing up on the edge of several hundred wooded acres, known to us as The Woods, we virtually lived out there. Summers we built tree houses and dams, explored, searched for agates and arrowheads, and biked on trails made by animals and off-road motorcycles. Winters we had fantastic sledding and could ice-skate for miles when the ice on the creek was good.

Across the shallow valley from us lived the Weber family. Mr. Weber was not only an unwitting supplier of tree house components but also a sheep rancher, and we could see his pastures from the large picture windows in the living room. In case you are not familiar with sheep, they are not as smart as they look. In fact, they are not even as smart as a clown looks.

More than once we witnessed a pack of six or eight wild dogs attack his flock. Other times we might not see the attack, but we'd find dead sheep in the pasture.

We were ice-skating one winter when we came upon God's favorite brainless critters. Four of them had wandered into the creek to, well, we don't know why they did that—did I mention they are brainless?—but there they were, and they were there so long their little legs froze in the newly formed ice. When we came upon them, they were bleating. When we finished skating and returned home, we told the owner about his furry morons.

The next day we passed the same spot. And stopped short. Sixteen bloody stumps were still stuck in the ice surrounded by hunks of wool and innards. The wild dogs had come and had their way with the sheep.

We encountered carcasses on a regular basis, and we could almost feel the eyes of the pack watching us as we examined their woolly spoils.

And then there was the horse that took ill. One day it was lying on the side of a hill, dead. The next day all its insides were eaten out. A fascinating science exhibit as well as a warning from the wild dogs.

The reality of the dog pack was quite enough to get our attention. Throw in the vivid imagination of a child, and this was scary business. I don't recall any of our lives being claimed by them, but the presence of this feral pack of hounds was a constant in our lives for years.

Many times we fled the woods, barking and baying dogs behind us. We never knew if they were actual wild dogs or just some officious farm dogs, but we weren't interested enough to find out.

What a relief to be safe in our home sweet home where our loving older siblings did everything in their powers to assuage our terror. Yeah, and I'm the Pope.

The older ones had us believing they had authority over the wild dogs and could summon them at will. When Mom and Dad were out, and anyone from Punky through Kevin was in charge, they frequently and convincingly threatened us younger ones with the wild dogs—sometimes for their personal entertainment and sometimes as a compliance tool.

Punky would say, "Okay, you guys, time for bed." The chorus replied, "Aw, c'mon, can't we watch the rest of *The Wonderful World of Disney?* The raccoons just broke into the cabin and—"

"No! Now!" She headed for the back door.

"But they just found the cupboard with the flour and—"

Opening the back door wide enough for, oddly enough, a pack of wild dogs to enter, she said, "I'm calling them, and they haven't eaten for a week. Oh, look, I can see them across the pasture, and I didn't even tell them yet. You know," she said smugly, "those wild dogs can read my mind, and they knew I needed them."

We barely heard that last part because by then we were in bed with our pillows and blankets over our heads, holding our breath until we fell asleep or passed out.

One Sunday morning, years later, I saw a huge dog come out of the barn. I shuddered, consumed by a case of the cumulative willies. That lone dog conjured up all the fears and memories of every wild hound that had traumatized me as a youth.

We always had an abundance of poultry—chickens, ducks, geese, guinea fowl, peacocks, and pheasants. The local foxes, opossums, and raccoons must have counted their blessings every time they helped themselves to our stock.

We set traps and generally caught several furry vermin each week, mostly opossums. These particular varmints make sheep look like intellectuals. Their very posture screams, "Look at me. I'm stupid."

I've read accounts of wild animals gnawing off their own paw to escape a trap, yet I've seen opossums sit complacently with nothing but the tip of their tail caught in the trap. We even caught opossums in traps with no bait. But I digress.

The dog was tall with slatted ribs, thick matted fur, and piercing yellow eyes. This time I was old enough to do something about it. I grabbed my twelve-gauge and headed to the barn. The archetypal dog and I squared off. We both had our hackles up. It bared its teeth and snarled at me. That was pretty much all the information I needed. I've wondered since if, in shooting that dog, I didn't kill all the dogs that bedeviled my childhood. Because ever since then, I haven't been quite so nervous.

As for the older siblings, they know nothing. "Wild dogs? What wild dogs?"

So Many Vines, So Few Watermelons
Mark

During the hot, sunny, steamy Iowa summers, Mother turned loose three of her boys on the neighborhood. We knew that if we kept away from the house and out of her sight, we could avoid being pressed into the service of string bean picking, or raspberry gathering, or garage sweeping, or bed making, or clean-clothes-putting-on, or hand and arm washing, or a host of other objectionable undertakings she would likely require from us. So we roamed the neighborhood. We were not bad boys, but we did not advertise our activities either.

I will call one neighbor family the Getouttadagartens. Clare and Cliff Getouttadagarten. That is not their real name, but since the statute of limitations may not have completely run its course, let us agree that none of this actually happened.

The Getouttadagarten family grew luscious strawberries—big, red, perfect, juicy, clean-and-ready-to-eat-immediately berries that a kid would be willing to spend time in the joint for.

In our case, the joint was a juvenile detention facility outside town euphemistically called the Boys Ranch. They had horses there. Could it really be hard time if they had horses? But we also knew they had a staff of "counselors" and "psychologists" who would ask us stupid personal questions about how we felt about this or that, and why we did evil things, and did we like girls, and so on. So it could get a little dicey. But we figured after years of practice with Mom and Dad, who themselves had decades of experience running inquisitions on the older siblings, we could easily withstand whatever questions the psychologists could drum up for us out at the Boys Ranch. Horses and a few questions—it would not be hard time. The strawberries were worth it.

The Getouttadagarten strawberries became the object of endless strategic planning meetings for my brothers and me: how to approach the strawberry patch from the adjoining soybean field (crouching? snake wiggling?), attack strategies, whether to eat them straight away (Paul Thomas) or collect them for later (Matthew), how to arrange lookouts in case one of the Getouttadagartens was home, and where to rendezvous on completion of the mission.

I admit that the Boys Ranch lurked all the time in the deeper reaches of my subconscious, or was it my unconscious? Is that my id or my ego? Are these Latin words? Why did Dad think Sigmund Freud was a dope? None of our older brothers and sisters would answer these questions for me—either they had no clue, or there was a dirty word involved. I wasn't sure which.

Preferring not to answer inane, personal questions put to us by a paid Freudian at the Boys Ranch, we did not want to get caught. We replayed our strawberry patch fallback and retreat strategies several times, discussing how (Mark) or whether (Paul Thomas) to extract a fallen brother should misfortune strike.

I can report—and we are still talking work of fiction here—that we had many a successful day of thieving in Getouttadagartens' strawberry patch. Long live the Queen; those strawberries were good. I must explain that we felt ethically justified in raiding that strawberry patch because both of the Getouttadagartens were bigots, if one defines that as folks who really dislike Catholics, Jews, and Blacks. They oftentimes cursed large Catholic families. What could they have been thinking?

At home, we had learned that bigotry and hatred were wrong, that they violated Christian teachings. So we concluded that stealing strawberries from bigots was an excellent way to apply some sort of cosmic morality to the situation. Stealing their strawberries became an important form of local justice.

We had at least two good years in the strawberry fields. Sometimes the anti-bigotry harvest was so large that we filled plastic bread sacks with berries for later consumption in our tree houses. As the summer got hotter, we got hungrier for the justice strawberries and became overconfident and emboldened in our daily raids. And you know what cometh after pride and an haughty spirit.

By this time, Cliff Getouttadagarten had determined that marauding songbirds had been feasting on his strawberries, so he put bird netting over the entire patch. Our initial consternation was followed by resolve; no bird net was going to stop us. And anyway, if we went back to the house for lunch, Mom would corral us and cause us to husk a basket of sweet corn or put on shoes or do something similarly outrageous. We needed those strawberries.

It happened in the late forenoon. We had stealthily crawled through the bean field and under that damn net, a-pickin' and a-chompin' and a-lip-lickin'. Then came a terrifying voice straight from the wilds of purgatory, "Hey, you boys! Get outta that garden!" Yikes! Cliff Getouttadagarten was on his porch hurriedly putting on his shoes and reaching for his shovel. We figured he intended to discriminate against us poor Catholic boys right then and there.

In the ensuing escape, only two of us cleared the net. Matthew did not, becoming entangled in it like a good-sized walleye with a crew cut, patched jeans, and a plastic bag of strawberries. What to do, what to do? Should we turn back and rescue our fallen comrade? And how about the bag of strawberries? Should we at least watch what Cliff Getouttadagarten does to Matthew?

"Caution is preferable to rash bravery," wrote William Shakespeare, who had undoubtedly gotten that quote from some other Brit with a ten-finger-discount habit. Our own personal discretion told us to get into a full gallop and head for the hills. Do not stop. Do not pass "Go." Do not go to jail.

To this day, I don't know how Matthew was freed from the net or what happened to him and his hide once he was unwrapped from the unholy net. Or if he was able to keep the bag of strawberries. We did not speak of such things.

In subsequent years, we learned the important lesson of that strawberry net. We turned our summertime attentions and appetites to a different neighborhood garden. This family we will call the Melonlookers. Orville and Joyce Melonlooker. We raided their watermelon patch with the same skill and zeal that we had applied to the Getouttadagartens' strawberries.

Every day, in season, Orville Melonlooker went out to his beautiful garden, searched for melons, and remarked to Dad, "Look at all these watermelon vines, and they're growing so well. You know, they blossom, but they don't seem to set fruit. I've looked and looked for watermelons, but I don't find any." To which Dad innocently replied, "Maybe they aren't getting pollinated by the bees."

They, of course, had no way of knowing that three little boys tracked the progress and location of each and every melon in the patch, from the time it was a little green egg up until it was the size of a feeder pig. When that perfect moment came and it was ready and ripe, full and heavy, we transported it out to the woods, to a tree house, to our barn, or to a secure, undisclosed location.

Illicit watermelon transport was carried out with great attention to both security and legal considerations, especially after the unfortunate incident with the strawberry net. Having studied the law as much as any twelve-year-old, I believed that the doctrine of hot pursuit did not apply across barbed wire fences so that once we arrived in our own horse pasture we were out of harm's way.

I am certain that Dad offered the bee pollination theory to the Melonlookers in all naïveté,. But I sometimes wonder if he was the one who came up with the songbirds-are-eating-the-strawberries theory for Cliff Getouttadagarten. It sounded like Dad.

....

We are each other's reference point at our turning points.—Elizabeth Fishel

....

Death in the Ditches
Matt

Pheasant hunting season began in late October and ended in early January, long enough to interfere with most major holidays. A thoroughgoing outdoorsman, Dad spent his off-hours working around the acreage with the land and animals, golfing, horseback riding, snowmobiling, fishing, and hunting.

During the 1960s, Dad drove a bright red Mustang, one of the first Mustangs in Iowa. Unfortunately, it seated four, and we were ten. We thought he'd made a pretty sly purchase, knowing that he'd never had to deal with more than three of us while driving his car. I often wondered how he got that past Mom. She knew how many kids she had.

With only three seats, there was much discussion about who went hunting and who got which seat ("shotgun" being the seat of choice). Wanting to be included in any car adventure, I always lobbied for a place, but lack of seniority denied me one for many years. When my time finally arrived, it was not what I had imagined.

I like to think that all those years the older ones were protecting me from this particular adventure. Hunting days began at dawn and, if you were lucky, ended sometime in the late afternoon. In between, you covered two hundred miles of desolate Iowa gravel roads. There was no breakfast or lunch as Dad apparently lived on air. For us, he packed a thermos with one cube of beef bouillon in lukewarm water and a package of saltine crackers. He occasionally stopped for a soda at a small-town tavern, the kind where you toss peanut shells on the floor. We were pathetically grateful for a glass of milk and lots of peanuts.

We were also grateful that Dad was a good shot because he wouldn't go home until he got his limit. And so there was bloodshed, and the car gradually filled up with dead bodies wrapped in newspaper.

Did I mention our hunting dog, Sheba? Fighting her for a window seat while keeping her away from the booty and the front seat and the guns required speed, agility, and a certain tolerance for dog breath.

To review, we had Dad, three of us boys, the dog, the dead birds, the "snack," the guns, and the ammunition all inside the little red Mustang. The temperature hovered right around zero during hunting season, so the windows frosted over, pretty much nullifying our job of pheasant spotting. That I suppose was a good thing because with Dad driving sixty miles per hour on icy gravel roads while we watched sideways out the windows produced carsickness in some of us. It might have been better if Dad hadn't been a cigar smoker at the time.

We looked forward to fence hunting, when we stopped the madness of driving and walked the roads with Sheba. Aside from the steep ditches, three feet of snow, falling through the ice on the creeks, and the barbed wire fencing hidden under the snow, this was a much preferred way to hunt.

I had missed all the clues about what really went on during these hunting trips. I used to wonder why Mom and my sisters never went, and why Pat and Ciccio looked so sick when they came home. I didn't listen when Kevin explained how the birds were blown to bits.

The aftermath—which the whole family got to share—wasn't much prettier as Dad butchered the birds on the kitchen table. He was thoughtful enough to lay old newspapers down first, but they were no match for what ensued. For an hour or so, the kitchen morphed into a setting for a horror movie: feet here, feathers there, blood, blood everywhere.

We amused ourselves the best we could by trying to figure out what the bird had just eaten by slicing open its gullet or gizzard or gimlet or something.

Mary imagined she was a puppeteer pulling tendons and sinews on the legs to make the feet dance or, after she got good, to make the feet grab our ears.

When it came to hunting, P.T. seemed to be the favored son. He was a good sport and a good shot, and I think he threw up less than Mark and I did. We were more than happy to let him have the shotgun seat and, in fact, we offered many times to stay home so that he and Dad could have more room in the car. Here is where I think Mom had some input. She wasn't about to let Dad go or do anything with one child and leave her with the other seven, so that offer never was accepted.

Mary and Punky saw some action on Sunday mornings. All ten of us were sardined into Mom's station wagon, rolling along the gravel roads to our little country church, dressed to the teeth when, wham, Dad slammed on the brakes, pulled a gun from who knows where, leaped out of the car, shot the bird, threw it in the car, and put the car back in "drive." Somehow it didn't seem quite right, the killing, I mean, on the way to church.

Every hunting season, we were very, very successful, which meant that we had to eat the things. I am fairly certain that Mom broke more than one tooth on hidden buckshot. Although she was quite well mannered at the table, it's hard to keep quiet when you've just hit a buckshot, which was even better hidden than the fine bones left behind in, let's say, the fish Dad caught and froze. At least fish bones didn't break teeth, and if a bone was caught in my throat, all I had to do was swallow a bread ball.

Soaking the birds in salt water to eliminate the gamy flavor is a rural myth. What with the unforgettably gamy flavor and the hidden buckshot, I spent most of our pheasant dinners trying to barter my share for anything on someone else's plate, even a bread ball.

E-mails

From: Ciccio
Subject: did you know . . . ?

I knew that! Did you just learn all those facts? We used to have quizzes on that stuff in second grade. It was a way to warm up after walking three miles to school in the blowing snow, with only one mitten and no boots.

✉✉✉

From: Mark
Subject: did you know . . . ?

Ciccio, I always got two mittens (matching) from Mom. I suppose she liked me better than, well, anyway, I had two mittens.

✉✉✉

From: Kevin
Subject: did you know . . . ?

I have never said anything until now, Mark, but I also had two mittens, leather boots, *and* they gave me a ride to school!

✉✉✉

From: P.T.
Subject: did you know . . . ?

Not only that, but they coached me on the answers for the third-grade quiz while we were driving to school (Dad used to let *me* drive).

✉✉✉

From: Mary
Subject: did you know . . . ?

I had my own bedroom.

✉✉✉

From: Ciccio
Subject: did you know . . . ?

Yes, you did. But you also had a 30-minute walk to get to the kitchen.

✉✉✉

From: P.T.
Subject: did you know . . . ?

Um, did you guys have socks? I had bread bags. Love, El Mismo

✉✉✉✉✉✉✉✉✉✉✉✉

From: Mark
Subject: gunman kills clowns in Colombian circus

BOGOTA, Colombia (Reuters)—Two clowns were shot and killed by an unidentified gunman during their performance at a traveling circus in the eastern Colombian town of Cucuta, police said Wednesday. The gunman burst into the Circo del Sol de Cali on Monday night and shot the clowns in front of an audience of 20 to 50 people, local police chief Jose Humberto Henao told Reuters.

"The killings had nothing to do with the show the victims were performing at the time of the incident," Henao said in a telephone interview. "We are investigating the motive."

Dear P.T., I knew this terrible story would attract your attention, what with your clown phobia and all. How do they know that the killings had nothing to do with the show? Did the investigators have to sit through the clown act?

I suppose there are a lot of folks like that gunman who *would* off a clown, if they *could* off a clown.

✉✉✉

From: P.T.
Subject: gunman kills clowns in Colombian circus

Omigod, Mark, where do you find this stuff? You must have access to professor-only websites. At least you're not one of those dreaded clown sympathizers who write articles that always start with, "The poor misunderstood fruit clown . . ."

I suppose one good thing to come out of this, being clowns, they probably died laughing. I remember Mom frequently shouting, "You kids quit clowning around!" Maybe she knew all along how dangerous it is to be a clown.

✉✉✉

From: Mary
Subject: gunman kills clowns in Colombian circus

I always wondered. Why Bozo the Clown? Are we going to confuse him with Bozo the Tax Attorney? Bozo the Pope?

✉✉✉

From: Pat
Subject: gunman kills clowns in Colombian circus

Mark, I am just riveted to my screen reading my siblings' comments, especially yours. This is top-drawer entertainment for me, your humble servant. What I'd like to (Anna Simpson's body is decomposing) say is to refer you to the classic foam or blinking rubber clown nose. I will share my favorite website with you but please do not disseminate it to others. From this site one can navigate to all sorts of clown noses. Hope to hear from those of you who like me are fascinated with this, my favorite site.

✉✉✉

From: P.T.
Subject: gunman kills clowns in Colombian circus

Pat! Those are *not* clown noses! Shame!

But that is interesting, very interesting. I think it was Sigmoid Freud who hypothesized the psychological correlation between the size of a man's Mr. Weasel and the size of his nose. It's an inverse relationship. Therefore men seeking to enhance the length and girth of their schnoz are possibly compensating for some other shortcoming. So given that, I guess I don't need to be so frightened by clowns anymore. And, anyway, from watching PBR (Professional Bull Riders) I discovered that rodeo clowns are boss!

⊠⊠⊠

From: Mark
Subject: gunman kills clowns in Colombian circus

Mary, Thanks for the clown picture you sent to illustrate our discussion. I can see why he is behind bars. He is wearing way, way too much make-up, even for a clown.

And thanks for the other great photos from Venice Beach. Mostly, thanks for not sending the usual Venice Beach photos of feminine men's butts. Their butts don't need any additional publicity.

Also, in case you saw any mimes causing trouble at Venice Beach, thanks too for not sending photos. They can be disconcerting because it's hard to know what a mime is thinking, if anything. Even photos of them can be pretty irritating when one is trying to calm down after a long day. m.

⊠⊠⊠

From: Kevin
Subject: gunman kills clowns in Colombian circus

Speaking of irritating, why is Jerry Lewis so beloved in France? Is it that he mostly mimes, like Marcel Marceau? I've never understood it. Love, Pierre

⊠⊠⊠

From: Mark
Subject: gunman kills clowns in Colombian circus

I can't stand watching Jerry Lewis. I think it is because Dad used to make us watch him when we were little.

mimes
clowns
Jerry Lewis
load 'em up
ship 'em all to France

⊠⊠⊠

From: P.T.
Subject: gunman kills clowns in Colombian circus

I'm so biased in my feelings for that guy, he'd have to invent time travel before I thought he was clever. Just me, I suppose. But if you have studied name origins, you would know that "Jerry" means "scratching" and "Lewis" means "on a chalk board."

⊠⊠⊠⊠⊠⊠⊠⊠⊠⊠⊠⊠

From: Mark
Subject: Rosalie as campus visitor

Dear All, If you go to the Luther College website you'll see a poster and announcement about Rosalie Maggio's visit to the campus ("Horse Mackerel: the Importance of Words and the Joy of Writing"). M.

⊠⊠⊠

From: Kevin
Subject: Rosalie as campus visitor

What a beautiful article, Punky and Mark. I've always loved horse mackerel, really, always. Love, M

⊠⊠⊠

From: P.T.
Subject: Rosalie as campus visitor

I like what Kevin said, so ditto for me, except for the horse mackerel.

I know the students will enjoy you. Dad's obituary got me thinking about my own. It will be able to be written on the back of a matchbook. Who will care that I loved my family (who doesn't?) or that I loved sports (that's deep). I'm just not a groupie kind of person. I don't like joining Rotary and Elks and churches. Hey, maybe that's what we can put in the obit: "He never liked joining groups." Or, is that a special thing? I guess I'm not living my life to create a posthumous r,sum, but I'm a slug compared to Dad. But, you know what, dambit, I pretty much like my life. So where were I? Oh yes, pace yourself during your stint at Luther. I want you to have enough energy left to give me a dance at the Sweetheart Ball! Gotta git. I love you, P.T.

⊠⊠⊠

From: Pat
Subject: Rosalie as campus visitor

I like everything P.T. said, and adopt it as if it were my very own.

⊠⊠⊠

From: Kevin
Subject: Rosalie as campus visitor

For those who haven't heard about the artist who painted his interpretation of Custer's Last Stand, it was a large picture of a green mountain prairie littered with Indians having sex all over the place. Floating in the air above the copulating Indians were large fish. When asked to explain this surreal picture, the artist said he was portraying Custer's last words: "Holy Mackerel! Look at all them fuckin' Indians!" Punky, maybe you could use this joke as an intro to your presentation at Luther about Horse Mackerel.

⊠⊠⊠

From: Mark
Subject: Rosalie as campus visitor

Kevin, What a good suggestion for Punky to tell the Mackerel-Indian story. That sounds like a good one to tell when she comes to Luther because it is a place that enjoys a good story.

Let's see if we can list the people it would offend:

Indians
Mackerels
People who fish (catch and release)
People who eat fish
Vegetarians
People who protect fish
People who have sex outdoors
People who have had sex with an Indian outdoors
Union Army supporters
Hindus
People who love mountain prairies
People who eat custard

That ought to do it, Punky.

✉✉✉

From: P.T.
Subject: Rosalie as campus visitor

Do it, Punky, do it, tell the joke, go ahead, what could it possibly hurt?

✉✉✉✉✉✉✉✉✉✉✉✉✉

From: Ciccio
Subject: mornings with Dad

Mark, I truly love you . . . wish I could have taken a class from you. You would have had one hell of a time trying to understand my lack of direction. Maybe because my days started out so poorly.

Dad's method of waking a teenager, such as me, was almost illegal. His index finger (similar to a 500-lb. jackhammer) tapping on the breastbone could have qualified as child abuse. But it was totally effective. I did want to get up, if for no other reason than that I could apply some undue pressure on his, well, his private parts. In the end, I have been a much better person thanks to his damn chest rap.

⊠⊠⊠

From: Kevin
Subject: mornings with Dad

And don't forget the "Sleeping Beauty" part of Dad's routine. While poking you in the chest repeatedly, he'd say, "Wake up, Sleeping Beauty! Sleeping Beauty, wake up! Sleeping Beauty! Sleeping Beauty!" He was forever puzzled by how you could sleep so soundly. I remember when you worked overtime at Glaser's, came home, slept for 12 hours, and then went back to work, seven days in a row.

⊠⊠⊠

From: P.T.
Subject: mornings with Dad

I have two memories to add. Besides the Sleeping Beauty command, Dad was also fond of "Up and at 'em!" I used to wonder who this Adam guy was. The other thing I remember is if you were ever told to wake up Ciccio it was wise to take with you a long pole and a garbage can lid.

⊠⊠⊠

From: Mark
Subject: mornings with Dad

Maggio, Dad did not say that "Sleeping Beauty" business to any of the others of us. Is this where you got your gender confusion?

⊠⊠⊠⊠⊠⊠⊠⊠⊠⊠⊠⊠⊠

CHAPTER 2

An Exciting Chapter in Which We Tell What We Did When Mom Told Us to Go Out and Play and Not Come Back Until She Rang the Train Bell, Which Could Be Heard for About Three Miles

Once Upon a Time There Were Tree Houses
Kevin

I learned to build tree houses from Ciccio and Pat when I was about seven. I was their gofer and was allowed to hang out with them as long as I kept running errands. A typical assignment might be a sortie to the house to sneak food, tools, or water.

Their first, biggest, and best tree house was in the ancient cottonwood on our land. It stood up out of a small, narrow ravine with a meager creek at its feet. These were Iowa woods, not Rocky Mountain forests, and everything was small-scale and sparse. This marvel of a full-fledged tree house boasted four sides, a roof that didn't leak, two entrances, and spy holes to see if anyone was coming. Anchored twenty-five feet above the ground, it was reached by steps nailed to the tree trunk—a precarious business because the steps wound around the tree looking for surfaces flat enough to take a board.

A great place to hang out, it was also close enough to home so that we could hear the dinner bell.

But our tree houses wouldn't have been half as amazing without the dump.

The dump squatted in a crevice, surrounded by trees and, farther out, acres of woods. It was thinly connected to the rest of the world by a mile-long dirt cow path that meandered through the cornfields.

The dump wasn't visible from anywhere, and in those days of unregulated landfills, only a few people knew about it. Even so, each week, five to ten cars disgorged themselves there, bringing in new materials for us to sort through.

The dump was lumberyard, hardware store, and furniture outlet for our tree houses. All the boards and wood we needed showed up there sooner or later. We recycled the nails, a difficult job for little kids. But where else would we get nails—from Dad's toolroom? Well, yes. Poor guy. But first we got what we could from the dump.

Carpet pieces were installed on the floors of our tree houses. Large sheets of plastic called Visqueen, when placed over the roofs, protected our tree houses from weather. Hoses served as urinals for the boys. Vases held wildflowers, and candlestick holders cradled misshapen candle stubs to give us light on moonless nights.

One day, when I was nine and Pat was eleven, he concocted a scheme involving the tree house, gasoline, and some rifle bullets. We made a wick out of old T-shirts, knotting them together until we had a five-foot-long kite tail. In the center of the tree house, we placed a pie tin filled with gasoline and about eight bullets. We doused the wick with gasoline, put one end in the pie tin, and draped the other end down the side of the tree. Once we were both on the ground, Pat lit the wick, and we plastered ourselves to the sides of the tree like Gumby figures. After waiting breathlessly for a few minutes, results! The crack-crack-crack of exploding bullets echoed around us. I've never been so scared and excited.

When Pat and Ciccio started getting more interested in girls than tree houses, the ownership and use of the "big tree house" defaulted to us younger kids. We added another way to get up the tree—two huge pulleys and a fat rope that Ciccio and Pat had "borrowed" from a neighbor's barn.

Anchoring those pulleys—one at the base of the tree and the other at the tree house door—was a major engineering feat. One day a little neighbor kid asked to try out the pulley system. He sat on a big knot we had tied in the up side of the rope and pulled himself up by pulling down on the other side of the rope. When he got to the top, he was so thrilled to see us that he punched the air with both hands. Of course, he fell all the way to the ground. Poor kid couldn't walk for a week.

For six years, I assumed the role of tree house crew chief based on what I'd learned from Ciccio and Pat and my own improvisations. I worked with Mary, P.T., when he got old enough, and our two best childhood friends, Leah and Licia. A spare neighbor kid had to be brought in from time to time.

The first step in building a tree house was to scout the woods for the perfect tree or trees. This sometimes took days or months because the tree houses were only one part of our life in the woods. We swam in the creeks, fished a little, made rope swings over the water, hiked endlessly, explored abandoned barns and homes, ate wild strawberries and raspberries, hunted small animals, rode our ponies through the woods, ice-skated and sledded in the winter, collected rocks, and rolled in the leaves in the fall—it was the best playground a kid could have.

A likely spot for a tree house was two oak trees eight feet apart, the right distance for some of the bigger boards from the dump. We'd nail two boards horizontally on each side of the trees as support beams for the floor and walls. The trees had to be sturdy, had to be branchless for at least ten to fifteen feet from the ground, and, again, branchless above the area chosen for the floor so we could install walls. The trunks had to be large enough to support steps and, lastly, the trees needed to be leafy enough to hide the tree house from our enemies.

Closer to home was a weird little finger of the forest that extended into the middle of a cornfield, but this was too close to civilization where kids lived who didn't build tree houses but liked to squat in them and leave matches and food and messes. The Cox family lived in the nearest house; so we used that as a reference for this area, as in, "Let's go over by the Coxes."

We built two tree houses over by the Coxes, both about fifteen feet high and in trees twenty feet apart. But the best part about these two tree houses was the thirty-foot roll of wire fencing I found at the dump and managed to run between the two tree houses—the fence lying flat in the air, horizontal to the ground. Now there was a bridge from one tree house to the other. It was a cool way to go back and forth instead of climbing down one tree and up the other. Unfortunately, the idea was cooler than the reality because if you didn't balance your weight just right, the fence would flip you off, and I'm not talking about hand gestures here. The other attractive feature about the bridge was that it provided a second exit from each tree house in case our enemies attacked us.

Speaking of enemies, we dug three holes in the ground, each about two feet by two feet by two feet. We covered them with small branches and handfuls of wild grasses, and spaced them along the paths because we figured our enemies would be too lazy to blaze through the jungle to get to our tree houses. We also put up a trip wire across one of the paths, but we took it down after a few weeks because we kept tripping ourselves. About five months after building the traps, we found one broken through to the bottom of the pit. We analyzed that hole like trackers and determined that the trap was crushed by a human foot and not a deer. We felt smug. We had bested our enemies.

During my tree house-building years, from about age seven to fourteen, my friends and I built one or two tree houses every summer. Once they were built, I quickly tired of them and began thinking about the next one. Even if building the next one was a year off, I could still evaluate likely trees during my hikes in the woods. Not everyone was this way. Ciccio and Pat built the big tree house, the best of all of them, and maintained it every year until they outgrew it. I don't think they ever built another one. P.T., Mark, and Matt became master tree house builders in their own right; but they were years younger than I, so I had outgrown tree houses by the time they reached their peak.

Building a tree house, like other endeavors in life, requires keeping an eye on both the process and the result. I have always been more interested in the process; there is nothing wrong with this imbalance—it is what it is. By contrast, Ciccio and Pat seemed to be more invested in results, and there's nothing wrong with that either.

I have been building tree houses throughout my adult life. My employment history illustrates this: my typical job has lasted three to five years. In a new job, I spend the first year on a huge learning curve. The second year is spent becoming more and more competent and successful. In the third year, boredom sets in because I know what I'm doing and find myself repeating tasks. I am then emotionally complete with the job and start scouting around for a new challenge. Unlike Dad, who did one thing well for sixty years, once I get good at my job, it's time to move on. It's hard to live this way because of the monumental learning curves, but I wouldn't and couldn't have it any other way.

In extracurricular activities, I've taken night classes and weekend seminars in everything from photography to hiking, Spanish, watercolors, spirituality, and nutrition. I stay with a subject long enough to know enough about it, whatever "enough" is for me, and then I start looking for something else.

I have not, however, built friendships like tree houses. They are deep and long-term. I nurture them liberally and never abandon them, a nice balance between process and results.

As a process person, I look at my spirituality more to learn about spiritual concepts than to reach conclusions. I build one tree house after another along my spiritual path, not staying in any one too long but striving for the next challenge. A spiritual "Aha!" will sustain me for months or years, and then I find myself outgrowing it and looking for a deeper context. My spiritual beliefs are a moving target, constantly changing as I learn more and more about them, never resting with the results of my inquiries for long. This is a hard way to be spiritual because I deny myself the comfort of feeling forever at home spiritually, but I have always liked building the next tree house.

....

We were a club, a society, a civilization all our own.—Annette, Cécile, Marie, and Yvonne Dionne

....

Chief Engineer
Mary

I had two tree houses that I was the chief engineer of. I had help with the boards, but the majority of the work was done by me. I scouted the trees, found the right place, located the wood for building, and checked with neighboring tree houses to make sure mine was up to code. We had maybe ten that were functional at one time.

One of my tree houses was a double-decker. Nothing fancy but it was eye-catching. I rarely used the top floor, but I always had bragging rights.

The first memory I have of my other tree house was five of us kids ranging in age from six to ten hauling a large steel horse watering trough about half a mile through the valley and up across a large field.

Who knows where you'd find a defunct watering trough lying around, but that bit of information is long gone by now. We built the wooden supports, which in itself was a remarkable job, and then somehow—that is the operative word, "somehow"—we hauled that trough up the tree and settled it on the supports. We nailed it down. Put a wooden roof over half of it. Sawed a hole through the bottom for our door. Turned back the edges so the door wouldn't saw us in half as we went in and out. As far inland as you could get in this country without beginning to come out the other side, we had our own ship's crow's nest.

Ciccio and Pat had the crème de la crème of tree houses. Great big thing in a great big cottonwood. It had a roof, door, pulley, swing, and I think smoking went on in there. I don't recall ever being invited up when they were there, so I can't say for sure.

The dump was our treasure trove. I never saw another kid there. I never saw a rat. I never caught any dread disease from it. Mark once cut his wrist on a rusty can, but I was wearing a bandanna, so I tied it around his wrist until we got home. He lived.

I don't think that we bragged about it much. Can you imagine telling someone who had the luxury of living in a center of culture like Fort Dodge that if they came out to play we could take them to the dump? So we didn't bruit it about, but a trip to the dump was the highlight of any summer day.

The dump was about fifteen miles from the house, or maybe a mile. It probably seemed far away because we were always hauling something on the return trip: fully functional Monopoly games, clean dolls with pretty dresses, shiny things, bowls, plates, cups, tables, chairs. We had barely conceived of a need for something when, presto, there it was at the dump. We roamed around on the top of people's refuse like mountain goats. We hopped, balanced, picked, culled, and hollered out our finds. Sometimes—and don't tell me I was the only one—we hid our finds from the others.

The best thing about the dump? It refreshed itself constantly. Each morning my first thought after waking was, "I wonder if anyone dropped anything off at the dump yesterday." My second thought was, "I wonder what I could find there that would take my tree house up to another level of wonderful?"

Finding Your Bliss
Paul

As kids, we grew up with a six-hundred-acre playground adjacent to our property. Mostly wooded, it had some meadows and a beautiful creek (that's "crick" where I come from). I remember how clever we thought we were to come up with the name of Snake Creek (did you ever see a creek that didn't "snake"?).

One of our main activities each summer was tree house construction. Sometimes we had one big one, and sometimes we each built our own smaller one. I remember the thrill of discovering the perfect oak tree to house our structure, with just the right configuration of branches.

We scavenged for building materials. My older brothers used to repair to our neighbor's barn at night and remove any wood or rope they deemed unnecessary to support the old behemoth. Eventually, Mr. Weber found out, and we lost our main supplier, along with our privileges around the house for a week or two.

Then there was the dump, an unsanctioned landfill at the edge of a cornfield next to the woods. We never headed to the tree house without first stopping by the dump to see what riches could be found. It must have been the cleanest dump in six counties by the end of summer. Nails were a particularly hot commodity. We spent hours pulling them out of old boards and sometimes out of each other's feet. We even resorted to begging. I remember the time I went with Dad to Town and Country Lumber when he was buying fencing. Once inside, I badgered him sufficiently that he relented and bought us a one-pound sack of sixteen-penny nails. Brand new nails. Life was good.

We spent all summer working on that tree house, beginning with the steps nailed to the side of the tree. The platform was next, followed by as many walls as materials would permit. One year somebody hauled the remains of a demolished house to our dump. What a bonanza! We were able to build a tree house with four walls and a roof with a trapdoor for entry. Not only that, but we shingled the entire outside of it to render it relatively impervious to weather. That worked out well enough until, after a week of rain, we found the inside covered with mold. There was even a frog in residence. The next summer it rotted and fell into a pile of itself beneath the tree.

We never seemed to just sit or play in the tree houses. We always had something to add or modify, activities that lasted precisely until the end of summer. When the next spring rolled around, the whole process began anew, even if last year's model was serviceable. We enjoyed the process of building, of achieving, and we enjoyed what we were achieving, so we were content. As Margot Fonteyn said, "Generally speaking, we are all happier when we are still striving for achievement than when the prize is in our hands."

I'm not saying that if you dash out and build yourself a tree house you can expect a lifetime of blissful happiness and contentment. You may certainly try that. What's the harm as long as it's not in the neighbor's tree? But if you think you can then smugly retreat to the friendly confines of your La-Z-Boy, thinking, "There! I'm all set," think again. As I see it, the problem with living a life of content is the possibility of lapsing into complacency. When you achieve something, it's good to be content. But if that contentment leads to complacency, then you will stop achieving, and the feeling of contentment will soon begin to wane. Sometimes I think a few of us adults could do with a challenging tree house project.

....

> We had codes
> In our house.—Louise Glück

....

Hangouts and Lookouts
Mary

For me, tree houses were tied with the barn for top childhood hangout.

Kevin, Licia, Leah, and I were a club. We held our meetings in the barn, and we each had an office, although now that I think about it, Leesh and I had to share a stall. Kevin was the president. Always. Leah, next oldest, was the vice president and treasurer. Always. And Leesh and I traded acting as secretary.

We swept the mud floors, outfitted three stalls with "office furniture" from the dump, and held meetings daily. Leesh and I were also lookouts. I don't know who we were looking out for, but we sat on a two-feet-by-two-feet platform at the apex of this huge barn and peered out the tiny window. I don't know why no one ever fell out that window. Had we fallen, we would have either lived, having landed on a sheep, or died, having landed on a boulder at the base of the barn. It was a long way down.

Kevin had a mirror in his office, a desk, a chair, a side table, a rug, a Monopoly game, paper, pencils, and pens. I don't think Leesh and I had much in our office, but we could spend all day in that stall pretending we did.

We ate a lot of peanut butter and jelly sandwiches and, as I recall, we made our own lunches once we were tall enough to reach the counter. So Leesh and I would make a lunch and take it to the barn, climb up to a rafter high above the mounded hay, and eat. What a treat. "Wanna have lunch in the barn today?" "Yeah. Good idea!" I don't know why our legs and hands weren't studded with slivers from climbing around on rough wood.

Leah and Licia were the grandkids of the guy who owned the big barn on the adjacent property. They and their parents lived in the house with Grandma and Grandpa. They were the only kids in their family, and their dad used to call us a tribe. I loved them. I still do. We used to call each other across the ravine, "Whoo, whoo, whoo." And back came the answer, "Whoo, whoo, whoo." Then we met at the ravine to plan our day. A trip to the dump was almost always on the agenda. Food from the garden was another given. Avoiding our Irish Catholic mothers was another. A trip to one barn or another was always indicated. Sometimes we walked to an abandoned schoolhouse and messed around in there. I climbed its windmill once. It wasn't easy but when I got to the top, there was a little board, about the size of a magazine, to sit on. I sat on it. What a view.

We had a little trouble keeping the horses out of the barn when we wanted to use it. But I learned one thing from horses. You could jump on their backs, and they didn't care.

Horses aside, I never met a barn I didn't like.

> Being a child is largely a flux of bold and furtive guesswork, fixed ideas continually dislodged by scrambling and tentative revision . . . . All our energy and cunning go into getting our bearings without letting on that we are ignorant and lost.—Fernanda Eberstadt

Radar Woman
Matt

Although we lived in the country, there were just enough neighbors within reach to make life more interesting. Much of our time was spent planning and executing raids on selected neighbors.

One home, fairly close to us, was a particular and perennial favorite. The couple had one apparently perfect child. Their yard appeared to have been groomed with a brush and comb (the father was in the men's garden club); and their garden was lush, thriving, and, we felt, way too fruitful for their small family.

If the mother had been just a little more agreeable, we might not have targeted their place, but she had a radar for the Maggio kids and was both vigilant and expeditious about reporting every run-of-the-mill infraction to Mother.

As we had a party line and as she spent most of her day listening to other people's telephone calls, she often overheard our conversations with friends and repeated everything to Mother. It took us a long time to figure out how Mom was privy to this information. For years, we simply assumed she was psychic.

Sometimes we lost a ball or Frisbee to the hungry roof of our house. Standing three feet from the roof's edge was our twenty-foot-high TV antenna, a ready-made ladder begging us to scamper up and retrieve the lost plaything.

Ring. Ring. "Irene, did you know your two little boys are up on the roof?"

We knew Lecture Number 132 by heart: "You get down from there right now, you could fall and break a leg, do you know how much it'll cost your father to fix that roof, that's not a playground up there, you know."

One day Mom sent Mark and me to our room for no good reason. Deciding it was grossly unjust, we escaped out the bedroom window.

Ring. Ring. "Irene, aren't your little boys supposed to be napping?"

For legal reasons, I don't like to say how we redressed the balance (always remembering that children going head-to-head with an adult are at a serious disadvantage and might need to rely on extraordinary measures), but I will say that Radar Woman, in the murky recesses of what passed for her brain, began associating, "Irene, did you know your little boys . . . ?" with inexplicable and unfortunate accidents to—but let us leave that to your imagination. And anyway, I might be making all this up.

The Untimely Demise of Clark Kevin

This story speaks to how we siblings were involved in each other's lives, sometimes in a caring way, sometimes in an intrusive way, and sometimes both. One of the dynamics of our family, as with most large families, is that we raised each other. Mom and Dad often knew nothing of the vignettes played out among us daily. I'm mostly grateful for the guidance and teachings of my older siblings about books, sports, animals, sex, cigarettes, cars, clothes, and more. I, in turn, was a quasi-parent in similar ways to my four younger siblings.

This story also shows how we integrated our strong Catholic upbringing into our daily lives, sometimes seriously and sometimes, um, not.

When Mark was five, he had a teddy bear named Clark, the finest teddy bear our family ever knew. Clark was only ten inches tall with curly golden fur, black plastic eyes, a triangular black cloth nose, and a red cloth tongue sticking out of a stitched mouth with a hint of a smile.

Clark went everywhere with Mark, not only to bed for naps and at night, but also outside to play, to the dinner table, and sometimes even to town.

But Clark was not immortal. First, he lost one eye, leaving black stitches in the shape of an X. His little cloth nose started to tear away. His tongue fell off and got lost. Patches of bare cloth started to show up where he used to have fur. And then the other eye fell off.

Mom, seeing the direction Clark was headed, bought Mark another bear. This bear was twice as big as Clark. He sported a red plaid Scottish bow tie; and his dark brown fur was made of a new material called polyester that felt unpleasantly slippery but was, on the upside, supposed to last forever. Mark named him Ted-Edward, Ted as in teddy bear and Edward as in Mark's middle name. Ted-Edward was a modern bear and perhaps had much to recommend him. But he was not Clark.

One day I decided that Clark's time was up, that he was really dead and that we should bury him. I was thirteen and a priest wannabe, so I thought about these things. I enlisted Mary's help. She was eleven and only moderately interested in the situation, but she did make some excellent suggestions. First of all, she pointed out that we couldn't bury Clark until he had been baptized, or he would spend eternal life in limbo. Mark, being baptized, would go to heaven or hell, depending on who was voting, but one thing was sure: he wouldn't go to limbo. An unbaptized Clark and a baptized Mark would have no chance of reuniting in the afterlife. At that point we nervously decided that Clark wasn't so dead after all. He had just enough life in him for a baptism, after which we could declare him officially dead.

The baptism was short and sweet. I wrapped a priestly looking cloth around my neck and shoulders. We blessed a jar of tap water, and Mary held it while I sprinkled it on Clark and said, "I now baptize you, Clark, in the name of the Father, the Son, and the Holy Ghost. Amen. You may now enter the gates of heaven."

I was good at baptisms. I learned from Ciccio and Pat. We lived on a major highway, and it was not unusual to find one of our dogs or cats, and sometimes even a pony, dead on the highway. Pat and Ciccio would rush out there with homemade holy water and sprinkle it on the dead animal. They determined that an ex post facto baptism was valid if it was done pretty quickly after the death, say, within a day. After such experiences, we went around the pastures baptizing the other animals so we wouldn't have to stretch the rules next time one of them died.

After Clark's baptism, Mary and I broke the news to Mark that Clark was dead and needed a good Catholic funeral. Mark was teary eyed but agreeable. It didn't take much of a nod from Mark to get me in gear. I was so anxious to officiate at my first funeral that I wasn't too particular about whether Mark really, really agreed.

And then Mary asked to be the priest. My answer was obvious. All priests were guys. But she said this wasn't a real funeral, so it didn't matter if she wasn't a real priest. My ego was offended at first. I had done baptisms, given mock Holy Communions, and was fully prepared to officiate at my first funeral. But Mary persisted, and in an iconoclastic mood we agreed that she would be the priest and I would be her altar boy.

A lot of thought goes into designing a meaningful ritual. We decided we needed professional mourners, and in the old tradition, at least what we thought was the old tradition, they should be paid since they were disinterested persons who had no reason to mourn for a bear they didn't even know. For mourners, we recruited brother P.T., age nine, along with our best friends and neighbors, Leah, age thirteen, and her sister, Licia, age ten. We paid them a nickel each.

Our property had two driveways—one leading to the garage and a long gravel road that went from the highway all the way past the house and on to the barns and pastures. The funeral procession began where the gravel road met the highway and ended one hundred feet farther down the road where we had chosen a burial plot.

As altar boy, I led the procession, holding high a cross made of two small branches tied together with wild grasses. Mark, the pallbearer, followed me carrying Clark's casket, which was actually a shoe box. Inside, Clark was wrapped from head to toe in a burial shroud, also known as an old rag from the toolshed. Mary, the be-shawled priest, sprinkled holy water left and right as we paraded down the gravel road. Bringing up the rear was P.T., who had the dual role of professional mourner and the guy who carried the shovel, and Leah and Licia, the paid professional mourners. They did such a good job of wailing that I almost cried myself.

At the burial site, P.T. solemnly handed me the shovel, and I dug the grave, sticking the cross in the small pile of dirt at the head. We took up a collection consisting of the three nickels we had given to the professional mourners. We whispered to them that they would get their nickels back afterward. I'll never forget Mary's brief, moving eulogy: "My dear brothers and sisters! Do not mourn for our dearly departed brother, Clark. Just pray for him and give more money to the church!"

A few weeks later, I became alarmed to see that the dirt over Clark's grave had been disturbed. Grave robbers or worse! I quickly dug up the shoe box and found Clark was still there. However, someone had pulled the burial shroud down from the top of his head to his neck so his face, or what was left of it, showed. I felt a twinge of guilt. Poor Mark. Clark wasn't so dead after all.

E-mails

From: Mark
Subject: Dad's television

I enjoyed my visit with Dad although I didn't get as much done as I'd hoped. We tried to watch a movie, but were confounded, as we are every week, by the most complex and poorly engineered TV installation in the northern part of the United States. Under the TV and the nearby table are dead and burned-out hulks of devices that were haute-couture or *au courant* (French for "dried currants") in 1982. We know they don't work, but we also know "we are not supposed" to discard them.

The television is electrically underserved (one ungrounded outlet for the entire living room, and it is wired through a lamp on a timer to an unknown wall .switch in Webster City) and under-cabled (one cable has three wires, yet there are three or four dozen ports on the backs of TV, VCR, DVD, and antenna—I was unable to persuade those three wires to serve the four dozen ports, no matter what I did or said to them).

Can someone help?

⊠⊠⊠

From: P.T.
Subject: Dad's television

That electronic wasteland is something to be reckoned with, just not by me! It reminds me of a slot machine. Every once in a while the cherries will line up and you can watch a movie but you never know why.

⊠⊠⊠

From: Pat
Subject: Dad's television

Marcus, Thank you for that detailed and sensitive summary. As you will soon see, I have no particular wise comment to inject into the mix. I think everyone is doing the best for Dad (short of giving him mind-altering medication at which time we could tell him he doesn't need his wheelchair and he would get up and exercise, walk, weed the garden, etc.). "We do all we can, when we can, and we can do no more" (circa 1956). I love this and think of it often as it tends to whittle down the guilt, remorse, and feelings of inadequacy we sometimes have when we look back on something and wish we had done it differently. If we really do all we can reasonably be expected to do, at the appropriate time, then we realistically can do no more and should be satisfied with what we did, even through the 20/20 vision of hindsight. So there! Love you.

⊠⊠⊠

From: Mark
Subject: Dad's television

My dear boy Paddy, Very philosophical and nice. Does this mean you'll fix the television? Mark

✉✉✉✉✉✉✉✉✉✉✉✉✉

From: Kevin
Subject: IQ test

Here's a one-question IQ test for your busy little brains.

A mute wants to buy a toothbrush. By imitating the action of brushing his teeth, he successfully expresses himself to the shopkeeper and the purchase is done. Now if there is a blind man who wishes to buy a pair of sunglasses, how should he express himself?

Think about it before scrolling down for the answer.

Answer: He says, "I would like to buy a pair of sunglasses."

If you got this wrong, turn off your computer and call it a day.

✉✉✉

From: P.T.
Subject: IQ test

Hey, I resemble that. My brain may be little but it ain't busy!

✉✉✉

From: Mark
Subject: IQ test

But, former Kevin, why would a mule want to buy a pair of sunglasses? And how could the mule "just ask" if he can't talk? Do you mean, like "Mr. Ed"?

I thought the answer was something related to woodchucks, and how much wood they could chuck.

Remember Dad's sworn enemies, the woodchucks in the barn? He never stopped talking about his traps, his theories about the arrangement of said traps, and the best bait (one year he was sure they wanted meaty/fatty things, the next year he was sure they wanted corny/veggie things). When I questioned him, he said, "I know woodchucks. That's all I can tell you." Mark

⊠⊠⊠

From: P.T.
Subject: IQ test

Mark, I think the mule was buying a toothbrush. It was the blond man who wanted sunglasses. The part that concerns me is when the mule exposes himself to the shopkeeper. I don't know why my firewall didn't catch that smut.

⊠⊠⊠

From: Matt
Subject: IQ test

In a marginally related story, did Dad ever tell you what happened one year during a cold snap? He was checking on the animals in the barn and spotted an opossum—one of a band of renegades who regularly ate our chickens. Dad didn't have a gun, so he got a scoop shovel and slowly, slowly tiptoed nearer. He was laughing to himself about how this would be the last time that one "played possum." With one mighty swing, he clobbered it. Boooiiiing! The opossum had died earlier and was frozen hard as a rock. The reverberations nearly broke Dad's wrist.

⊠⊠⊠

From: Kevin
Subject: IQ test

Matt made up that story.

⊠⊠⊠

From: Ciccio
Subject: IQ test

No, that's a true story. At least Dad thought it was true.

Mark, I have recently been impressed with your comments, stories, etc. But with your last e-mail, I am having second thoughts. I think that the woodchucks and the groundhogs needed neither a toothbrush nor a pair of sunglasses. On the other hand, and maybe this is the connection, Mom had lots of sunglasses and Dad believed in toothbrushes. Also I can't imagine Dad making the statement, "That's all I can tell you." He never arrived at the point when he could not tell more.

So, I am wondering if it is this new job that has caused you to deviate from the e-mail thread about a guy with dirty teeth and another who lost his sunglasses. None of this has anything to do with barnyard varmints.

I look forward to your explanation.

⊠⊠⊠

From: Mark
Subject: IQ test

Ciccio, This is the time of year when every good professor is up to his ass in alligators.

Many of the alligators are trying to graduate from college two weeks from now.

And my ass seems to be in their way.

That's my excuse.

⊠⊠⊠

From: Ciccio
Subject: IQ test

Mark, Why not just fail some of the good students and give As to the lowest group? It would be interesting to see how that would affect them in the future. Go ahead and do it. Later, you could write a book about the suicides, failures, etc.

✉✉✉

From: P.T.
Subject: IQ test

Yes, Mark, this idea has merit. What a study in social engineering! See if you can turn the good students into loser winos or politicians and the bad students into successful contributors to society. Then, as Ciccio said, write a book or even a movie like Eddie Murphy's "Trading Places."

✉✉✉

From: Pat
Subject: IQ test

It's times like this that one wonders what one ever did to deserve being part of a family like this . . .

BTW, Mark, did you do okay on the other I.Q. test?

✉✉✉

From: Mark
Subject: IQ test

Aye, Paddy, I got 88% on the first try and 100% on the second. But I cheated because I did it when my brain was already awake. You see, I have 119 sheep and lambs. So every morning, I traipse out into the Iowa sunrise, and I start my day with the following brain exercise:

Sheep, sheep, sheep, lamb, sheep, lamb, black sheep, sheep, sheep, lamb, lamb, lamb, oh dammit. Start over.

Sheep, black sheep, sheep, lamb, sheep, lamb, sheep, sheep, sheep, lamb, lamb lamb, oh dammit. Stand still. Start over.

Sheep, sheep, lamb, sheep, lamb, sheep, lamb, sheep, lamb, black sheep, oh dammit. Shit. Start over.

I keep doing this until I have counted all 119 as they should be. My doctor friends are evenly split on whether this retards the onset of Alzheimer's disease, as does your brain exercise, or actually encourages it.

Wait, what did you want to know?

✉✉✉

From: Pat
Subject: IQ test

Ciccio and Mark, you guys crack me up.

✉✉✉

From: P.T.
Subject: IQ test

What about me?

✉✉✉✉✉✉✉✉✉✉✉✉✉

From: Mary
Subject: Papa Bear

Hello Buoys and Gulls, The eye doctor told Dad he had good news and bad news. The good news: the doc could fix his vision so both his eyes would be 20-25. The bad news: he wouldn't get to see the doctor anymore. Dad laughed and patted the doc's shoulder to show he appreciated the humor. He looks so good! You won't believe he's going to be 91.

I scolded him about his swollen legs and he told me to calm down. I would have laughed but I was pointing out a red sore that was splitting open, and it looked to me, Dr. Mary, like one of those leg ulcers that never heal.

Dad reads everything you might care to send. He's totally current on the news whether it's Fort Dodge or the world. His memory is better than mine. That's not saying much, I guess. Then let me say, his memory is better than a lot of people in their 54s.

Mike went for a walk this morning and saw a mother deer and baby and my encounter with wildlife today was to have a hummingbird so close to me I could see its tongue! And its little toenails. Also, I spoke a few words to a turkey this morning as it ambled through the yard. And no, the turkey was not Mike.

Dad's computer is really irritating. I have taken it into Joe twice now. And I had Frontiernet out here. Each says it's the other's fault, but both agree it's the computer's fault. I asked if they could put aside their differences and find a solution for this poor old dying man who uses it as his main and nearly only connection to his concerned and loving children. In the meantime, I will be at the pawn shop looking for a used bazooka. In case no one else can fix it, I will.

I probably have more to say but you need to be patient. When the time is right, I will release more info. (When I remember is when the time is right.) Love, MMM

✉✉✉

From: Mark
Subject: Papa Bear

Mary, Mary, Why was the hummingbird sticking out its tongue at you? What did you say to it? Why can't you just let these things go, with the animals? Why does it always have to end like this?

✉✉✉✉✉✉✉✉✉✉✉✉✉

From: Ciccio
Subject: rabbits

Hi. Everything is good at Route 4. The only bad thing is that Mary canceled the cable TV service so I can't watch FOX News.

P.T., you would be shocked at the audacity of the local rabbits. They must've gotten word that all the guns had been removed from the property. There were no less than six of them sunning themselves in the back yard today. I could tell by the looks on their little faces that they felt quite safe. Love, Ciccio

⊠⊠⊠

From: P.T.
Subject: rabbits

Dear Ciccio,

Those rabbits are a bunch of greedy little opportunistic bastards. Wait until they find out the new owner's husband is none other than Major Monzo, a retired Navy Seal with too much time on his hands and a trunkful of explosives. It won't be long before those freeloading bark-biters pack it in and move to Story City.

⊠⊠⊠

From: Mark
Subject: chocolate Easter bunnies

I am distressed to think you would wish them on me. I don't even like chocolate Easter bunnies. And those spherical shapes are Easter Bunny eggs, laid by Christian rabbits at this time of the year. If you break them open, you will find that they are chocolate inside.

They are considered a sign of dental decay, and remind us of the importance of the "seasonal" aisle at Wal-mart.

People think rabbits are "cute" but in actuality they are a race of vicious, wanton baby tree-killers.

Knowing that some of your branches of the family take kindly to rabbits, I will not go into detail about my efforts to punish them for their devilish evil ways. Suffice it to say that my Book of Rabbit Punishments and Recipes was handed down from Dad, and from his dad before him, in the original Italian.

✉✉✉

From: Matt
Subject: rabbits

I must agree with your assessment, Mark. We got an adorable Minilop rabbit for Jack. It was supposed to be a girl rabbit and it was supposed to reach the size of a guinea pig. Well, it's a boy rabbit and it is nearly as big as our Golden Retriever. It has long floppy ears—its only redeeming quality—and a nasty disposition. We are fortunate not to have been sued by people who've put their hand in the cage to pet it. I'm thinking of releasing it in the wild where, with any luck, something bigger will take care of it.

In fact, since we just got back from vacation, we have retrieved the retriever, the cat, and the rabbit. Kitty was declawed and spayed while we were gone. Would like to have had some sort of surgery on the rabbit, but couldn't think of any electives.

✉✉✉

From: P.T.
Subject: rabbits

Dear Mark, I surmise from the tone of your e-mail that you have become disenchanted with rabbits. Or perhaps your most recent harey problem has served to arouse a preexisting subliminal bile towards our hoppy little friends.

You must understand that these misguided lagomorphs mean no personal affront to you or your trees. It is quite simply a matter of survival for them.

I did a little research to see what, if any, solutions might be available for this gnawing issue. There were many ideas purported to keep bunnies from eating pine trees.

By far the most successful approach is quite straightforward. You need only mix coyotes in with your mulch (one coyote per ten yards of mulch is most efficacious). That should keep the rabbits away. Don't thank me until you have tried this. I have my doubts about the practicality of this method. But go ahead, see for yourself.

⊠⊠⊠

From: Mark
Subject: rabbits

Maggio, I am very sorry about your job. I don't use the word "sucks" in the colloquial meaning, and I encourage my students to avoid it because it is filthy and noncreative, but if I did, I would say that the world sucks.

At least you're not a rabbit. This is a notice from my college:

"The Vet Tech Program is looking for rabbit volunteers for an exotics class. The vet tech students will be practicing rabbit handling, physical examinations, and blood draws. If you have a rabbit that would like to volunteer, please call 555-1234."

My concern, if I were a rabbit—apart from how they knew I "would like to volunteer"—would not become urgent until I got past the "rabbit handling" part. That would be okay. I believe my concern would become more animated when we got to the "practice blood draws" part of the morning.

So there you have it. At least we are not rabbits. The world sucks for them, too. Allahu Akbar!

Punky, could you kindly forward this to your Katie and Jason and Liz? Rabbit lovers everywhere will be aghast.

⊠⊠⊠

From: P.T.
Subject: rabbits

Okay, guys, this is a true story.

One of my assistants took her four-year-old nephew to Mass on Good Friday. As a part of the service they were acting out The Passion. The little fella was soaking it all in and would ask her questions every now and then. He seemed to really like the part when they all shouted, "Release Barabbus!" A little later she asked if he was doing okay. He said, "Yes, but when do they release the rabbits?"

⊠⊠⊠

From: Pat
Subject: rabbits

After reading all the rabbit e-mails, I recalled that when Punky used to get mad at me (like when I ate the bottoms off her newly baked cupcakes and neatly replaced the frosting tops) she would banish me to my room and with great emphasis she would say, "You wrabbit." What was that about?

⊠⊠⊠

From: Punky
Subject: what I am up against . . .

See attached photo showing a ruined canister of "rabbit repellant granules."

That was a brand-new canister. The rabbits ate nearly all the granules as well as most of the canister.

I tend to think they are also sending me a message, along the lines of "up yours."

Mark. You said mothballs would keep them away. Despite buying a fortune's worth of mothballs, there isn't a mothball left in the yard. Not one. Overnight they carry them away to their burrows. Keeping moths out of their fur coats, no doubt.

I'm going to have to start trapping them and then find some ethnic group that likes to eat rabbit or that will do work in exchange for some chubby rabbits. Or, hey, it's okay—they don't have to work. Just take the rabbits.

⋈⋈⋈

From: Pat
Subject: what I am up against . . .

OMG, you're so cute. I laughed and laughed . . . and then you drop the ethnic bomb.

⋈⋈⋈

From: Kevin
Subject: what I am up against . . .

Why don't you simply give them back their land? K

⋈⋈⋈

From: Ciccio
Subject: rabbits

Ro, Calm down. And no more coffee tonight!

⋈⋈⋈

From: P.T.
Subject: what I am up against . . .

Bastards! All of them! I went out and bought some fox urine (I had to meet a fox in an alley and he went behind a dumpster with a cup) in an attempt to save my flora. The idea is to make them think there is a stinky fox predator so they move away. The other thing I would try is to put the mothballs in the neighbors yard.

This is P.T. Maggio and I approve this message.

⊠⊠⊠

From: Mark
Subject: what I am up against . . .

Dear Punky, I think Monty Python did a documentary about the vicious rabbits.

Now as for Jason, who is an in-law, at most, I have forwarded his "explosives" solution to the Department of Homeland Security for their clearance and information.

His other viciously anti-rabbit statements have been forwarded to the southern California PETA league. Their e-mail sent an auto-reply. Evidently, they are busy sweeping up after the pit-bull they turned loose in Santa Monica found the minks they turned loose in the Valley. The "meet-up" was not pretty. Their auto-reply said Cody, Director of Rabbit Anti-Defamation, would get back to us in a few days, or after all the minks have been eaten by the pit-bull, whichever comes first.

⊠⊠⊠

From: P.T.
Subject: what I am up against . . .

I have had to cancel the remainder of my appointments today because I can't stop laughing. You knuckleheads!

⊠⊠⊠⊠⊠⊠⊠⊠⊠⊠⊠⊠⊠

From: Mark
Subject: crocodile pictures

Mary, Some of your photos of birds and storks and vultures and crocodiles are so good they almost look real.

However, my students have taught me that nothing in society is real anymore. Every real thing is actually a virtual thing. Even real things aren't really real, like people I thought were 12-year-old girls in Boone are actually 35-year-old

Internet male pedophiles in San Francisco. My students taught me about photoshopping and shopphotographing and photographicshopping on the computer, and facebook and bookoffaces and faceshopping and photobooking and facebookshopping and MySpace and MyFaceBook and My-photo-shop-face, and so on. After they were done explaining it all to me, I realized that none of them were actually my students. I just thought they were. A few of the larger ones said they were interested in learning how to read and write and cipher, and they wondered if I was that kind of teacher.

So is the croc real or virtually real?

✉✉✉

From: Punky
Subject: was this photoshopped?

And what about these donkeys and zebras? Are they photoshopped? Or do I believe my own lying eyes?

✉✉✉

From: Mark
Subject: was this photoshopped?

Dear Punky, This photo was most assuredly not done in the photoshop. Neither donkeys nor zebras have the cloven hoof, so when they go to the photoshop they can't get the door open. I would have thought you could figure that out on your own. You can see their hooves in the photo.

I suppose they must have developed the film themselves. I'm not sure.

✉✉✉

From: Matt
Subject: attachments

How sad that I couldn't open this attachment. It's even sadder that I cannot open many attachments. Most sad that I can barely function on a computer.

Thanks for the thought though. I hope and pray that your attachments are things that a good Christian would like to see. If you can format them differently, I would be much obliged.

⊠⊠⊠

From: Pat
Subject: attachments

I too had a little trouble opening "Why I Like Florida" and "Nary a Tanline," Matt. Both wholesome family-rated clips. The trouble was I just couldn't open them fast enough. Was that your problem, too?

⊠⊠⊠

From: Ciccio
Subject: attachments

The item downloaded and opened, but there were no pictures. I let my imagination run rampant for a while, but it would be better if you resent it. Thanks, C.

⊠⊠⊠

From: Matt
Subject: attachments

But where would we be without e-mails? For one thing, we cannot interrupt each other this way.

⊠⊠⊠

From: P.T.
Subject: attachments

Why are you people all so dear and so damn funny. Matt, you are correct, this e-mailing is a great thing. I anticipate each day with gusto because of what I might find in my inbox.

Hey, me and the wif are going to be in Bloomington over the weekend when Kedin graces us with his presence. I know you guys are busier than a zipper on Prom night but . . . ?

⊠⊠⊠

From: Kevin
Subject: attachments

I see that my resent, revised e-mail did not "send." I'm ready to get out the bazooka and blow up my computer. A day without a three-hour phone chat with a techie in India would be like a day without, oh, I don't know, a knitting needle in my temple.

⊠⊠⊠

From: P.T.
Subject: computers

Buenos dias! Can I borrow your bazooka when you're done?

I downloaded a simulcast thing from MSNBC so I could follow the Iowa-Creighton game at the office. It worked really cool-like for a while, but then the unthinkable happened.

The big gray box appeared and said something to the effect, "Paul, you ignorant moron, you brainless cretin, you are dumb beyond stupid. What makes you think you can use this computer for the purpose for which it is intended? You just earned yourself a FATAL ERROR, bucko! You better close every program you have open, or have ever opened, or have ever even thought about opening, or plan to open in the future."

I took the hint and clicked on close. To my consternation, the same box appeared again, this time with a knife sticking out of a heart with blood running out of it. At this point everything locked up tighter than a new jar of pickles. My mouse was having a D-Con OD. I finally had to shut down the power and, of all heinous acts, close windows improperly. I ran every defrag, scan disk, troubleshooting mother I could find. I deleted all temporary Internet files, said three rosaries and four novenas, and finally I think it's okay. Last time I ever download *that* program.

✉✉✉

From: Mark
Subject: and then there's Facebook

Dear Punky, I went to the bookstore to buy the FACEBOOK to see Peppe's face, as you instructed, but the 12-year-old clerk said she does not sell it. She said you just have to open it. "How can I open it if you don't have it?" I inquired. She said it's not really a book; they just call it a book. "Well, if it's not a book, how can I open it?" She said they had it but it was on their computer. I asked her to get it down from the computer and let me look at it. Now she was getting that irritated-12-year-old-clerk look on her face. It's not a book. You don't open it, she said, you just subscribe to it. "And they'll send it to me?" I asked plaintively. No, there's nothing to send! Just subscribe to it and open it! I told her I want to read the FACEBOOK so I can have more friends. Especially friends whom I have never met and who might be lying about their age, gender, and felony conviction record. I told her I need more social networking and that this FACEBOOK would give me more social networking friends, but I would never have to be in the same room with them, or actually meet them, unless we could meet with a police detective at a cheap motel . . .

As you can see, I never got the FACEBOOK. Just send me a photo of Peppe, okay?

✉✉✉

From: Matt
Subject: and then there's Facebook

What a FUN E-MAIL, THANKS. hAD A REAL NICE WEEKEND, hate the Caps lock.

✉✉✉

From: Ciccio
Subject: caps lock

Someone needs to step up and move the "Caps Lock" button to somewhere south of hell. Not only is it a totally useless command, but the location of the button is some nerd's dirty trick of a legacy.

The only one of us who doesn't give a hoot is Punky. She is capable of typing 150 characters a second with duct tape around her eyes, ears, fingers, and knees. Her aside, I think we should get the Caps LOCK BUTTON MOVED. Damn it! We need to let the whole Country know the truth . . . the bUSH aDMINISTRATION SET tHE INTERNET uP SO THAT wE ALL WOULD hAVE TO DEAL WITH THE cAPS lock FUNCTION. tHIS WILL KEEP A LOT OF lIBERALS BUSY.

✉✉✉

From: P.T.
Subject: caps lock

dEAR frank, I wish just for once you'd tell us how you really feel.
I was glad to know that I'm not the only one who thinks that the "Caps Lock" button should be in the next room.

iN c%se you AREE wond^^^ig, I haave been usingv a sVedish key&bort all dees yars. vUrks for*** me.

✉✉✉✉✉✉✉✉✉✉✉✉✉✉

CHAPTER 3

A Questionable Chapter in Which We Are Hazy on the Distinction Between Memoir and Big Fat Lies

Haircuts and Hats
Paul

In the infancy of dentistry as a profession, it was common for a dentist not only to fix and pull teeth but also to cut hair and maybe even shoe horses on the side. Once they bought that contraption of a dental chair, they must have wanted to make it pay off—although the guy who came up with the misguided notion he could use it to work on horses probably regretted it.

Today dentists restrict themselves to doing treatment specific to the oral cavity. In fact, the profession has become so sophisticated that there are more than eight types of specialists to deal with an area no bigger than your mouth.

Dad embraced dentistry around the time that dentists began concentrating on doing only the job they were trained for. But Dad must have been cut from the same mold as those old-time dentists because he raised horses and ponies on the side, was frequently the farrier's assistant when our horses needed shoes, and even pitched a mean horseshoe.

He also harbored another, more sinister connection to his predecessors. He believed he was meant to give haircuts.

Dad kept a mysterious shoe box in the cupboard above the refrigerator. When we saw him going for that box, we disappeared like mice through a crack.

Sooner or later, perhaps by trickery, he'd corner one of us six boys and position us on a chair in the kitchen. The box was now sitting on the counter, and we were able to glimpse its contents. The most ominous item was a thick black electrical cord attached to a shiny silver device about the size of a good pair of brass knuckles. On the end opposite the cord protruded something that looked like a hedge trimmer only with sharper teeth. We could also see scissors, the kind that were once silver but were now brown either due to oxidation or dried blood. Some of the other articles in the box might have been left over from the days when dentists shod horses. So when he asked, "Are you ready to get your ears lowered?" you wanted to answer, "No, but I *am* ready to change my pants."

A couple of the less threatening items in the shoe box were the container of talcum powder and the barber's brush. I actually liked both of them because they were soft, and when he used them, you knew the session was nearly over. In the bottom of the box was the plastic apron, which was as much a restraining device as anything else.

After sitting shirtless under that handy apron for half an hour, we'd get so sweaty that when the apron came off and he shook it, voilà—! we were breaded in our own hair clippings. That created the collateral trauma of knowing we'd need a shower sometime in the next week.

Dad's time in the military must have influenced his barbering philosophy because when he finished, there wasn't a hair left standing. On the upside, it promised months between haircuts. He usually discovered a wood tick or two once he got down to the scalp, and of course, there was no cover for head lice. Once when I fell and put a nice gash in the back of my head, the doctor didn't even have to shave my head to stitch me up. So it wasn't all bad.

Once you were talcumed and brushed, there was one more thing to do before crawling into bed. Dad sent us to find another head for his hungry clippers, in the way perhaps that Dr. Frankenstein might have said to his assistant, "Igor, find me another head for my monster."

In time Dad worked his magic on all six of us. We'd mope around for the next week with the forlorn look of freshly shorn sheep. Everyone except for me, that is. I had discovered hats.

Once that lightbulb came on, I was rarely hatless. I felt naked when I couldn't wear a hat to school or church—the very times when you needed one the most.

Today, if I'm not in the office or at a dress-up affair, odds are I'll be wearing a hat. I never thought much about it until a friend said, nodding toward my baseball cap, "Gee, Doc, for a year after I met you, I thought you had male-pattern baldness." As the years have passed, the ozone layer has thinned, and the experts are telling us to wear hats. I thank Dad for giving me a head start.

....

What one loves in childhood stays in the heart forever.—Mary Jo Putney

....

Desperately Seeking Sugar Paul and Mark

Sweets were a real treat to us. We lived miles from the candy stores in town, and with a dentist for a father, we didn't have any around the house. Halloween was consequently considered a holy day to us and was preceded by a reverent anticipation.

For the entire month leading up to this glorious day of days, we worked on perfecting our costumes. The possibilities were endless, as long as you wanted to be a bum, a pirate, or a pirate bum. We gathered the necessary makeup supplies, which consisted solely of charcoal, and rifled through the large storage room for props.

Sometimes we trick-or-treated the entire neighborhood, sneaked back into the basement, changed costumes, and went around again.

We were giddy with our haul. Like a cat bringing a dead mouse to its master, we dutifully went straight to the living room and disgorged our bags onto the floor at Mom's feet.

We never seemed to learn, or perhaps we thought this was how the game was played, but inevitably Mom used her powers of eminent domain to confiscate what we believed was personal property. And once Mom got the candy, it went into some black hole.

We never saw it again, never tasted its sugary waste calories, never saw anyone eating it, never found wrappers in the trash—nothing. Mom was good. She left no tracks. To this day, we don't know if she was looking out for our health or if she had some nefarious destination for the candy stash.

When any of us found ourselves alone in the kitchen, we climbed on the counters and rummaged through the cupboards, just in case a change of policy had left them rife with treats.

I once found a huge package of chocolate: the mother lode. I looked over both shoulders to see if anyone was watching. That was standard operating procedure because in a family of ten there was always somebody pussyfooting around.

The coast clear, I noiselessly teased open the package and broke off a smooth dark square. I sank my teeth into it—and was rewarded with the most bitter of disappointments. Damn if I hadn't found Baker's unsweetened chocolate. Fortunately, the antidote was nearby in the form of shredded coconut, the sweetest thing in the house.

So that's what we'd find: Baker's chocolate, coconut, a rogue marshmallow now and then, and, in the later years, artificial sweeteners like saccharin and industrial sweets like marshmallow "fluff" whose ingredients have still not been disclosed to the government.

Soda pop was expressly prohibited, although 7 Up was sometimes available for medicinal purposes. "Mom, I don't feel good. My stomach hurts."

"Here. Take one cup of 7 Up and call me in the morning."

If you were feeling really not good, she'd dump a tablespoon of baking soda in the 7 Up and let you shoot it down at the moment of greatest fulmination. Eventually, there would be an enormous egress of gas from the drinker's mouth, and they would feel better. Or maybe not.

We had two possibilities of gaining access to real candy. The drive-in theater just down the road had a dandy snack parade, and if we talked nice to the ticket person, she let us in without a ticket for the sole purpose of buying candy. It was a dangerous mission though, so whoever drew the short straw took orders and collected money. They had to get out of the house and off the property undetected. Ride their bike on busy Highway 169 at night, in the dark, without lights, wearing black clothes. Sweet-talk the ticket lady. Buy the snacks—and you better get the order right. Return home without being hit by a car, or caught by a mom and scheduled for a rehabilitation session.

There was also Otho Corners, a rudimentary predecessor to today's convenience stores. The sorties here involved many of the same risks as the drive-in theater, except that we could go there in daylight, we could go as a group, and we didn't have to ride on the highway. On the downside, it was four miles by gravel road.

Given all this, you can perhaps appreciate our feelings about what happened one summer in the mid-1960s.

One of our neighbors was a bit of an entrepreneur. He had a regular job, but he also bought, sold, hatched, raised, butchered, traded, fed, ate, and cared for hundreds of small farm animals and poultry contained under a huge syntax of chicken wire fencing. We liked him, within reason, because he taught us a lot about raising poultry and operating incubators.

Eventually, he branched out, opening a Dixie Cream Donuts store in town. Business was good. There weren't many places locally to buy doughnuts, and he had a nice product.

One day when Dad sent Matt, Mark, and me to borrow some chicken equipment from that neighbor, we found him in his garage. What we also found in his garage were boxes of doughnuts stacked in a corner. I believe Mark let out an audible gasp. It seemed our neighbor brought home all the day-old doughnuts from the Dixie Cream shop and fed them to his ducks and pheasants and sheep.

As it happened, they liked sugary and fatty treats as much as we did but, being in cages and pens, they had trouble getting a sugar fix on their own. We were sympathetic. To a point.

The three of us had but a single thought: plunder, pillage, and loot! Back at home base—the basement—we established our strategy (loosely, KISS) and time frame (loosely, ASAP).

In line with Keep It Simple, Stupid, as soon as darkness fell and the coast was clear, we ran like hell into that garage, grabbed some doughnuts, and ran like hell back to the toolshed (it was thought unwise to risk the doughnuts in the house).

We were careful to leave enough doughnuts of each variety, like the chocolate-frosted ones, the peanut-covered long johns, and so on, just in case our neighbor was feeding a certain type of doughnut to a particular group of chickens or ducks. Even so, each sortie provided a plentiful assortment of doughnuts. We became so complacent we didn't even bother with the boring doughy parts. We just lapped up the toppings and cream fillings, then discarded the dregs.

We occasionally brought in help, posting a neighbor boy as lookout, but this created problems in dividing our spoils. How many doughnuts exactly was a lookout boy worth? Issues of compensation, inventory, and equity were involved.

Although the raids continued all summer, the chickens and ducks still grew big and fat. Had we not eaten all those day-old doughnuts, some of those ducks would have developed coronary artery disease. All in all, helping ourselves to those doughnuts was the best thing for everyone involved. In the years since, we've never found doughnuts to equal them.

....

"Which one are you?" is a question the members of big families hear all the time . . . . Growing up in a big family you're surrounded by people a lot like you—you share rooms and friends, take the same bus to school, learn to swim or ski or sing together; your voices sound alike; people say you have the same hair or eyes. Despite what some may think, group identity can be very liberating. It allows you to focus on the things that are unique to you . . . . Being in a big family forces you to develop those special traits early. After all, who will you say you are if someone asks?—Julie, Liz, Sheila, Monica, and Lian Dolan

....

Hey, Do You Kids Need Three Hundred Wild Ducks?
Mark

One of Dad's patients—a farmer we'll call Mr. Polachek—came in for some dental work. Well, actually, to get his tongue trimmed. As he got older, Mr. Polachek was sure his tongue was swelling up. It felt as if it filled his entire mouth. He could feel areas on his tongue that needed to be trimmed off.

Dad told him there was nothing wrong with his tongue. "Just stop thinking about it," he said.

Dad loved his farmer patients, so after the dental (and lingual) activities were completed, there was always a little visiting. Mr. Polachek told Dad that three hundred wild mallard ducks had taken up residence in his cattle loafing shed, without being invited. They loved it there because there were no cattle in the shed just now, there was a duck-friendly swampy area nearby, and spilled corn in the loafing shed allowed the ducks to gorge on it, as ducks will do. It was the perfect home for them.

But whenever Mr. Polachek entered the shed—where he expected to put cattle one of these days—huge flocks of ducks exploded in a dusty, furious, flapping barrage of swearing and quacking. After flying around excitedly outside, they came right back into the shed. Mr. Polachek naturally wondered how his cattle could get any loafing done with the duck hubbub.

He generously said Dad could have the ducks if he wanted them.

That evening, Dad approached Matt and me, who were in the business of buying and selling chickens, ducks, geese, and other assorted fowls. We saw ourselves as poultry barons—the Rockefeller of Cornish-Rocks, the JP Morgan of mallards. "Do you guys need three hundred wild ducks?" Dad asked. "They're free."

"Yes, we do," was our immediate answer.

"What are you going to do with them?" Dad asked.

We told him we'd have to think about it and that our people would get back to his people in the morning—whereupon we commenced figuring out what to do with three hundred free wild ducks.

Matt and I sold ducklings and mature ducks to folks who wanted to raise them, but we also had many inquiries from people who wanted tasty free-range ducks for their home freezer. We scoured our customer records and decided we could probably sell all three hundred ducks if we could catch them and get them butchered and packaged and frozen.

The closest duck butcher was in Swea City, seventy-five miles away. We got a duck appointment and enlisted Dad's help in catching the wild ducks and driving them up to Swea City.

The butcher told us that if his people had to package the ducks, it would cost an extra ten cents per duck. A dime a duck was nothing to sneeze at, so Dad came up with an idea. When a friend's local meatpacking plant had gone out of business, Dad had taken home a stack of heavy-duty, plastic, food-grade bags printed "Gus Glaser's Bavarian Ring Bologna." With a large family, Dad bought in bulk and against future contingencies. He knew that one day we would need ring bologna bags. That day was here.

At the appointed time, a cool Iowa autumn morning well before daybreak, Dad and Matt and I plodded through the swampy areas of Mr. Polachek's cattle yard toward the intruder ducks. Inside the loafing shed, the wild ducks were gorging themselves on leftover corn, just as we expected. They looked peaceable and dispassionate. Matt and I gave each other a look: so far, so good. I'm not sure what Dad, being older and wiser, thought at that moment.

What followed in the next hour does not lend itself readily to the written word. Until now, history has no record of any mass "wild duck in barn" captures, and my own memory has selectively forgotten much of the violence.

We sensibly began by herding them into a corner, the better to catch them. Showing their displeasure, they detonated upward in a blast of multi-duck flight. Wings and currents flipped us over into the cow pies, which the cattle had so thoughtlessly left in our way.

When we managed to catch a duck, it beat us about the head and chin with strong—and surprisingly bony—wings. Whack, whack, whack. A nice rhythmic beating is what I remember. Duck after duck, every one just beat the daylights out of me. Some of them got you in the esophagus—bang, bang, bang, right on the old Adam's apple. Others went for your private parts. Say no more. I wanted morphine. And I was only twelve.

Some ducks seemed able to gain altitude if their wings were free, even if we were holding on to their body. I was not a very heavy little boy, and I am pretty sure I lifted off a couple of times.

Discussing the episode later, we decided the ducks must have seen Daffy Duck cartoons. Just as I dove to grab a duck, it smiled and stepped to the side, causing me to crash headlong into a wall or a post and bounce off. Just like the cartoons. With my head flattened, no less. And then there was the old duck standby, the bill to the eye. As I tried to catch a duck, it aimed at my head, like a Boeing 747 planning to fly right through my brain. Instead, at the last minute, its pointy little bill would drill into my eye. I was punk'd and pok'd.

I'm leaving out the part about what ducks do when they get excited or nervous or, actually, when they are just being ducks. But our clothes and shoes were ruined, and later I took a boot scraper into the shower with me.

We managed to catch them all, dress them, bag them, freeze them, and ultimately deliver them to folks for their Sunday dinner. We made good money on the deal and, except for the injuries we sustained, we saw it as a success. Although . . .

"I wanted a duck, not ring bologna," said Mrs. Schlichtensteiner.

"I assure you that it is a duck, Mrs. Schlichtensteiner."

"But it says, 'Bavarian Ring Bologna.' It's not a duck."

"You've got to trust me, Mrs. Schlichtensteiner, I'm a twelve-year-old boy, and I swear to you, it's a duck. It looks like a duck and feels like a duck, doesn't it?"

"Well, we do like ring bologna too."

For Less Than Twenty-five Dollars
Rosalie

When we were growing up, horses seemed like a good idea to someone. Mother? Dad? I don't know if it was a case of keeping us busy and out of the house or an attempt to tire us out. I'm also fuzzy about how the first horse came to live with us. Was the barn built and then needed horses? Or did the horses start arriving and need a barn? What's clearer to me are the years when the pasture was dotted with Dad's bargain-basement horses.

He used to go to the sale barn on Friday nights and bring home any equine that (a) still had all four legs and could switch its tail and (b) cost less than twenty-five dollars. Way less. Dad figured he had done well if the horse didn't die on the way home.

With his standards, "horses" was a ragged saddle blanket of a term that covered a disparate group of highly individual and generally ill-behaved animals.

Meriweather, a miniature pony (and imagine how small that would be) had only one working eye—the other eye was glass and was not a good match at that.

The swaybacked Tennessee Walker had huge growths on the inside of her forelegs—fairly off-putting unless you were too many kids with too few horses, in which case Duchess looked pretty good.

Duchess achieved family-legend status the day Mother invited all the nuns to an end-of-the-school-year picnic at our house. When you have eight kids trotting through a school system, you feel it incumbent on you to make nice with those who suffer with them all year. Mother's annual hospitality was at once an act of penitence for the past and a down payment on the future.

It was only slightly windy the day that Duchess and the nuns crossed paths, but there was enough of a breeze to flirt with the nuns' long black veils. Duchess, who had two good eyes but, as horses do, on opposite sides of the head, turned her head left and saw something disturbing up in the yard. When her other eye confirmed the nearby presence of black-robed creatures, parts of which were twitching, fluttering, and waving, she was certain that her life depended upon getting over a fence taller than she was. We were staggered by what, in other circumstances, would be called a levitation, a miracle, a Lipizzan-like astonishment.

We enjoyed Duchess's performance rather too much and were sent to our rooms for riffing on the incident. "We *told* you those nuns are scary. Even a dumb horse . . ."

Blaze, an unbroken quarter horse, broke Dad's thumb. Beauty (we had all read *Black Beauty*, but our hopes for a silky black horse that had been mistreated and that we would redeem were never realized, so we had to make do with calling the stocky pinto Beauty) never saw a rider that she didn't immediately free-associate with "tree." We got to be pretty good at holding up the offside leg when she tried to brush us off on the apricot tree, the apple tree, the mulberry tree, the . . . well, any tree. If a visiting child annoyed us, we helpfully boosted them up onto Beauty.

Beulah was probably the meanest-tempered buckskin in six counties, but she had legs, she moved, and if you were tenacious and conscious every minute of where her teeth were, she wasn't a bad ride.

Our tack was also sale-barn bargain material with the advantage that it was in such bad shape we never had to clean it, and anyway, riding bareback was easier and quicker than saddling something.

I actually had a decent horse once—a registered American Saddle Horse, officially named Princess Red Cloud, informally called Lady. She was my companion and my ride on endless explorations of empty country gravel roads where I could practice being cool. By that I mean smoking. I wasn't sure whether I wanted anyone to see me or not, trotting along on Lady while puffing on a Lark. But I was cool.

Lady died while I was in college, and although they told me it was colic, I always suspected it was secondhand smoke.

....

Valentine's Day e-mail from Mom:

Dear loved ones, sending all our love with this note, for
the nice things you do & say. You are all so thoughtful
and fun to laugh with & talk to & to share your good
news with. Thanks for your lifelong love and we'll pray
your loved ones will be as good to you.

....

God Loves Him Even If He Does Have Bedbugs
Mark

A constant irritant and massive waste of time in my youth was riding the
big orange school bus. For many years, we spent two or three hours a day,
every day, on the bus. It stunted my human development. In fact, when I
got to college, I got a C—in Human Development.

Riding the bus all those mind-numbing hours caused an across-the-board
dumbing down of the kids confined by its tedious route. By the time we
reached school, the teachers had all they could do to get us back to the level
of thinking we had possessed when we left the breakfast table.

Every couple of years, we convinced Mom to mount an objection to the bus
schedule and its implicit encouragement of stupidity. She called numerous
nameless school bureaucrats to ask politely if there was any way to reduce
our dumbing down time or if we could be put on the foul orange conveyance
at any point later in the route.

The responses were not encouraging. "You live out in the country. You are
at the beginning of the route in the morning. But strangely enough, you
are end of the route in the afternoon. You live on a paved road. You live on
the wrong side of town. Your kids might be in the wrong school. The bus
can only drive on the right-hand side of the road, if you are the driver. We
cannot change the route because the door is on the wrong side of the bus.
We don't know why that is. Your house is on the left-hand side of the road,
but only after the winter solstice. The bus has to go south before it goes north

because of the rotation of the Earth. We will be happy to change the route if you ever have one girl in fourth grade and three boys all in seventh grade at the same time. The bus schedule and route is set forth in the Constitution and cannot be changed except by a vote of two-thirds of the States."

Mom gave up for another year or two before asking the same question. Bureaucracy, we were told, carries within it the seeds of its own destruction, or so we hoped. We became childhood fans of limited government.

But it was on that awful bus that we came into contact with kids from neighborhoods and home environments different from our own.

Sometimes we reported what we saw and heard to the authorities (Mom and Dad) but most often, wanting to avoid the stool pigeon label, we kept our own confidence. One boy, whom I will call Hugo Winterhalter (not the conductor and musician), was from a poor family who lived in a ramshackle house on our big orange bus route. Members of this family were not known to bathe or shower too often. This boy Hugo was of interest to us because he was bullied as often as we were, and we wanted to take his "side" in the violent, but daily, bus fights. However, there were a few details about Hugo that we wanted to clarify before proposing any cooperative arrangements or mutual understandings.

"Mom, Hugo has open sores and boils on the back of his neck and his arms. Should we still be his friends?" She called the school nurse who said, "Don't worry, they are just bedbug bites that got infected. Your boys won't get those sores."

Hugo confirmed that he had many bedbugs, and this satisfied us. But then we got to wondering. Why don't we have any bedbugs at our house? Our teacher, Mrs. Finekettle, explained, "Don't worry, the only reason he has bedbugs is because he wets the bed so often. You don't wet the bed anymore, so you won't get bedbugs from Hugo." Again, that satisfied Matthew and me, in the way that only little boys can be satisfied.

Upon further reflection, however, we began to wonder. Why is Hugo still wetting the bed even though we are all well into the long-pants phase of our lives? Putting that question to Mother, she replied that he was still wetting the bed because every day on the bus the bullies were beating him into a semi-liquid pulp. We wondered whether we should be his friends—nonbathing, bed-wetting, bedbugged, boiled, infected, beaten as he was. "What do you think, Mom, should we be his friends?"

Mom drew from her strong Christian upbringing; and in remarks that seemed to have been inspired by the Sermon on the Mount, except maybe the bed-wetting part, she summed up her feelings on the subject: "God created Hugo just as He created you. Hugo is a child of God, as you are."

"What about the bedbugs?"

"God loves you all just the same. It doesn't matter whether the Winterhalters live in a big mansion or a shack. I think you should be nice to Hugo and be his friend when you can."

That was about as clear a doctrinal statement as a fourth-grader was going to get. So we befriended Hugo as best we could. We were bullied and beaten, our lunches and our wallets were taken, and through it all we tried to be nice to Hugo, based on Saint Paul's First Letter to the Corinthians, et cetera.

Then one day on the bus, we noticed that Hugo's family had a quarantine notice posted on their house. They had tuberculosis, which could have been a dirty word or a private part because Mother and Dad always referred to it as TB. We weren't sure.

And so round 15 of the questioning began. "Mom, Hugo has TB. Should we still be his friends?"

Saving the Younger Children From Danger
Mary

P.T. and I were babysitting Matt and Mark one sunny summer afternoon while Mom was at her bridge club and Dad was at work. The others were gone.

Mark and Matt came running up to the house, waving their arms, screaming and yelling and pointing toward the toolshed. They managed to gasp that there were two humongous snakes lounging on the cement dog run in the enclosed dog kennel. P.T. and I went to look. We came running up to the house, waving our arms, screaming and yelling and pointing toward the toolshed. But it turned out that we were the oldest ones home that day. There was no one older to tell. Oops.

First, we grabbed the ever-handy multipurpose machete. Never leave home without it was our motto. We also got a large heavy crowbar, a big ol' sledgehammer, a shovel, a spade, maybe a trowel or two, a few regular hammers, some bricks, a claw hammer, an assortment of our own personal pocketknives, an oversize rasp, and one of those horse toenail clippers with the long handles. Some of these tools weighed more than we did, but we dragged them down to the reconnaissance spot.

The snakes were still basking as if it were their own kennel. Adults and the faint of heart may want to shut their eyes here. That's what we did.

Next, we tried to prod them with a long-handled shovel. After poking them, we ran like hell. Five minutes later, we cautiously approached, armed to the teeth, and there they were, just as if nothing had happened. In the meantime, Dad's hunting dog, Sheba, was going nuts, upping the tension considerably. She was barking out the door of her doghouse at the deaf snakes.

And then it finally dawned on us. Maybe they were dead. Yeah, that's it. They're dead. Ha! Stupid snakes. We weren't really afraid of them. We just didn't want Matt and Mark to get hurt.

We helped Matt and Mark up onto the roof of the toolshed where they'd be safe. Armed with the machete, the sledgehammer, and the toenail clippers, P.T. and I advanced. Looking brave on the outside, we opened the kennel gate, a chain-link affair like the rest of the kennel. The snakes were coiled tightly in a circle as big as a family-size pizza. Two of them, each about five inches around. Wait until everyone heard about this. The first rattlesnakes found in north-central Iowa!

Our antennae were stretched to the max, watching for movement. None seen. I poked the nearest snake with the sledgehammer, and lordy, lordy, it moved.

After a while, Mark and Matt yelled to us (we were up on the hill by then) that the snakes were still there and still not moving, and it was safe for us to return. We came back ready to kill or be killed in the name of our poor frightened brothers.

With the sledgehammer, we took turns hammering those snakes until they were up under that great railroad tie in the sky. Why we did what we did next, I'll never know.

We determined to hang those snakes from a tree, and we worked like devils for the rest of the afternoon toward that end. We tied a string around one's neck and tried to drag it up the hill to the tree that was right between the house and Dad's barbecue pit. I remember the twine kept breaking or slipping off the snake, so we had to use the versatile toenail clippers to hold on to the snake as we dragged it up the hill. Several hours of work finally saw the two beaten snakes hanging upside down from the tree limb. That tree was a bear to climb because it had no low branches, but we "got 'er done."

Mom and Dad came home at the same time and looked out the kitchen window to see two long things hanging from the tree with black balls around them. The black balls turned out to be flies. Can you believe it? They made us take our trophies down.

We Pass On Our Wisdom
Kevin

One autumn, the grown-up Pat and I drove from Colorado to visit Dad and, while there, decided to visit our old playground in the woods.

Matt and Laura's boys, Sam and Jack, were ten and nine at the time, the perfect age, we thought, to accompany us. Matt had taken them on numerous nature, hiking, and camping adventures; so they had some good outdoor skills.

We had heard about the knives, of course, so it wasn't surprising that when we invited them, we could read but a single thought in their eyes: The Knives.

89

After years of begging for their own pocketknives, they had gotten Matt and Laura to agree that they could have pocketknives if they used them under close supervision. Sam and Jack liked to push the envelope and, when in doubt, erred on the side of risk rather than caution. Consequently, the knives were kept in Matt's private office at his dental clinic, so the boys wouldn't have access to them.

When the question arose of the boys accompanying us, and their knives accompanying them, Laura and Matt said the boys could take their pocketknives with them but only if (a) Pat and I were one-on-one with Sam and Jack every minute and (b) the boys were given a solid grounding in the safe and proper handling of the knives.

We all went to Matt's office for a solemn rite of passage, Matt removing the two small knives from his desk drawer, entrusting them and his boys to us, and telling us again how one couldn't be too careful when Sam and Jack were involved.

Back at Dad's house, I asked Pat to give the boys the knife talk. Pat had been in Scouts with his son Cass from the time Cass was a little bitty Scout until he obtained his Eagle Scout award, so Pat had excellent wilderness skills. Dad joined the four of us at the round kitchen table as Pat and I took the knives out of their boxes, set them in the middle of the table, and carefully and dramatically opened them up.

Sam and Jack could hardly sit still.

I gave a short intro for Pat, telling the boys the ground rules their parents had set down and that Pat would begin their safety lessons now at the table with more to follow in the woods. We were all silent, not looking at Pat but mesmerized by the shiny new knives in the center of the table.

Pat is quite a talker—always has been—but he outdid himself that day. He spun an elaborate yarn that had the boys wide-eyed with awe and trepidation and Dad and me choking back our laughter.

He began it by saying solemnly, "Boys, I want to tell you the story of Three-Fingered Joe."

E-mails

From: Matt
Subject: plantings

I went out to Route 4 today and was sad to find no one there. I'm glad no one was there, because there wasn't supposed to be anyone there. Still, I was sad that none of you were there.

It dawned on me that plants might be moved to my office or home—lilac, peony, hazelnut, fern, floribunda rose, asparagus, hostas. They're all plentiful and could be separated without leaving a void. Any takers?

⊠⊠⊠

From: P.T.
Subject: plantings

Dear Matmandu, I would love to snag some asparagus from Dad's garden. His stuff is hardy and prolific (not unlike its late gardener).

Did you ever try to grow asparagus from scratch? I never, ever saw so much as a sprig. Show me a sign, Lord. Here is the deal, you buy these dried-out old plant carcasses that look like they came from King Tut's tomb, very gnarly. Now, you dig a trench not less than 5.98" deep and not more than 6.13" deep. The angle of the trench walls shall be no more or no less than 32 degrees. The soil has to be solid yet not clay-like, sandy yet not porous, rich yet not fertile, well-drained yet not too dry, dark yet not too dark. This plant likes full sun which is partly shaded from 10 till noon and again from 3:15 to 3:28. It can take winds of between 4 and 4.5 knots, no more, no less. Fertilize only on garbage day yet not with garbage. Insert the plant into the ground only on a day when the sun doesn't shine and the moon is full. For best results check on the apposition of Venus and Uranus in the seventh hour of harmonic karma. Now all you have to do is sit back and wait. I have been waiting for close to 20 years. I would like some of that already-started asparagus.

Bah for now, I love you, P.T.

✉✉✉

From: Ciccio
Subject: plantings

P.T., All of us agree that you can take as many of those asparagus plants as you want. If you dig them up with a big dirt ball around them, they will grow anywhere. Ciccio

✉✉✉

From: P.T.
Subject: plantings

Ciccio, where are you, son? Hey, thanks for the green light on the asparagus. You said I have to "dig them up with a big dirt ball around." Do you think Kenny Roberts would be available to help? Love, Gardener Guy Peet

✉✉✉

From: Matt
Subject: plantings

Forgot to say how great the house looked, Mary. You did a stellar job of organizing and cleaning and donating and throwing. There's much more to be done, but it's manageable now. Many thanks.

✉✉✉

From: Ciccio
Subject: plantings

Mary, I want to join Matt in thanking you for all that you've done in that house. I purposely didn't send this e-mail to everyone as I didn't want them to know how much you have made on the sale of all that stuff. What the heck, more power to you. And what they don't know won't hurt them.

✉✉✉✉✉✉✉✉✉✉✉✉✉

From: Matt
Subject: does everyone know Pat was made partner in his law firm?

Congratulations, Pat! I've heard of this distinction for most of my life, but it remains shrouded in mystery, much like the acronym for PEO. (Does anyone know what PEO stands for?)

I know many attorneys never attain this level of distinction. By the way, would you please clarify just what level of distinction we are discussing?

⊠⊠⊠

From: Kevin
Subject: does everyone know Pat was made partner in his law firm?

I join Matt with my congratulations. Although, since I already knew about this, I'm just giving him one congratulation.

⊠⊠⊠

From: Ciccio
Subject: does everyone know Pat was made partner in his law firm?

I think we should never talk to Pat again for not telling about this. After all, this is something we should know so we can treat him differently. No more Mr. Black Sheep.

Since Pat kept this a secret from me, I am going to keep a secret from him. No, this is not about the gun and the bullets and Grandma Nash and the vise. Actually, I am going to keep it from everyone so no one can tell him. I think I will keep the secret for about 30 years. So there.

⊠⊠⊠

From: Mary
Subject: does everyone know Pat was made partner in his law firm?

In a mysterious coincidence, Ciccio received 250,000 points just as Mary learned the secret Ciccio's not going to tell Pat or anyone else.

In another breaking story, a man who had been caught embezzling millions from his employer went to a lawyer seeking defense. He didn't want to go to jail. But his lawyer told him, "Don't worry. You'll never have to go to jail with all that money. And the lawyer was right. When the man was sent to prison, he didn't have a dime.

⊠⊠⊠

From: Pat
Subject: does everyone know Pat was made partner in his law firm?

Mary, It's e-mails like this that got your transmission torched. This joke is like all the bad lawyer jokes. After you disseminate so many (no one knows the magic number) your Karma bag is drained, your tranny goes south, and who knows what other bad things happen to you pursuant to the Karma "butterfly effect." Hope this helps as I am a helpful person. Love you.

⊠⊠⊠

From: P.T.
Subject: does everyone know Pat was made partner in his law firm?

PEO? I was just reading the January issue of *Modern Sheep* and they use PEO to describe the gastric disorder of Putrid Evacuation by Ovines. Commonly referred to as Sheeparrhea.

⊠⊠⊠

From: Mark
Subject: does everyone know Pat was made partner in his law firm?

P.T. or Pat or whoever you are, I have a sheep veterinary medicine manual, and on page 1 they start off with the obligatory medical advice: "A sick sheep is a dead sheep."

On page 2 they present your sheeparrhea (PEO).

Page 3 discusses common psychiatric disorders of sheep, for example, I-Want-to-Be-Alone disease. Sheep are flock beasties. No healthy sheep worth her weight in wool wants to be alone.

That's pretty much the whole manual, although there is a brief Index to Topics Covered on page 4, which can be helpful, like if you forget where the section on a sick sheep is a dead sheep was located in the text.

I am glad you know of our troubles with sheep.

N.B. You are aware, I am sure, of the current debate raging in the sheep community as to whether the "I Want To Be Alone" sheep disorder is really a disorder or not. Some are claiming it is not a disorder at all, that they were born this way, and had no choice in the matter.

⋈⋈⋈⋈⋈⋈⋈⋈⋈⋈⋈⋈⋈⋈

From: Ciccio
Subject: satellite photos of the earth

That's really cool. But the Red Sea is darker than the Black Sea. And the Black Sea isn't black, it's blue!

⋈⋈⋈

From: P.T.
Subject: satellite photos of the earth

Fine, then. I shall cease sending shots of seas since I see you can see seas better than most.

⋈⋈⋈⋈⋈⋈⋈⋈⋈⋈⋈⋈⋈⋈

From: Pat
Subject: stingrays

Dear Sibs, I will be in Alcatraz starting tomorrow returning late Saturday night. My return is conditioned on the hope that prison officials do not get wind that I am an attorney.

In the meantime, I've been up all night worrying about P.T. and Terry as I know they spend a good deal of time on their boat, which is not rated to withstand stingrays.

✉✉✉

From: P.T.
Subject: stingrays

Yes, yes, I once fought a stingray off the coast of Gibraltar. Now he's just a ray.

✉✉✉✉✉✉✉✉✉✉✉✉✉

From: P.T.
Subject: football game

Dear Mr. Answer Man, I was watching a football game and one of the players pulled a muscle. The announcer said they would take him to the locker room and put some mice on it. Have you heard of this before? Signed, Longtime Reader

✉✉✉

From: Mary
Subject: football game

What are you smokin' out there?

✉✉✉

From: Kevin
Subject: football game

They used to put some meat on pulled muscles but found out some mice is better. Answer Man

✉✉✉

From: Pat
Subject: football game

You nutcases. I am ROFLMAO. (No, wait a minute. That's a bit of an exaggeration. I am LMAO.)

✉✉✉

From: P.T.
Subject: football game

Kevin, U R 2 quick. I think they still do use some meat and then alternate with some mice.

✉✉✉

From: Matt
Subject: football game

I love waking up to this stuff. It's better than coffee.

✉✉✉

From: Ciccio
Subject: football game

And my day was going so well . . .

✉✉✉✉✉✉✉✉✉✉✉✉✉

From: Mark
Subject: Ciccio's visit to the farm

get out of the car cut down a giant old dead ash tree go get a new chain for the chainsaw fill it up with gas go to the garage for a nippers cut log into giant chunks quick lift those logs is that a vertebrae sticking out of your back time to feed the sheep warm up the two lamb bottles with sheep's milk go to the barn tell the sheep to quiet down throw several bales of hay into bunk don't forget that water bucket that one sheep is still trying get into the oat bin quick close that gate oh well she's in there now run back up to the house get another infrared bulb because that one ewe bit the bulb out of her heat lamp milk that sheep okay now there's time to wash the lamb bottle tote that bale lift that bundle get the old blue truck and the ladder climb the apple tree and when you get up there cut off the top three and a half feet quick did you drop your pruning hook now hammer your swords into plowshares I mean pruning hooks watch out for that steel post did it denut you now get the other ladder out of the truck go to the barn for chores again didn't we just feed these sheep a few hours ago quick grab little broken leg and brother of broken leg and give them a bottle can you carry two buckets of water at once don't forget those two friendly rams over there they will want oats too did you remember to bring them hay tote that barge lift that bale swing low sweet chariot milk that sheep did you forget to trim the trees around the Christmas tree farm grab that branch hold on and I will cut it off was that your leg how did you get into the crotch of that tree sorry to use the word crotch after the denutting incident tie this come along strap quick around that branch and I will pull it down to earth with the truck how did your leg get tangled up in the strap are you still alive hurry time to chore the sheep again pick that cotton when the two-ton grain bin falls you hold on to the wagon to make sure it does not move did the wagon move is that your leg under the wheel tote that barge I'm gonna lay down my troubles down by the riverside comin for to carry me home don't forget to clean up the workshop rewire those heat lamps oh should I not have plugged in that cord did you feel it or did it just startle you did you remember to pile up the logs in the barn lift that log you are breathing pretty hard a band of angel comin after me comin for to carry me home time to do the vet work on those lambs grab that sheep can't you hold her she is only 240 pounds you should be able to take her did you forget to play with skunky run to town ask for parts can you pay for them I forget my wallet hurry up and pile those logs over there sweep out the kitchen I'm gonna lay down my ball and chain down by the riverside swing low sweet chariot comin for to carry me home Ciccio where did you go

From: Ciccio
Subject: Ciccio's visit to the farm

Thanks for the synopsis of our time together. I had a great time with you although I would suggest that your visitors be under the age of 30 and in superior physical condition. I had 12 hours of sleep last night and for 11 hours of that time, I dreamed of flying out of ash trees and landing in sheep poop. Hired Hand

⊠⊠⊠

From: P.T.
Subject: barn

Hi Dr. Marco Polo, So I clicked on the link you gave me and I saw everything Craig ever tried to sell from Aardvarks to Zzebras but for some reason I couldn't find bbarns. I would love to bid on your bbarn but I couldn't find the listing and, anaway (isn't that how farmers say it?), I just don't know where I'd keep it. Don't get me wrong, it's a regal and historic structure but I already have more buildings than I care to support. Buildings are almost as expensive as kids, except buildings generally don't want to go to college. Some do, like I bet those Smithsonian buildings had some secondary education, but most are happy to just be sheds and bbarns. Anaway, I wish you the best of luck in selling your bbarn.

⊠⊠⊠

From: Kevin
Subject: speaking of barns

Remember jumping off the barn in the summer? Ouch! And then there were Dad's rabbits in the old barn—lots of small screen hutches bursting with babies. Anybody know why we had all those rabbits?

I still think Mom torched the old barn. It's too suspicious. Dad talked about getting rid of it for quite a while. Then one night Mom woke me at 3 a.m. and she was very excited. "Come see! Come see!" A classmate of Punky's was driving home from a night shift, saw the blaze, and allegedly woke Mom—I think she was already up. She loved fires.

⊠⊠⊠

From: P.T.
Subject: speaking of barns

Mom was involved in the destruction of that barn, Maggio, but she didn't set it ablaze. I was told that Nikita Kruschev got wind of mom's fondness for JFK and ordered a missile strike on Dad's little rabbit shack. He meant it as a warning but due to an incapable translator they ended up hitting the rabbit warren. They thought he said to send a warren shot.

I also have memories of jumping off the barn. It usually happened just after I was shoved. El Mismo

⊠⊠⊠

From: Mary
Subject: speaking of barns

You jumped right after you were pushed? How smart of you.

⊠⊠⊠

From: Ciccio
Subject: speaking of barns

Did you know that, in the end, the old barn was worth about $37.50? The insurance paid off on the spare automotive parts stored in the barn—short blocks, tires, seats, etc. Of course, all that stuff was mine. You're welcome.

The guy who spotted the fire was a really good friend of Rosalie's. He thought he might get her hand in marriage, or something, for reporting the fire. I think he also liked Mom. And, yes, Kevin, Mom was enough of a fire bug to be considered as the cause. We are all fortunate to have crossed her path in life.

⊠⊠⊠⊠⊠⊠⊠⊠⊠⊠⊠⊠⊠

From: Pat
Subject: the Shadow

You ran into a retired FBI agent who kept the Shadow under surveillance in 1968 in Iowa City?

✉✉✉

From: Matt
Subject: the Shadow

One of you was formerly known as "The Shadow." I know who, but want to know why.

✉✉✉

From: Kevin
Subject: the Shadow

The Shadow was a handle given to Pat by his frat brothers. Further affiant sayeth not.

✉✉✉

From: Pat
Subject: the Shadow

Kevin and I had a blood pact. I promised I would never publish his driving record and he promised to take the bar exam for me under the assumed name of Patrick. In light of these recent attacks about my former Shadow life, I must reassess whether I am still bound by that pledge of silence.

✉✉✉

From: Kevin
Subject: the Shadow

Speaking of which or whom, I had dinner with the Shadow last night and it was very enjoyable. Anon. K

✉✉✉

From: P.T.
Subject: the Shadow

Dear Anon. K,

Did you change your name again? I must have missed it. I like it though. I think it is a popular pen name.

✉✉✉✉✉✉✉✉✉✉✉✉✉

CHAPTER 4

A Literary Chapter in Which We Explain That When Mom Said, "Half a Dozen of You, Get Out of Here!" She Was Using a Figure of Speech

Thanksgiving Day 1959
Kevin

Thanksgiving, Christmas, and Easter dinners at our house looked like Norman Rockwell paintings. Although Mom did all the hard work, she was dressed up throughout the day: an attractive dress, lipstick, hairdo, and a pretty apron (the only time she wore one).

Since she spent most of the day in the kitchen cooking, and we spent most of the day trying to get a taste of whatever she was cooking, she was obliged to say several times, "Half a dozen of you, get out of here!" She said this whether there were two or three or six of us in the kitchen and, occasionally, when only one of us was there.

For Thanksgiving 1959, Mother's priest brother, Father Tom, joined us. Whenever he visited, every one of us including Mom and Dad dropped to our knees and received his blessing. Same thing when he left. In between, he entertained us with jokes and interesting stories—and he also listened to us. This time he'd brought something with which to astound us: a tape recorder the size of a suitcase. The technology was primitive, but none of us had ever seen one, so we were easily pleased.

We were still experimenting with it when Mother called us to the table. Noting our pleasure in the new machine and our unwillingness to leave it, even for Thanksgiving dinner, Father Tom suggested we run the tape while we were eating.

We were a little self-conscious at first, but eventually forgot about the recorder as we said grace, watched Dad wield his carving tools, and focused on the spirited conversation that always came of eating in the fancy dining room and being on our best behavior.

For the past couple of years, at every holiday meal, six-year-old P.T. had asked for a piece of the gizzard. We always told him he was too young—our lame excuse to keep more of it for the big kids. The gizzard became his fruit of the poisonous tree. The more he couldn't have it, the more he wanted it. And so he took advantage of the circulating platters of victuals to sneak a piece without asking. His goal was to eat it as fast as he could before anyone saw him.

The conversation was lively:

"Pass the potatoes."
"Can I have some cranberries?"
"Quick, take these beans, the dish is hot."
"Eh, eh."
"Let's go to the big tree house after dinner."
"Have you seen Uncle Kevin and Skip lately?"
"Pass the rolls, please."
"No, pass them clockwise."
"Eehh."
"Who wants dark meat?"
"Eecckk!"
"P.T., stop making that noise and eat your dinner."
"Aaccck!"
"Whoever's on dishes today is in luck because we'll all help."
"Acckk, eehh, ack!"
"Mom, tell P.T. to stop making noises."
"Father Tom, did you know—uuggh-ack-ack—our priest used to be an electrician?"
"Hack, hack, hack."
"Honey, your wine is the best ever."
"Arruggga-eck-eck."
"I want to watch *Superman* after dinner."
"Gggguh, guh, guh, huck, ack, errrgg, aaa."
"You can't, it's not on today because it's a holiday."

"Kkk, huk!"
"Mom, P.T.'s turning purple."
"Ch-ch-ch-kkkk-uuggg-crcratack!"
"Oh my god."
"Honey, I think he's choking!"
"P.T., let me see what's in your mouth!"

Suddenly, Mom and Dad were serious while we were scared or crying or both.

"Honey, pat him on the back! Harder!"
"I think there's something stuck in his throat!"
"Turn him upside down! Hurry!"
"He's not breathing!"
"Hit his back while he's upside down. Again! Harder! Shake him!"

Meanwhile, the juvenile Greek chorus gave voice:

"He's dying!"
"P.T.'s dying!"
"Don't say that!"
"He's not breathing!"
"He's turning purple!"
"Our brother is dying right in front of us!"
"I can't watch!"
"Stop crying, that won't help!"
"Be quiet so Mom and Dad can hear each other!"
"Oh noooo, I think he's dead!"
"His eyes aren't moving!"
"Look how still he is!"
"Save him!"
"Somebody, help!"

And then while Dad was shaking purple P.T. upside down with Mom's finger in his mouth, a piece of gizzard came flying out. "Ack! Ekk! Uck! Uck!" We surrounded P.T. while he tried to catch his breath, touching him and whispering to him that he was all right. Mom cradled him in her arms for a while before she and Dad decided to put him to bed; someone would check on him every few minutes. Afterward, Mom came back to the table and said P.T. fell asleep the second his head hit the pillow. Dad talked about how fortunate we were that God was watching over us and saved little P.T.'s life and what a thing to be thankful for on Thanksgiving Day. We finished eating with a certain thoughtful solemnity.

After dessert, we were sitting around the table, too full to move, when Father Tom said, "Oh my garsh, Reenie, I forgot we tape-recorded the whole meal!" We were stunned. The horror, the trauma, the near tragedy that we just experienced was on tape and we could relive it if we dared.

Later, after the table was cleared, the kitchen was clean, and we were all relaxing in the living room, feeling almost normal again, we decided to listen to the tape.

As the spool replayed our meal, we heard light conversation, punctuated with a few quiet interruptions by P.T. choking, more conversation, louder choking noises, still more conversation, guttural sounds unlike anything we had ever heard, and then the emergency-room dialogue of Mom and Dad, with the kids' counterpoint crying for P.T.'s life, all in choppy, surreal voices due to the inferior quality of the recorder.

About halfway through the taped near-death experience of our little brother, one of the kids struggled, hand over mouth, to stifle a chuckle. A muffled snort was heard from someone else, a few embarrassed laughs from others. When we noticed Mom and Dad and Father Tom trying not to laugh, our laughter turned to hysteria. We rolled on the floor, holding our stomachs, trying to catch our breath, tears streaming down our faces, open hands slapping on the carpet, laughing, laughing, laughing!

We replayed the tape a dozen times, laughing harder every time until finally we had enough. Even though we had no school the next day and could have stayed up late, we settled into our beds early, exhausted from so much joy at all of us being alive.

··

Laughing together is as close as you can get to another person without touching, and sometimes it represents a closer tie than touching ever could.—Regina Barreca

··

The Caste System
Matt

Fort Dodge, a prosperous Midwestern town of twenty-eight thousand, was founded in 1848. A frontier outpost, it was originally named Mineral City for the large deposits of clay, coal, limestone, and gypsum. The area cropland is considered the richest agricultural land in the country. With the nearest good-size town sixty miles away, Fort Dodge serves as a hub of activity in north-central Iowa. The relative isolation lends itself to some provincialism, as well as to strong family, religious, and community ties—curiously, much like our family home but on a larger scale.

We had a mini-community of our own: ten people, a roomy ranch-style house, two barns, and two smaller sheds. Over the years, we were home to ponies, horses, sheep, goats, geese, ducks, chickens, peacocks, guinea hens, dogs, cats, guinea pigs, goldfish (indoor and outdoor), and parakeets.

On the grounds, Dad had a huge vegetable garden as well as a grape arbor, a rhubarb patch, rows and rows of raspberries, hazelnut trees, and mulberry, cherry, apple, plum, and apricot trees. I can still taste Mom's jellies and jams. With our willing help (okay, I was kidding about "willing"), she canned and froze monumental quantities of food each year. Preparing and freezing sweet corn, which was the only thing Dad didn't need to grow, thanks to farming friends, was the pinnacle of the canning season and required lots of help. Winter meals delivered more savor because we had sweat equity in most of what was on our plates.

Nearly two thousand feet of manicured privet hedge bordered the front of the property. Dad's pride and joy, its maintenance was one of the few chores he wouldn't allow us to do. After we cared for the animals, mowed the yard, cleaned our rooms, and helped with meals, laundry, and dishes, we were free to play.

We rarely went to the movies, roller-skating, after-school events, or shopping as that meant "another trip to town." As I grew older, I realized it wasn't the distance that kept us from going to and from town but Mom and Dad's perspective that it was generally a waste of time and money. Occasionally I felt isolated, but we had each other, and we had bikes. It was three miles to the gas station where we could buy a soda, two miles to a goldfish pond for fishing, and several miles to the homes of farm friends where a whole day could pass in an instant.

The mostly undisputed caste system in our tree house community carried through into the rest of our lives. The oldest set the rules, and the rest followed nicely. We had our wars but, in the end, we each knew where we stood, and we learned to be team players. I respected the older ones' authority. In return, I enjoyed a general sense of well-being along with the security of belonging, fun, and friendship. In another trade-off, there were smaller groupings in which everyone got a chance to be the "oldest" of seven, six, five, etc., siblings (Mark had only one junior, me, but I like to think I kept him busy)—and everyone had their moment as the youngest of the family. One of us retains that privilege to this day.

Eating Wasn't Always Fun
Mary

For most of my growing-up years, we had cornflakes for breakfast. Actually, here are the four things I remember ever having for breakfast: cornflakes, corn mush, raw eggs, oatmeal. We must have had pancakes, but I don't remember them. And sometimes, as a special treat, we had fried bread dough with syrup.

After Dad mixed his flour and dry yeast and warm water and dash of salt in a huge spaghetti bowl, he punched it for a few minutes and let it rest. All of us have requested his recipe. The response was uniformly, "Come over here and watch me." Only Matt has managed to replicate the Italian-beyond-Italian freshly baked bread and its forerunner, fried bread dough.

As the dough rose, we sneaked into the kitchen to tear off puffy, raw bits of it. It was pure love, a panacea for any ailment. And you could play with it before you ate it. Dad must have seen all the little pinches and camouflaging folds we made in his dough, but he never said a word. When the dough was "ready" (only he seemed to know this), he pulled off sticky hunks and fried it in a cast-iron pan. Heaven.

Dad was the morning herder. (I don't remember where Mom was. She was the evening herder.) He'd poke us in the sternum to wake us because no one can sleep through that. Then he'd get food on the table. Dad was always in a hurry. He used to boil eggs, crack them in a bowl, mix them up with saltines, and yum, yum. That's sarcasm. I like to think that instead of boiling the eggs, he just ran them under hot water. To this day, I cannot eat a soft egg. They have to be hard enough to walk on.

Another food I didn't care for, primarily because I was sure I'd need the last rites if I ever got them all down, was green beans. The ones we grew and ate late in the summer had strings that give new meaning to "string beans."

You'd chew and chew one of those beans—and they were big, end-of-season, not-safe-to-eat beans—and be left with a mass of cellulose in your mouth. No way did God mean for us to swallow that, but Mom meant for us to. And so there was lots of gagging toward the end of the meal, which was when everyone got around to eating their string beans.

If you were clever and could distract the person next to you and if they were younger or in any way weaker than you, you could stuff the wad of cellulose under their plate. When the table was cleared, Mom would see the hunk of stuff and make that person eat it no matter how many times they said it wasn't theirs. I did that quite often with green bean cellulose and gristle. I remember being able to dish out this particular scheme, but rarely did I have to take it because I guarded my plate carefully. And I was short, so I was really close to my plate.

The lives of most practicing Italians revolve around the word "Mangia!" ("Eat!")! We learned this at Nonna's while we were still very young.

Nonna was always about ninety years old. She wore faded blue shapeless dresses that felt like a baby's skin. She smelled like anise or spaghetti. I always get those two mixed up. About four feet tall, with silver hair in a bun (I once saw it loose, and it fell all the way to the floor), she was warm and soft and holy. She was so holy, in fact, that we were certain she had a direct line to God . . . until she got talking in noisy, excitable Italian with Dad. Then I used to size up the space under Aunt Margaret's couch, in case I needed to take cover.

On rare occasions, I accompanied Nonna to her bedroom to find something she wanted to show us (usually a holy card). It was scary. She raised snails to eat, and they crawled all over the walls and curtains of her bedroom, disdaining their milk-carton homes.

Every Sunday, barring snowstorms or measles, we went to Mass, to Nonna's, and in the summer, to Jim Kempley's ice cream stand. In that order. I don't remember Mom being with us. She may have been home taking care of the newest baby of the family.

Nonna greeted us at the door of the house where she lived with Aunt Margaret and her family. We lined up in no particular order and shuffled into the house, giving Nonna a big hug and a kiss and getting our cheeks pinched. While she was pinching cheeks, she said a bunch of stuff in Italian that always ended with, "Che d'oro! Che d'oro!" For years, I thought she was saying "Kay Doro" and wondered what she had to do with us. It means "such gold!" That was us. Imagine.

We all found a place to sit in the living room, which seemed to shrink as we piled in. She nodded and smiled at us. We smiled and nodded back. After a few minutes of this, she and Dad and Aunt Margaret would get into it in Italian. This part made us nervous. Later we found out they were talking about their tomatoes or a cure for blisters or a letter from a cousin in Sicily but, watching them, we were trying to figure when we should bring in the police.

Before we left, we always had to eat something. "Mangia! Mangia! Mangia!" All the while, Nonna and Aunt Margaret were stuffing cookies into our faces or hands. After twenty minutes of this, brushing crumbs off our clothes, we lined up for our good-byes. But even on our way to the car, our sticky hands would be finding cookies in pockets and hankies and waistbands. From behind us came the good-bye cries—hard to make out the exact words but probably "Mangia! Mangia!"

....

> It was only among your own people that you didn't need to shine, because that wasn't what mattered. Your own people were your own people. You could take them for granted, and be taken for granted by them. The bosom of the family was an extraordinarily restful place.—Patricia Wentworth

....

The Government Is Here to Help Us
Mark

An amateur conservationist, Dad decided one spring to plant a sheep pasture with trees and shrubs to help hold the soil and to provide some habitat for birds. He planted olive bushes on the slopes and walnut trees on the more level areas. He pointed out that in forty or fifty years the walnut trees would be valuable lumber trees, and someone could collect a pretty penny at harvest time.

We all helped plant and water one hundred little walnut trees. After a couple of weeks, the sheep grew impatient to reclaim their pasture. Commensurate with their impatience, the grass and clover in that pasture grew rapidly and needed mowing or grazing by someone, human or animal. When we asked Dad if we could turn the sheep out into the walnut tree field, he said not yet as he didn't know if the sheep would eat the little trees.

We looked at the sheep. Why were they licking their lips? Was it the lush grass and clover that had not been grazed down for several weeks? Or was it the neatly planted rows of leafy little walnut trees? They were playing their cards close to their chests. All we could pick up from their body language was, "Let us in there!"

Dad decided to ask the county extension agent. He was a government man. He got paid to know this kind of thing.

The county extension agent said this was a challenging and complex question, that it had never come up before, that there were a number of dimensions to this question, and that he would have to consult with headquarters and get back to us.

A week or so later, the agent reported that walnut trees exuded juglone, a tannin or poison that kills everything growing nearby. Sheep would not be interested in its acidic, yucky taste.

Confident that his government had spoken, Dad instructed us to check the fences and turn the sheep into the walnut tree pasture.

"Don't worry," Dad told us. "The government man says those sheep won't lay a glove on the little walnut trees."

Within days the sheep laid waste to the trees. They breakfasted, lunched, dined, and snacked on walnut trees. Fresh walnut leaves with a side order of walnut bark. Stripped and pulled walnut tenderloin, topped with a light sprinkling of walnut branches. Whole roast walnut tree for Sunday dinner.

As horrified as he was by this conservationist's catastrophe, Dad was even more horrified to realize that the government man was wrong. He didn't want to think that the one thing he had ever asked from his government, his one little question, could have met with such incompetence.

In some small place within, Dad still wanted to believe in his government. So he called the county extension agent and reported the sheepish mayhem and the very real possibility of their polishing off the entire field. The government man said, "Quick, put little chicken wire fences around each tree. That will keep the sheep away from them."

Dad protested that this seemed insignificant protection from the onslaught of a determined flock of sheep. No, the government man insisted, chicken wire fencing would keep those trees safe.

So we made a hundred little chicken wire fences and staked them down. The sheep watched us through the fence, snickering and laughing, especially the old ewes who had been around the block. They seemed to be getting quite a bit of enjoyment—in a dark, evil sheep sort of way—out of watching us kids make those little fences.

We put the fences up and turned the sheep loose.

They immediately assaulted the one hundred little fences surrounding the one hundred little walnut trees, hoofing and stepping and pummeling the fences, leaving wads of chicken wire at the base of each tree. Walnut tree sandwich time! Nutty! Delicious!

Dad wanted to call the government man and tell him how wrong he was—again. That he did not know sheep or walnut trees. That government should try harder to serve the people. But about that time, President Nixon was going south on us, and the Watergate hearings were steaming ahead. First the walnut trees, and now Nixon. The winds of government failure and corruption had reached our little homestead. Dad's faith in government was shaken beyond repair. Nothing Nixon or the government man could say would bring back those little walnut trees.

Miracles and Catechisms
Rosalie

The dead horse was supposed to dry like the snakes did, but we hadn't factored in the difference in their sizes. What did we know?

Horse and snakes aside, the eight of us were like all other Catholic kids (we could memorize). And we were like none of them.

For one thing, we had our own personal family chapel. When Mother and Dad built the house in 1950, they designed a chapel right into it. No one else in any of the three parishes in Fort Dodge (we're talking heyday of the Church here) had a chapel in their home. We weren't sure what this meant. But it seemed a point in our favor, if anyone was keeping score. And, by golly, if you went to Catholic schools, you knew there were scorekeepers. Big-time.

Dad rescued the discarded side altar from a nearby country parish. Painted white and gold, it was a miniature church itself, with Gothic spires and arches. There was one kneeler in the chapel. I can't remember seeing anyone ever use it, though certainly Mother's brother and sister, Father Tom and Sister Grace, were holy enough. When we were called to the rosary every night during May and October by the big train bell in the backyard, there was no question but that it was knees to hard wooden floor for us.

As proud as we were of the chapel, we came to take it for granted. On the few occasions that friends came out from town, they always wanted to see the chapel when what we wanted to show them was our collection of snakeskins.

For another thing, we had our own personal, family saint. Dad's sister, Margaret Mary Maggio (1911-1924), was up for beatification and she had her own holy cards.

We knew, as soon as we could understand English, that people could be levitated right off the ground, that stone angels could cry, that disfiguring full-body burn scars could disappear overnight. We didn't just believe this. We knew this.

The best part was that Margaret Mary was able to perform these miracles without having had to deal with torture, stigmata, severed body parts, or lions (she died of scarlet fever at the age of thirteen). She was a domestic saint, a companionable age-mate for us. Her particular interest was in shepherding the immigrant Italian children of Boone to the Catholic grade school across the tracks. Trains ran hard and often in those days. Margaret Mary assured the worried parents that the Blessed Virgin would be with the children. Eventually, they believed her. All the Catholic kids went to Sacred Heart School on the other side of the tracks.

Counterweighting the chapel, Margaret Mary, the Catholic schools, the Baltimore Catechism, and Sister Mary Theophilus and her sistren was the fact that during all our childhood we "ran wild." That's the way the neighbors put it when they complained. The Israelites had nothing on us for disobedience and false gods and hardening of hearts when we heard God's voice (as at Meribah).

A few years before I was born, Antonia White wrote, "Catholicism isn't a religion, it's a nationality." It's both, of course. And like any ethnic group, Catholics come in all the human forms while sharing a second language (and I don't mean Latin). If you were a Catholic child who never made a ball of Wonder Bread, pressed it flat, and played communion with it, I have to question how Catholic you really were.

Our own bread rose with the flour and yeast of Catholicism, but the extra ingredients were what made it nourishing for us. The flavor was sometimes soda bread and sometimes focaccia.

Mother was 100 percent Irish. She too was one of eight children, and her parents had been rewarded with the ultimate Catholic blessing: a priest and a nun in the family. We always knew how lucky we were.

Edna O'Brien says, "Irish Catholicism is very much founded on the stone of fear and of punishment." Good point. In any case, it has its own characteristic face.

Dad was 100 percent Sicilian, which is a bit different from Italian, but that's another story. I was named after my grandmother, who was named after the patron saint of the Palermo province, Santa Rosalia.

In 1624, when Palermo was ravaged by the plague, she instructed (well, she was long dead by then but if you're Catholic, you know how these appearances work) a shepherd (okay, we don't actually know, but they're usually shepherds) to find her bones and carry them around the city three times. The results were good. And so to this day, believers venerate her bones in the kitschy damp cave at the top of Monte Pellegrino where, according to legend, she lived centuries ago. The damp part is important because the dripping water, collected in ugly zinc gutters, is miraculous. Or is considered miraculous, which comes to the same thing.

Some years ago, the bones were discovered to be the bones of a goat. What I want to tell you about Italian Catholicism is that people still motor or hotfoot it up that winding mountain road to the shrine. If you can judge by the number of stalls outside the grotto selling gold plastic framed pictures, rosaries in every color of the rainbow, and religious dime-store art, St. Rosalia is more popular than ever.

When you aren't distracted by the stunning views as you wind up the mountain road, you'll see a path dating from the seventeenth century paralleling the road. This was used by the devout going up to see St. Rosalia on foot or knee (our very own Nonna made a pilgrimage on her knees in the early days of the last century).

Rudolph Vecoli points out that "Italian Catholics are only nominally Catholic." What we have is more of a folk religion, "a fusion of animism, polytheism and sorcery, with the sacraments of the church thrown in." Possibly.

Back to the horse. We hadn't done anything to it, although P.T. and Mary had killed the snakes. Dad told us to bury the horse, but we had another, better idea. It was hard work pulling that huge dead horse out to the woods but—oh, tell the truth. It was just a pony. But sweaty work nonetheless.

Ropes. A pulley. About six of us working. We suspended the dead pony from a cottonwood tree. In theory, the flesh would fall away, leaving us a pure white skeleton hanging in the air. Can you see it?

I'll skip the part about the smell, the flies, the falling chunks of horse. It wasn't one of our successes. But for a few hours we were goal-driven visionaries—purposeful, creative, and united. That's the part I remember.

Thus we toggled from the conventional indoctrination and practice of Catholicism (and hey, we were all A students—did we know our religion, or what?) to the lawless, insular, self-created world we inhabited the rest of the time.

(In case you were wondering, the police were called only once. A babysitter reported a missing three-year-old, but Mary was actually clinging to the springs on the underside of a bed. She was quite an acrobat. Mother would have known better than to call the police.)

Little by little, we noticed something. Lightning did not strike. The dead did not come forth from their graves to reproach us. We smelled no eternal fires. In short, God was probably not a punitive God.

Eventually, this led to other realizations. God had, perhaps, a great sense of humor. God was a lot bigger and nicer and more interesting than they'd told us. God was ours, and we were God's. Safe.

We were more comfortable in church than we should have been. It wasn't that much different from our chapel. Father Tom—he later became a monsignor—got up to give a homily at Corpus Christi one Sunday, and the ten of us, seated in the first two pews, raised our deeply bowed heads to look at him. We were each wearing a pair of Groucho Marx glasses with matching mustache. Yes, Mother and Dad were wearing them too. We didn't just come out of nowhere, you know.

Somewhere between miracles and catechisms, Irish guilt and Italian superstition, our irreverent childhood subculture and mid-twentieth-century conventions, we became the people we were meant to be. Believers all, today our spirituality is as varied as it is ferociously rooted. Wherever we are on Sunday mornings, each of us is Irish and Italian and, at some perhaps cellular level, mysteriously Catholic.

....

E-mail from Dad
"True Story"

My Guardian Angel appeared to me last week. I have hesitated telling you this for fear that it would be pushed aside as an old man's dream or wish, but it really happened. I awakened sitting on the edge of my bed. I glanced up and saw a figure rushing at me from the doorway. It all happened quick as a flash. His disappearance was as fast as his appearance. But I was able to see his bright smiling face and head covered with long black flowing hair. The sight of him was breathtaking and frightening.

When I recovered my composure, I contemplated within myself and pondered whether he had come to get me or whether he wanted to let me know that he was still at my side after all these years.

I have always believed in angels, but the impact on me of this visit has strengthened my belief immensely—so much so, that I now pray daily that the angels the Lord has assigned to my children and to their children for generations infinitive will deliver them from all evil and guard them from all harm as my guardian has done.

Please believe and keep your faith in the Good Lord and His angels and saints so that you will be loved and cared for forever and ever.

Dad

....

Pieces of Eight
Mark

Brother Paul Thomas, the clever one, has been identified and fingered as the child who sought to acquire the family's Wheat pennies, Mercury dimes, gold foil stamp collection, and other shiny valuable objects. However, although accused of it and although his coin lust was weighty and loathsome, Paul Thomas never did get the family pennies.

As a little boy and capitalist, I greatly feared the sacking and pillaging of my silver coin collection by my larger sibling (Paul Thomas) or by my smarter sibling (Matthew). It is not insignificant that Matthew was also a coin collector, a competitor for the odd silver coin that Dad found in his change. It would not be beneath either brother, in the early years that could be counted on one hand, to pirate my coins.

I think I was also a prepubescent conservative because I vaguely feared that somehow Big Government would begin to tax us little children, and on some Orwellian pretense, they would come and confiscate my coin collection. So I devised a benevolent and protective plan to keep my coins safe.

Whenever I filled up a little oval-shaped plastic coin purse with World War II lead pennies or silver dimes or silver quarters or, yea verily, silver fifty-cent pieces, I stashed it on top of the supporting brick masonry work underneath the living room wood fireplace mantel.

And what was I doing in the living room, you wonder? This was at a point in my youthful life where I had not yet offended Mother enough to be banished from it, and so I still had daily access to the living room. I had—while teething—mightily chewed the windowsills in that room, but no one ever hung that one on me (no living witnesses), so Mother continued to allow me carte blanche in there.

And so, when no one was looking, I sneaked into the living room and shoved my little coin purses up under the mantel.

From time to time, as my schedule and personal safety allowed, I crept back into the living room and retrieved the coin purses for long, happy minutes of fondling.

But then, as with all boys (I suppose even more so for boys nowadays who take their daily steroids), my fingers started to fatten up, and upon attempting to retrieve my coin purses, I couldn't gain hold of them, and I ended up pushing them too far in, whereupon they evidently fell down behind the masonry brickwork.

I actually continued mine efforts until four or five coin purses had been pushed over the nonnegotiable edge of oblivion down into the fireplace. I know what you are thinking. Repeating the same action and expecting different results is insanity. But I didn't actually repeat the same mistake five times. Each time, I tried a different retrieval method: coat hanger, bent fork, glue on my fingertips, and so on.

As a child, I always had many questions, hundreds of them, I seem to remember. Few of them were answered with anything but, "Did you finish your homework?" In a triumph of hope over experience, I went to Dad to question him about retrieving my hoard. We had a friendly but unproductive talk. It consisted largely of comments like, "Didn't you know that fireplaces are hollow?" "Why did you keep doing it when they continued to fall inside?" "There's nothing we can do about it." "Just forget about it." He must have been interested in my unusual problem, however, because he didn't ask me if I'd finished my homework.

And so my hopes for rescue were dashed. Like a good little entrepreneur and conservative, I deducted the lost coins on my schedule of capital gains and losses for my tax return that year.

E-mails

From: Mark
Subject: ferrets

Does anyone else find the announcement below vaguely unnerving?

Of greatest concern to me are the statements, "Your ferrets will be treated well" and "the students will be practicing restraint."

As I read the announcement, I had a kind of gut reaction, like, where is my .22 rifle, do I have shells, are they on the shelf, will the ferret be gone by the time I get there? Mark

Vet Tech Program Needs Ferrets

The Vet Tech Program Exotics class is looking for ferrets to borrow. If you have a ferret that would be willing to participate in their class, please call Phoebe at 555-5555. Your ferrets will be treated well. The students will be practicing restraint, performing physical exams, administering gas anesthesia, monitoring vital signs and then drawing blood samples.

⊠⊠⊠

From: P.T.
Subject: ferrets

That ad is a classic, hard to believe it's for real. Especially for me. The last time I let someone use my ferret I never got it back.

⊠⊠⊠

From: Kevin
Subject: ferrets

Once I bought a house in Aurora from an old woman who had two ferrets. The house looked really nice when I viewed it with all her furnishings in it. But when she moved out and I moved in, there were huge brown spots on the carpet where the big furniture had been, like the sofa and loveseat. I was puzzled and told my new neighbor about it. He said, didn't I know that ferrets don't have to arch their backs when they shit so they can shit horizontally? No, I didn't know that. Well, yes, they like dark places so they sit under the furniture all day shitting sideways. K

⊠⊠⊠

From: Pat
Subject: ferrets

I am diligently reading, summarizing, and thoroughly enjoying all of your recent e-mail activity. In the meantime, I made a note to self: add to the proprietary universal lawyer dirty trick list the shit sideways. I haven't yet thought through how I can use it to take advantage of someone or to sucker-punch someone, but hope to soon. Love youse guys!

⊠⊠⊠

From: Mark
Subject: ferrets

P.T., Sorry you never got that ferret back. I think he was the one eating my chickens. Just before I pulled the trigger, I said a little prayer to Saint Peter at the Pearly Gates, asking him to be wary of any ferrets coming up to Gates, and reminding him how ferrets fabricate.

I know an old fellow here who is a retired machinist. He is quite famous locally, known as the inventor of the first mink opener. It is a simple device, not well appreciated by minks and ferrets and weasels and ermine. I am not allowed to describe it online (PETA, etc.) but let's just say that this device assists the mink rancher with an essential chore at harvest time.

⊠⊠⊠

From: Mary
Subject: ferrets

This is the only ferret joke I know: Two ferrets are sitting on a bar stool. One starts to insult the other one. He screams, "I slept with your mother!" The bar gets quiet as all the other ferrets listen to see what the second ferret will do. The first one yells again, "I slept with your mother!" The other says, "Go home, Dad, you're drunk."

⊠⊠⊠

From: Mark
Subject: ferrets

While we're on the subject, have you ever heard of ferret banging? This practice originated on a small farm in north-central Iowa. It involves waiting until the ferret has one of your chickens by the neck. Tighten your belt, and go get the emergency sand shovel. Then, bang the ferret repeatedly about his fur-bearin' carcass with said sand shovel, until he drops the hen. Keep banging the ferret, and you can see who lasts the longest. Ferret banging should not be confused with ferret bagging. The former practice is not pleasurable for most ferrets, whereas the latter practice is quite enjoyed by ferrets everywhere, regardless of their sexual orientation.

⊠⊠⊠⊠⊠⊠⊠⊠⊠⊠⊠⊠⊠

From: Matt
Subject: photo

Dear Family, Laura and I sent all of you copies of the photo of Mom that hung in the living room in a gold oval frame. You can note on the back: "May 1947, winner of the Mrs. Webster County beauty pageant." Enjoy!

⊠⊠⊠

From: Kevin
Subject: photo

Wow, Matt, how thoughtful. Thanks so much. By the way, our brother Ditto was in utero at the time. Kevin

⊠⊠⊠

From: P.T.
Subject: photo

I always thought his name was Shut The Hell Up.

⊠⊠⊠

From: Mary
Subject: photo

You should talk, Get The Hell Out Of Here.

⊠⊠⊠

From: Pat
Subject: photo

Hey. I represent that!

⊠⊠⊠

From: Kevin
Subject: photo

Only a lawyer would say "I represent that!" A normal person would say, "I resemble that!

⊠⊠⊠

From: Mark
Subject: photo

I re-send all your inferences.

⊠⊠⊠

From: Pat
Subject: photo

Markus, It is always good to hear from you. But you have to imagine that the written word does not always mean to me what it appears to say. For example, when you wrote this cute phrase: "I re-send all your inferences" I actually saw "Buy rolled oats for emergency use."

⊠⊠⊠

From: Mark
Subject: photo

It's my e-mail system that makes me re-sendful.

⊠⊠⊠

From: Mary
Subject: photo

What the heck is going on here? All that stuff you guys wrote is going in
your permanent records.

⊠⊠⊠⊠⊠⊠⊠⊠⊠⊠⊠⊠⊠

From: Kevin
Subject: Katie and Jason's wedding

Hello, All. I thought you'd like to know that niece Katie and her intended,
Jason, have asked me to officiate at their wedding. After serious consideration
I have agreed. It's an honor and a huge responsibility.

Each of you has a unique and deep spiritual life, which I respect, and this
may be a stretch for you as it is for me. Feel free to let me know what you
think, and also feel free to help me feel comfortable in this role. The wedding
is, of course, about Katie and Jason, but officiating has put a new edge on
it for me.

I had a long talk with Katie and Jason today and they are well-prepared.
Their emphasis seems to be less on themselves and more on being gracious
hosts to the community of family and friends who will come from near and
far to celebrate their marriage with them. Looks to be enjoyable for all of
us in many ways. Much love, Kevin

⊠⊠⊠

From: P.T.
Subject: Katie and Jason's wedding

I knew they were going to ask you. They asked me first but I have a
conflict.

⊠⊠⊠

From: Mark
Subject: Katie and Jason's wedding

Actually, they asked me before they asked P.T. I was going to do it, but since I am a never-married, I thought it might look bad.

⊠⊠⊠

From: Pat
Subject: Katie and Jason's wedding

Hi Mark, You funny guy. It is always good to hear from you. In fact, in my humble opinion, you rank in the top seven people (siblings) I like to hear from. I must rise to refute your comment about serving as the WO. I think you'd be an awesome WO. Regarding the never-married moniker, I think time has dulled the memory a bit. Remember Egypt and Vietnam? Love you.

⊠⊠⊠

From: Ciccio
Subject: Katie and Jason's wedding

I don't think they asked P.T. as they don't trust him. He kills pheasants.

⊠⊠⊠

From: Pat
Subject: Katie and Jason's wedding

Kevin, Congrats on being asked to officiate. The only advice I can think of is be absolutely certain you don't say: "And now I pronounce you *man* and wife."

As I approach the wedding, I am sure I will have more thoughts to share with you, Bro. Love you.

⊠⊠⊠

From: Matt
Subject: Katie and Jason's wedding

Dear Kevin, That is such an honor! Laura and I were reminiscing about our uncle presiding at our wedding. Actually, didn't Father Tom preside at Punky's, Ciccio's, Pat's, and Mary's weddings too?

We are sad that we will not be able to be with you all. Our cruise gets back on June 1st, and we cannot see our way to extending our time there long enough to make the wedding.

⊠⊠⊠

From: Jason
Subject: Katie and Jason's wedding

Dear RM, I do worry about how you introduce me (blind) to your people. "Well, Katie is happy, and, um, he shows some potential." Or, "We're confident that, in some way, he'll show his mettle."

⊠⊠⊠

From: Mark
Subject: Katie and Jason's wedding

I don't think there's any real reason for the male relatives to see Jason's mettle. If he wants to show it to the women, well, that's his business, quite literally. But I have no interest in seeing it. Let's just assume he has a sufficient mettle, and leave it at that.

⊠⊠⊠

From: Mary
Subject: Katie and Jason's wedding

Darn it, Jason, I don't care what Punky says about you, I like you.

And, Matt, it will be totally impossible to have a really good time at the wedding without your family. I plan on pouting for at least a couple of hours.

I agree, you might want to get into Mark's house while he's at the wedding and upend furniture, turn on faucets, and stuff like that. I bet he'd think that was funny. I hope he doesn't see this e-mail though because then there goes the surprise.

Punky and Mark are trying to outdo each other with wedding costumes. I plan on the traditional Batman suit. Must find my whoopee cushion too. I always think that's hilarious during the ceremony.

Speaking of which, do you think we have to call Kevin "Brother Maggio" now? We could otherwise call him Cletus. That's sort of an ecclesiastical name. Love, MMM

✉✉✉

From: Punky
Subject: Katie and Jason's wedding

Kevin calls Katie and Jason every Saturday to talk about things that engaged couples should be thinking about. We really appreciate his doing this. It's a sacrifice for him, as he had another wedding scheduled that day.

✉✉✉

From: Mark
Subject: Katie and Jason's wedding

What was he planning to sacrifice at the weddings? I didn't know we still did that sort of thing.

P.S. I bought a new fat suit for the wedding. I know I am fat, but for some reason, the coat makes me look even fatter. Maybe I am just now getting in touch with my feminine side.

✉✉✉

From: Mary
Subject: Katie and Jason's wedding

Yes, Jason, you are now in The Family. You are a made man; you are not just a friend anymore. This means we can borrow money from you.

And Katie, this marriage means your aunts will induct you into the Sisterhood the next time we're together but you must bring a toenail clipping from Jason and a sample of his handwriting.

This poem is by my good friend, Ogden, and it is entitled "A Word To Husbands":

To keep your marriage brimming
With love in the loving cup,
Whenever you're wrong, admit it;
Whenever you're right, shut up.

Love to you all! MMM

✉✉✉✉✉✉✉✉✉✉✉✉✉

From: Pat
Subject: ditto

Although most of my e-mails are downright worthless, this one isn't. I rise, Mr. Chair-human, to enthusiastically, exuberantly, emotionally, and wholeheartedly ditto nearly everything P.T. said. Except the part about the earwig.

And, Matt, please write Mary and tell her how much you are looking forward to seeing her on the left coast so that I can ditto. Thanks.

✉✉✉

From: Pat
Subject: ditto

Hey, Mary, I received your photos. Thanks for including me. They were wonde; quite beaut; impres; stunni. It was not only interes but fascina to get your unique perspec. You have an amaz eye and are a mos sensiti photogr.

I apologize as none of the other sibs have written to compliment you, which means I am having trouble coming up with my own compliments. I typically ditto yet there is nothing yet to ditto. I will wait a bit and write again later.

As my dearest and may I say favorite younger sister, you probably think I am a laze yerk and a bum for adopting others' compliments, but actually I am a little ADD and AADD and dyslexic and left-handed and DLP/LCD and underhanded and, more than anything else, a lawyer. Love you.

✉✉✉

From: Matt
Subject: ditto

Ditto. That's all the time I have today. Call me "Pat" if you like. In fact, I ditto myself. I think dittos are acceptable as long as I am dittoing myself.

✉✉✉

From: Pat
Subject: ditto

Mary, As you can clearly see, the Bro Doc Matt without license or permission used my "ditto." Pls. credit my account with the amount of his points commensurate with such an egregious infraction. Danke.

✉✉✉

From: Matt
Subject: ditto

Punky, have you come across any random dittos? A ditto that was unaccounted for maybe?

✉✉✉

From: Pat
Subject: ditto

MMM, I was disheartened, disappointed, and otherwise distraught to see you using the word "ditto." Within the family context, I am the only one with sufficient legal rights to the repeated use of that word. The bro Maggio used it several months ago, but since he still maintains his law license, I was fearful of challenging him.

⊠⊠⊠

From: P.T.
Subject: ditto

I mimeo that. (Is that okay, Pat?)

⊠⊠⊠

From: Pat
Subject: ditto

Dearest Prolific Ro, Thanks for your great e-mails of late. I am a besmirched runt for not thanking you sooner. Sitting in my rocking chair, waiting for some of the sibs to thank you so I can ditto them, is just not cutting it.

Bro Maggio suggested that I could wean myself of my ditto complex by cutting and pasting complimentary language from others. In this way my compliments would take on a more personal flavor. I'll be doing that as soon as someone else says something nice to you.

⊠⊠⊠

From: P.T.
Subject: ditto

Dear Padraigh, I have always been so proud of my big brother earning his JD degree. Only now, years later, have I come to realize you in fact earned a Juris Ditto degree. I am no less impressed by this accomplishment. You, sir, are a master dittoer!

I can't help wondering how that plays out in the courtroom. Judge Meanie: "I hereby sentence this lowly perp to 800 years of hard time for failing to pay that damn parking ticket." Pat: "Ditto, your honor." And then you could say, as you say every evening when you walk in your back door and set down your briefcase on the lamp table, "I rest my case." I like it.

✉✉✉

From: Matt
Subject: ditto

I would have to agree with all that has been said up to this point. MJM

✉✉✉

From: P.T.
Subject: ditto

That's a veiled ditto if I ever saw one.

By the way, Pat is supposed to leave the country today unless he's sleeping on an airport floor in Colorado. In either case, I think we can get away with using ditto while he is gone. Watch this . . . ditto ditto ditto . . . see, nothing happened to . . . what the heck . . . aarrrrrgghghh . . .

✉✉✉✉✉✉✉✉✉✉✉✉✉

From: Audrey
Subject: Maggio family correspondence

Hello. It appears that you all have inadvertently included me in your e-mail correspondence. If you doublecheck your e-mail addresses you'll find that newsed.com should be newsed.net or newsed.org. Audrey

✉✉✉

From: Frank
Subject: Maggio family correspondence

Audrey, Could you tell me who's been sending them to you? Thanks. We'll get it taken care of.

⊠⊠⊠

From: Audrey
Subject: Maggio family correspondence

Waaah, I want back in the family! You all seem to be a wonderful, loving group, which made it hard to do the "right" thing and not read your e-mails. (I did the wrong thing, and read them, okay?) By the way, Mary takes great photos! I love the landscapes that capture the amazing beauty of the Midwest.

Best wishes to you all—I kinda miss you already! Audrey

⊠⊠⊠

From: Mark
Subject: Maggio family correspondence

Did anyone else notice that that "newsed" e-mail address has crept back into this deliberation like an old coyote at the new moon?

⊠⊠⊠

From: Audrey
Subject: I leave you people alone for a few weeks . . .

. . . and all of a sudden you are eating each other's blankets and beaning blackbirds! The winter must be getting long back there. I've missed you all! Best, Audrey

⊠⊠⊠

From: Pat
Subject: points

Who is Audrey? How did she get into our e-mails? A person not properly authorized to participate in the Maggio Upper Echelon Inner Circle (MUEIC) is an interloper and should be kicked to the curb.

Mary, please send me 10,000 points for my watchdog-like e-mail.

✉✉✉

From: P.T.
Subject: points

I knew I'd get points after I put in my last e-mail, "Especially Mary."

✉✉✉

From: Pat
Subject: points

Mary, I recommend giving Kevin 2 or 3 points and me the remaining 250,000 on the remembering-significant-dates schedule. Here is why. Although he first sent a congratulatory e-mail on the awesome Laura and Matt's 23 years of marriage, I have known of this marriage and important date for 23 years and I attended that ceremony and I remember lots things about it. I just didn't put it in an e-mail yesterday.

Congratulations Laura and Matt!

P.S. Pssst, Kevin! What important dates (besides the inauguration) are coming up next? Send me a PM (personal message just to me).

✉✉✉

From: Matt
Subject: points

Thanks for all your anniversary greetings. I have about 50 billion points now, but I cannot for the life of me remember where they are. Maybe I gifted them to the kids or put them in a foreign account?

⊠⊠⊠

From: Ciccio
Subject: points

What exactly IS the score these days?

⊠⊠⊠

From: Mark
Subject: points

Mary, I am filing a political objection to Pat getting any points based on his status as the Black Sheep of the Family.

At the farm, I am custodian-ad-litem for two (2) actual (not figurative) black sheep. If I am awarded, as legal custodian, their points, then I drop my objection to Pat getting the Black Sheep points.

In other words, my objection to Pat getting the points is not very principled. As long as I get some, you can give him some as well.

Since you can issue any number of points and point-debt-obligations and deficit-point-bonds and federal-reserve-points (fiat points) without Constitutional authorization, like a drunken sailor, on shore leave, no less, why don't you just issue Pat, and me—as legal custodian for two actual black sheep, the black sheep points. And be quick about it. We've got an economic emergency on our hands here.

⊠⊠⊠

From: Kevin
Subject: points

Hi, Mary. As you know, any points less than half are rounded to 0. I see no reason not to give points to Pat and Mark wantonly and recklessly as long as they're less than 0.50. Points appear larger if decimals are used rather than fractions. For example, 0.4375 points seems like a lot more than 7/16ths of a point so this decimal number could be awarded to Pat and/or Mark for being a black sheep or for being the custodian of black sheep. Thus and therefore, in brief sum, and for the sole eleemosynary purpose of aggrandizing Pat's and Mark's self-esteem, I encourage you to dispense many, many points to them on account of their similar but different black sheepnesses. As to the exact decimals per brother, I leave that up to your impeccable capriciousness. What do you think of this approach? Beowolf.

✉✉✉

From: Mary
Subject: points

Dear Beo, You are, as always, spot on. The devil is in the decimals. Only me, Felty

✉✉✉

From: Mark
Subject: points

Dear K-Michael, Who is this "we" that has agreed to the point system? Have you got a mouse in your pocket?

✉✉✉

From: Pat
Subject: points

Mark, I am going to say this once and once only. You should be a writer. MPGMAMP! (Mary Please Give Me All Mark's Points!)

✉✉✉

From: Mark
Subject: points

Mary, Pat wrote, "MPGMAMP," which I looked up in the Urban Dictionary (I told them I live in a big city), and they said what Pat means is: Mary Please Give Mark All My Points (MPGMAMP).

Now that Pat has ceded all his points to me, I have decided to cash them in and quit the game. I want that can opener you promised me. I have had my eye on it for many months. If there are any points left over, I would also be interested in the Chia Pet Armadillo that you offer.

Now send the damn can opener.

✉✉✉

From: P.T.
Subject: points

Mary, You need to give Mark *all* the points. Even Pat's. Do it NOW!

✉✉✉

From: Kevin
Subject: points

Yes, I've got a dead mouse in my pocket. But as for the point system, Mary and I assumed the responsibility in college when no one else wanted the job, and now, by default, we are irreversibly ensconced as Keepers of the Points. Also, I had no idea 7/16ths would be rounded off to zero. Thanks, Pat. Sorry, Ciccio. K

✉✉✉

From: Mary
Subject: points

Who said? Who agreed? What means this? Who said is me. I'll see your floundering and raise you two blusters.

By questioning my administrative abilities, you lost all capability of gaining any points for two days. Right, Beowolf?

This system of points has been in place long before there even were points. It's an extremely intricate and convoluted system. The lineage of overseers, the Faustian point structure, the bantam nuances of resolution (sometimes vindication), these things cannot just be picked up by anyone in New Dork.

One of the greatest truths is that once an egg has been scrambled, well, you get my drift. You don't get to do points. Only Kevin and P.T. and I do, but Kevin and P.T. don't happen to have very many points right now so I am the overseer.

The rest of you have not sent in your accounts so I don't know where you stand point-wise but, Pat, remember, you can't buy points.

Ciccio, I will write you a separate e-mail for why you are so far in the hole.

Only me,
Felty

✉✉✉

From: Kevin
Subject: points

Mary, you can't make me do anything.

✉✉✉

From: P.T.
Subject: points

That's right, Kedin, she's not the boss of you!

⊠⊠⊠

From: Pat
Subject: points

I cracked up watching the "lost luggage" video. Classic. Have watched it three times now. It is hard to tell because my e-mails are mixed up, but I think Pat sent that video so, Mary, please credit him with 500 points.

Also, Paul's story about the skunk and Kevin's story about Mom and the license may deserve more points. So, Mary, please send 500 points to Kevin, P.T., and me. Regards.

P.S. I notice, parenthetically, that the more juicy e-mails have circumvented me. Mary, please transfer 10,000 points to my friend, Patrick. Thanks.

⊠⊠⊠

From: Mary
Subject: points

Pat, you were doing so well! You had over fifty points after you sent me that money. But this bottomless begging for points has resulted in negative numbers for you. Sorry.

⊠⊠⊠

From: Pat
Subject: points

Confidential: Ciccio Only

Hey Ciccio, Why don't we team up like we did when we were kids and scare the bejesus out of Mary to shake her down for a truckload of points? I think she is still scarred over your threats to lock her in the well pit. Perhaps we can use that again. Once we get our points we're off to the Giggling Marlin in Cabo! Call me.

✉✉✉✉✉✉✉✉✉✉✉✉✉

From: Kevin
Subject: pagan baby certificates?

For my next class reunion, someone's asking if any of us have a real live Pagan Baby Adoption Certificate from our days at Corpus Christi. I thought I had one around here somewhere but can't find it. Does anyone have one?

✉✉✉

From: Ciccio
Subject: pagan baby certificates?

I found some and sent you all copies several years ago.

✉✉✉

From: Mark
Subject: pagan baby certificates?

Kevin Michael, The last time I had a look at a Pagan Baby Certificate, they still had the Reverse Retrograde Inclusion clause in it (look on the back of the certificate, in small letters, near the bottom).

The Reverse Retrograde Inclusion clause provides, as you will recall, that if said Pagan Baby does not expressly affirm and claim his or her Pagan status with a Court of competent jurisdiction by the age of five (5), then said Pagan Baby reverts to, and is indeed from that point onward, a Christian. Loss or destruction of said Certificate does not in any way impede the operation of or negate the Reverse Retrograde Inclusion clause.

God uses many channels to claim His faithful. Mark

P.S. If the baby is a Presbyterian, I think you can get your money back.

⊠⊠⊠

From: Kevin
Subject: pagan baby certificates?

Hi, Mark. Thank you for your biased views. The conundrum for pagan babies is that, if they died before being baptized, they were to spend eternity in limbo (but not on their knees since they were just babies). Since limbo has been abolished, no one knows where those pagan babies are or where pagan babies go who died after limbo was expunged from the canon.

In my childhood we adopted many pagan babies for a ransom of $5 apiece or three for $10, often with names like "Kevin Michael," "Mary Margaret," and "Patrick Joseph." Where are they now? K

⊠⊠⊠

From: P.T.
Subject: pagan baby certificates?

I must agree with what Mark said. I don't know what half those words mean, so apparently he makes a good point. The only Pagan Baby Certificate (PBC) I have seen is the one I use for my passport. I merely filled out the form on the back of a Wheaties box. It works in any airport except for those with international flights.

Now, Mark, I happen to know that you are in possession of a number of sheep. I believe you even claim flock status. It is flock, isn't it? I'd hate to say "flock of sheep" if it is supposed to be "pride of sheep," "covey of sheep," or, God forbid, an "exaltation of sheep."

At any rate I surmise the sheep to be nondenominational and therefore possibly pagan. I suggest you look into this matter because your sheep will need PBCs if you plan to travel with them. On a side note, about the travel, I have witnessed passengers trying to load various farm animals into the overhead bins. I don't know about sheep, but horses don't fit and neither do Brahma bulls. Rabbits and some of the smaller turkeys go in just fine.

I hope I have been helpful. Mahzutmah be praised, P.T.

⊠⊠⊠

From: Matt
Subject: pagan baby certificates?

Was there just the one pagan baby? I seem to remember more than one, but my memory has gone the way of the carrier pigeons.

⊠⊠⊠

From: P.T.
Subject: pagan baby certificates?

Does anybody want to take up a collection and buy Mary? She is not exactly a baby anymore but she makes a good pagan.

⊠⊠⊠

From: Mark
Subject: to everyone but Pat

We should be more sensitive when we talk about this subject around our brother Pat. I mean, Pat *was* the pagan baby. I saw the certificate. Kevin held it over him for years during childhood.

Mom and Dad had to take delivery on him in 1948, after the orphanage in Portugal refused the pagan-in-a-basket, and now we have little Pat as a blessing to us all.

I think that the basic legal dispute at the time of his infancy probably affected his career choice.

We must respect Pat for following the great Benedictine mandate, "Do Not Speak, But Work and Pray."

⊠⊠⊠

From: P.T.
Subject: to everyone but Pat

Dear Marky Bird, I seriously appreciate your comments, but I fear you have misunderestimated Paddy's affliction with The Dyslexia.

For example, he may have become confused when you said Pat *was* the baby pagan because, of course, he certainly read it as Pat *saw* the pagan baby. Even though that may or yam not be true, he will probably never know if he actually *was* the pagan baby or merely *saw* it.

You must remember that our sweet brother lives in a world of palindromes and reverse images. So maybe you should slack him some cut and break the boy a give. But for now I think the perfect namenick might be something like Radar. Even better would be Otto out of respect for the number of siblings in our family. You make the call.

✉︎✉︎✉︎

From: Pat
Subject: to everyone but Pat

P.S. from P.T.: I and every patient I have ever had thinks Pat is the most awesome person, so much so that I and all my friends just can't find the words to describe how cool he really is. Love you all. El Mismo

P.P.S. And, as if I could even get my arms around it, but I will try, he also is my very favorite sibling.

✉︎✉︎✉︎✉︎✉︎✉︎✉︎✉︎✉︎✉︎✉︎✉︎✉︎

From: P.T.
Subject: Jim F.'s funeral

Dear Mateo, Thanks for letting us know. I remember he always wore white sox. Mom said he had an allergy to sox (Pat, not sex). But why did all the lawyers come to his funeral? Was his death the result of product liability, malpractice, wrongful termination?

Jim was my football coach in 7th and 8th grade. I was a strapping 43-pounder and I couldn't figure out why he wouldn't put me in more often. Probably because he couldn't see me. He may have thought I was just a pile of some big guy's equipment lying on the ground. I became the dog on the pant leg, following him up and down the sidelines lobbying for a chance to get in the game. He'd shake his pant leg and say something like, "Damn those mosquitoes!" I've always thought if he had given me a chance I could have ended up playing in the NFL and I'd have a cool nickname like Scooter. But I'm over that now . . . mostly.

Ciao babies, Paolo

⊠⊠⊠

From: Punky
Subject: names

But Paul Thomas is a fine name. You're the only one of us named after Dad.

⊠⊠⊠

From: P.T.
Subject: names

It would seem I was named after Dad but, in fact, they named me after the Pope.

By the way, I'm not sure which one of you knuckleheads to thank, but ever since my staff attended Dad's funeral they think it's real fun to call me Peetey.

⊠⊠⊠

From: Mark
Subject: names

P.T., Are you sure you were named after Pope Paul? His middle name was "The Sixth" whereas your middle name is "Thomas." Other than that, I think you are probably right.

⊠⊠⊠

From: P.T.
Subject: names

Actually, no, I'm not sure about that. It seemed plausible until you pointed out that number thing.

For my confirmation name, I ended up using Francis after they told me my first choice, Satan, was unacceptable.

⊠⊠⊠⊠⊠⊠⊠⊠⊠⊠⊠⊠

CHAPTER 5

An Embarrassing Chapter in Which We Confess That We Were Not Always Hardly Ever Little Angels

The Development of Moral Thinking
Frank

In 1950, when I was five years old and there were four children, the half-completed Dr. Paul and Irene Maggio family moved to a four-acre plot about three miles outside town. Even though Dad was a great dentist, he didn't have a secret stockpile of money, so he and Mom were quite frugal. They figured we'd be better off raising our own food than depending on a grocery store.

By the time I was in first grade, we had a number of things in a vast and productive garden that were required to be picked, cleaned, smashed, and canned to feed our hungry little faces throughout the year. Every summer morning, Mom gave the able pickers (anyone who had learned to walk) a pot with instructions to go pick something, anything, until the pot was full. This could have been beans, peas, raspberries, strawberries, peppers, tomatoes, mulberries, or rhubarb.

Classically, in the case, for example, of raspberries, we picked three raspberries, ate four, picked two, ate four, ate five more, ate six. Eventually, we came to our senses and remembered Who was planning on us returning with full bowls. None of us liked this part of the day, but once it was done, we were free. Mother felt that healthy children did not belong indoors in the summer, so after handing in our buckets, we knew we needed to be outside doing something. And that was pure fun.

We had ponies as far back as I can remember and, as we got older, we had horses. Behind our four acres were about eight hundred acres of beautiful wooded land with generous hills and valleys, complete with a creek that flowed all the way to the Des Moines River. We spent countless hours on horseback or foot playing and exploring in the woods.

The summer after fifth grade, I found myself in dire need of pocket change. Mom suggested I ask the farmer next door if I could work for him. I thought that was a great idea, so I asked, and he said I could split logs for him. This was done with a metal wedge and a sledgehammer, neither of which I could easily lift. I had split logs from ten in the morning until around three in the afternoon (no lunch) when he came out to say I'd done enough and could quit for the day. At that point he reached out and gave me a quarter, thanked me, and walked away. I was not happy and would not forget this.

By the next summer, Pat and I had become proficient at building tree houses and rigging up tree swings, and decided we were ready to build the mother of all tree houses.

We desperately needed a good strong rope, with pulleys, to hoist our building materials up into a huge cottonwood tree. I remembered where I had seen such a rope. In the barn of the farmer next door.

To gain access to the upper level of the barn for hay or straw storage, the whole top half of one end of the barn could fold down. This was done by attaching a rope to the top of the "door" and running the rope along the apex of the barn roof all the way to the other end of the barn. The rope descended that wall and stretched along the floor of the barn all the way back to the other end. If the latches on that "door" were released, a horse or tractor could slowly pull the rope forward and let that giant door open out and fold down. When it was time to close it up, the tractor pulled back, and the rope running through the barn pulled the door back into place.

That rope was exactly what we needed.

I worked my way to the top of the door, carrying saw, hammer, and nails. About two feet from the point where the rope was attached to the door, I firmly nailed the rope to the apex of the roof. Then I cut the rope. This way, the barn door wouldn't flap down when I cut it.

What a rope! It was so long and so heavy (at least an inch in diameter) we thought we wouldn't be able to drag it out to the building site. But we were nothing if not stubborn and determined. That rope served us well for many years on many projects. And I got it for splitting wood for five hours.

Never mind the ethics of that equation. I was probably below the "age of reason" at the time. Yeah, yeah, that's right. And they thought I wasn't listening in catechism class.

Boris and Natasha
Pat

Living in the shadows of a brilliant person (my older sister) and an athletic person (my older brother) was not without its dark side. At night, the following phrase cycled endlessly through my brain: "He who is first shall be last. He who is last shall be first." I kept waiting to be first, but it never came to pass.

Difficult to admit, but it was depressing being third in succession to the throne, behind these two gifted siblings. I kept jumping. They kept raising the bar. I did not have the IQ to compete with my sister or the athletic ability to compete with my brother, but what I did have was a truckload of resourcefulness.

Being an orderly person, I started with my sister. I designed and sketched out a wholly satisfactory consequence for her: a hole in the backyard, three feet deep and three feet in diameter. I planned to cover it with mosquito screening from the basement door camouflaged by grass clippings. At the bottom of the hole, the plans called for sharpened bamboo branches protruding from the ground. My plan was an excellent plan, conceptually.

Shortly before I was to blow out ten candles on my birthday cake, Dad caught me working on the basement screen door and kindly inquired about my activities. Because this happened years before my lawyering days, I could only tell the truth. I disclosed every wretched hand-wringing detail to him. He decided I'd feel a lot better if I took the pitchfork and cleaned all the manure and straw mix out of Lady's barn stall. Lady was the prized American Saddle

Horse gifted, by my parents, to none other than their number 1 daughter (in case you've lost the thread here, the target of my jealousy).

But I didn't forget the other one. In Iowa, when I was a kid, fireworks were the precursors to the typical M16 assault rifle kids carry around today. We conspired, from sunup to sundown, to acquire anything from a ladyfinger to a cherry bomb. You could easily distinguish those who didn't like fireworks and thought they were dangerous from those kids who had made a buy—the latter stood taller and walked smartly.

One Saturday evening, shortly after I voluntarily walked away from the plot on my brainy sister (perhaps I am mistaken about this, but she used to read at least one nonfiction and one fiction book a day), I was walking very tall and stepping very smartly. Yes, I had made a buy, from neighborhood doofus Minny Minnuso. This buy was specially tailored to serve as the chief ingredient in my plan to bring down my athletic brother, a.k.a. "favorite son."

The firecracker was about the size of a kidney bean but had a boom not unlike that of a five-hundred-pound World War II bomb. When you jerked the strings in opposite directions, the firecracker gave you its all. I derived so much pleasure from seeing the little eight-inch strings sticking out of each end of the firecracker that I nearly abandoned the plan just so I could continue to drool. I didn't ask for much out of life.

Romeo, or I mean my brother Ciccio, was quite the party boy and usually stayed out until the wee hours on a Saturday night. Being the favorite son, he got a pass from the folks on curfews. It reminded me of the way they'd given Lady to Punky. It didn't matter. I tied the firecracker to the heater on one side of the path he took to his bed and tied the other string to his nightstand. He'd walk to his bed with that smile on his face, the result of whatever he did on those Saturday nights, catch his foot on the firecracker, and set off an explosion. I felt I was ahead of my time, the van Gogh of personal revenge.

From my position under the dresser, I was wired with anticipation, barely able to control myself when I heard the boom of the tripped firecracker.

On a pain scale of zero to ten, zero being not much pain, I'd say ten barely covers what I suffered after big brother heard me snort and fished me out from under the dresser.

One wonders, yes, one wonders, why the oldest three siblings live thousands of miles apart. Ciccio lives in Manhattan, Punky is in California. And I? Colorado isn't precisely halfway between, but it's close enough to allow me to sleep at night.

The Innocent and the Guilty
Frank

On my last day at the Catholic high school, I accepted a ride home from a classmate. He is now deceased, but I still don't want to use his name. This was a guy Mom told me to stay away from. She said he was not a good person, and I should have no contact with him. I had my own thoughts about that.

He had a 1960 Pontiac, manual drive, that was so fast he could lay rubber in third gear. So he was cool. And one night when I was supposed to be staying with a friend, he and I drove up to Lake Okoboji and broke speed records doing it. So he was very cool.

Getting back to the incident, we drove around town, not thinking of anything special and picking up a few other guys. Then suddenly, there was the Goodyear store, complete with a display out by the street of tires for sale. Someone in the car said, "Let's take one of those!" No sooner said than done.

We drove around the block, pulled up next to the display, and I jumped out and grabbed a tire and pulled it into the backseat with me. The driver took off like a bat out of hell (I don't know where you come from, but that expression is pure Iowa). A little later they dropped me off at home, and that was the end of that.

The next day, Saturday, Dad and I took a break from trimming hedges. While Dad was enjoying a beer in the kitchen, the phone rang, and I answered it. It was the chief of police, and he wanted to talk to Dad. I thought this might be something I should not overhear, so I went into the other room. When the conversation was over, Dad said, "That was the chief of police, and he wants us to go to the station house regarding a tire stolen yesterday from the Goodyear store. Do you know anything about this?"

I said that I didn't and that I would be happy to go see the chief of police right now.

Dad, Mom, and I drove into town, not without a lot of questioning. I maintained that I knew nothing about anything. I expressed astonishment that my name was connected to a missing tire.

When we arrived at the police station, the chief had the three of us sit for thirty minutes in a private room. Of course, during that time I maintained my attitude of not only innocence but also of wonderment as to why I was there.

The chief finally entered the room and said that a tire had been stolen from the Goodyear store on the previous day at approximately 4:00 p.m. and did I know anything about it.

I said, "Yes, I took it."

If Mom and Dad had been the types to fall off their chairs, that would have been the time. They were bewildered, disappointed, and speechless. The police chief said, "You took it?"

I said, "Yes, I took it."

He questioned me about why I needed it and what I was going to do with it. I had no answers for him. He expressed a certain dissatisfaction that I would steal something that I didn't desperately need. This thought has lasted a lifetime.

As it turned out, they had already caught the other culprits and knew I was involved. The police had been trying for some time to pin something on my "friend." Having found stolen property in his glove compartment and trunk, they now had what they needed to nail him. But the police were upset that I was involved. My parents' position and sterling reputation in Fort Dodge saved me from being brought up on serious charges.

I was told to return the tire and apologize to the store manager. Can you imagine such an easy out to a bad situation?

In a related story, a friend and I were cruising down Main Street, as was our adolescent custom and pleasure. I got out of my 1924 Ford Model A roadster and stood on the running board and manipulated the speed of the car by using the spark control. My mission was to go the entire thirteen blocks without needing to use the brake. When we got down to Seventh Avenue, it was obvious that the light would not change in time, so I jumped inside the car and hit the brake. You know what comes next. The cop car.

He pulled up alongside me so that we were only two feet from each other. He asked me if my dad knew where I was. That was upsetting. How did he know who my dad was? I told him that I was supposed to be at Denny's house. He told me to go there at once, and if he saw me again, he'd put me in jail.

Living in a small town with parents who are admired and respected has had a lot to do with the fact that I am not serving a life sentence for something.

....

We know one another's faults, virtues, catastrophes, mortifications, triumphs, rivalries, desires, and how long we can each hang by our hands to a bar. We have been banded together under pack codes and tribal laws.—Rose Macaulay

....

The Black Sheep
Pat

Pride, the first of the seven deadly sins, can be a driving force and an endless source of energy, or it can be wickedly corrosive.

Beginning when I reached the age of reason up until the time I was held back a year in school, in second grade, I was so proud that I couldn't or wouldn't ask any of my knowledgeable brothers and sisters whether being labeled the black sheep of the family was a good thing or a bad thing.

In a way, I was blessed. Seldom did someone tell me that I was a doofus for flunking my math test. Seldom did anyone state that I was a psycho for putting a large tack on Sister Mary Generosa's chair. I was always simply told, "You are the black sheep."

Although no one would admit it, many secretly admired my bravado in running up to the front of my sixth-grade classroom and placing the tack on Sister's chair. I was ridiculed only for admitting it. She said, "Whoever put this tack on my seat, stand up." Thirty-one right arms pointed immediately at me. So I stood up.

Dad was widely known for imparting a good deal of wisdom not only to his children but also to others. When I went to him for help because I was not sleeping at night, he suggested that I count sheep to fall asleep quickly. It didn't work. First, the sheep jumping over the fence startled me because they were all black. Second, four of us shared a basement bedroom. So we were close enough to know when one brother wet his bed or when others cursed or told dirty stories. These sounds and smells, like the unexpected sight of black sheep, kept me awake. I had just begun to get control over these external stimulants when Ciccio drafted me into a conspiracy.

Every night, about 1:00 a.m., we went upstairs, in the dark, shaking like leaves in case Mom had her night surveillance on, and ate as much ice cream as we could and gnawed the bottoms out of as many cupcakes as we could. Then we pushed the car out of the garage onto the highway, started it, and were off to town.

When we returned from our little excursions, I was so frightened of being caught I *really* couldn't sleep. For some reason, Ciccio wasn't similarly afflicted. I have a couple of theories on that, but not now. Eventually, the folks caught on, and I was called the black sheep for being so deranged. I never knew why Ciccio always seemed to get a pass on things like that.

I generally had good ideas about what naughty things I could do when inadequately supervised. Being "inadequately supervised" was any time I was not actually in restraints.

When my parents brought in my maternal grandmother to "babysit" (we weren't babies) and then left for a trip to Texas, I had the gestalt to place a live rifle shell in the toolroom vise (Ciccio helped me tighten it in there) and to hammer it so we could see what would happen.

What happened was about what you'd expect. From the top of the basement stairs, Grandma's voice rose in alarm: "Boys? What was that noise?"

The predictable answer. "Nothing."

Ciccio and I were also reported for sneaking into the drive-in movie theater down the road. The rest of the kids virtuously watched the show from on top of the barn, compensating for the lack of speakers by each taking a role and making up the dialogue. Does that sound like a good time to you? Me neither.

But we harbored feelings about the tattletale neighbor. One night we sneaked down the road with a can of gasoline and wrote on his lawn. Imagine our joy as we rode past in the school bus each day and watched the grass turn brown. The brown part spelled "f—."

The neighbor replaced the dead grass. Now, when we rode past on the school bus, "f—" was spelled out in the distinctive bright green of new sod. And this was the Catholic school bus, mind you.

As an adult, I am not so ashamed of being the black sheep. White sheep follow one another around mindlessly. If one white sheep winks, they all wink. Not so with black sheep. First, there is just one black sheep, so you've got some status there in the rarity thing. Second, black sheep do stupid things before anyone else does stupid things. So there is some glory in being the first. Last, it could be argued that black sheep are leaders. You never see one trying to build a consensus. They are crazy all by themselves. It brings to mind Margaret Thatcher's words, perhaps prompted by her keen observation of black sheep behavior, "Consensus building is the death knell to leadership." I couldn't have said it any better.

Poor Mrs. Clark
Kevin

She wasn't always "poor Mrs. Clark" in my memory. At first she was simply the music teacher at Corpus Christi Grade School Academy. She was an anomaly not only because she was one of the few lay teachers at that time but also because of her appearance, a stark contrast to that of the nuns.

An older heavyset woman from Texas, she wore lots of costume jewelry, red lipstick, red nail polish, and skimpy summer dresses with large flower patterns and lots of cleavage. Her long red hair was pinned up in weird patterns on the top and back of her head. Being kids, we couldn't help being fascinated by the noticeable wattle under her chin and the way her voice warbled.

Mrs. Clark had only one child, Sonny Boy, a twenty-something who lived in Texas. She worshipped him and regaled her captive classroom audiences with many unutterably boring stories about him, hand over her heart, tears in her eyes.

The fourth floor of the academy was generally off-limits because it was not structurally sound enough to hold more than a few bodies at a time. It had a dusty old stage, storage and classrooms, lots of old furniture, and—the coup de grâce—large class pictures of all the previous graduates. We used to go up there and sneak a peek at Mom and her siblings and, yes, at that time, even Grandma's picture was there.

Mrs. Clark had a funky room up there where she gave voice and piano lessons—and where Mary and I rehearsed our famous P.T.A numbers like "Playmates" and "Sunbonnet Sally and Overall Jim."

One beautiful spring day, Pat rushed into Mrs. Clark's studio and breathlessly announced that Sonny Boy had driven all the way from Texas to see her. He was waiting for her in the parking lot below right now! Mrs. Clark hustled her large body—bracelets and necklaces jangling—down four double flights of wooden stairs, warbling to herself all the while about the virtues of Sonny Boy and how wasn't it just like him to surprise her with a visit. Pat was following closely behind.

When Mrs. Clark got down to the parking lot, she looked left, she looked right, she looked left again. But Sonny Boy was nowhere to be seen. Pat was laughing so hard he barely managed to get out, "April fool! April fool!"

Poor Mrs. Clark.

....
Heirlooms we don't have in our family.
But stories we've got.—Rose Chernin
....

The Exploding Toilet
Frank

In the early stage of being a grown-up, when my wife Mary, son Mike, and I lived in St. Paul, we were visited by most of my brothers and sisters. I particularly recall winter break of 1969-1970 when Pat and Kevin traveled from Iowa to ski in Minnesota.

Pat was in his first year at Drake Law School, and Kevin was a junior at the University of Iowa, with his eye on law school.

Kevin was the almost-perfect student, not just in the matter of grades (he graduated Phi Beta Kappa) but in holding class offices and participating in multiple extracurricular activities. There is no doubt that he had an eye on the presidency of the United States. He had never been in trouble. Quite an accomplishment. He should have kept his eye on that ball when he agreed to join Pat on this trip.

Pat was an above-average student who was not afraid to take chances and who saw no problem with getting into trouble now and then. He once told me that he made the decision in college to become a lawyer. His other choice was to be some kind of crook. As it turned out, he's an exceptional lawyer and human being. But that is now. This was then.

Other than some possible frostbite, their first day on the slopes was uneventful. They begged me to go with them the second day, but they had used up every bit of my winter clothing in an effort to keep themselves from freezing. I had a wife and child, so I couldn't take the risk of freezing with them.

As darkness fell—that would be 4:00 p.m. MWT (Minnesota Winter Time)—we began preparations for thawing out the skiers. But the hour grew late, and they didn't return. Since that was pre-cell phone, we had no way of knowing their whereabouts. We figured that if they were in the morgue (1) someone would call us and (2) they would not have to be put on ice. Mary went to bed while I waited up until I fell asleep around 3:00 a.m.

At 4:30 a.m., they came in the front door, very quietly. They were awake and coherent and didn't even look frozen, thawed, or tired. Kevin went straight to bed without as much as a word. Pat tried the same thing, but I was able to coax him into telling me a little about their activities. The story went something like this:

After skiing all day in below-zero temperatures and a strong wind, they decided to repair to a bar in Hudson, Wisconsin—only twenty minutes from St. Paul and an easier state in which to buy beer.

After transferring some quantity of beer from the bartender's supplies to their bellies, Pat departed to the bathroom. While in there, he lit a cherry bomb and flushed it down the toilet. As luck would have it, this toilet was a slow flush, and the cherry bomb went off prior to going down into the pipe.

The toilet bowl exploded.

A quick-thinking fellow, Pat immediately dropped his pants around his ankles and ran out of the restroom screaming, "Someone tried to blow me up!"

What a shock for Kevin. There was his ski pal brother in the middle of the bar, naked from the waist down! Some nasty drunk just tried to blow him up in the restroom!

Pat continued his noisy expostulations as the bouncer helped him put his pants back on. However, the bouncer soon realized that Pat and Kevin had been drinking together and that absolutely no one else had been anywhere near the restroom.

It was well after 1:00 a.m., but that didn't stop the wheels of justice. The sheriff drove them to the home of the local justice of the peace, who was not happy to be awakened at that hour. His thoughts ran along the lines of pressing charges, jailing both of them, and returning to bed.

Pat wasn't having any of it. "Look, if you jail us, we'll both be kicked out of school. We can't pay the fine plus damages, so we'll spend some time in your good jail where you will have to feed us. In the morning, that poor bar owner is going to have to call a plumber to fix the toilet, and he will be stuck with the bill. On the other hand, if you don't press charges, we will pay right now for the toilet repair, and we would have enough left over for a donation to the police fund."

That, of course, is a much-abbreviated version of Pat's position. After a great deal of this, the JP realized that the BS wouldn't end until sunrise, so he accepted Pat's proposal and let them go.

Kevin walked on eggs for years afterward and, to my knowledge, has never discussed the episode in public. Pat took it in stride. I am still laughing.

....

My brothers, the dragon slayers, capable and strong.—Patricia Penton Leimbach

....

The Exploding Toilet
Kevin

Every once in a while, something happens in my life that has no particular meaning, no deep lesson, no spiritual message, no personal growth opportunity, no nada, nothing. It leaves me scratching my head and wondering, "What the heck was that all about?" This is such a story.

It happened during Christmas break when I was a junior at the University of Iowa and Pat was in his first year of law school at Drake. Besides being in law school, Pat also managed a twenty-five-unit apartment complex in Des Moines. He and I had been home in Fort Dodge for Christmas and decided to spend a few days with Ciccio and Mary Claire and their wonder baby Michael.

One night after skiing, Pat and I had dates with Karen and Katie (nowhere near their real names), but since they were only twenty years old and too young to drink in Minnesota, we headed across the Mississippi where the Wisconsin beer-drinking age was eighteen.

We found a lone bar out in the countryside. The building looked like a little old brick warehouse, but inside crowds of college kids like us were shouting over a jukebox, drunk or trying to get that way. Pat and I sat on one side of our booth facing our dates. After a few pitchers of beer, Pat tapped me on the arm and pointed to his coat pocket, which was lying on the seat and out of view of our dates. In it was a handful of M-80 firecrackers. I was drunk; I laughed.

Pat had to cup his hands over my ear and shout for about ten minutes to explain what he had in mind. The wick on an M-80 was waterproof, he said, and took about a minute to burn. If it exploded inside a pipe, it had a much bigger impact because of some concussive factor. He said a guy could light an M-80 and flush it down the toilet on the eleventh floor of a dormitory, and the guy who was sitting on the can on the fourth floor would shoot up in the air on a geyser of toilet-bowl water.

I don't pretend to understand or accept vandalism, but I'm embarrassed to say that Pat's plan for the bar restroom had a certain boozy appeal for me.

The bathroom was down a long, narrow, unlit hallway with a right-angled turn in the middle. The bathroom itself was a large empty room with two urinals on one wall, two sinks on another, and two freestanding toilets against another wall with no stalls around them. We waited until we had it all to ourselves for one mad moment.

My job was simply to flush the toilet when Pat said to. After Pat lit the M-80 and threw it in as I flushed the toilet, Pat said we needed to leave pronto.

As I was turning to leave, I noticed the water in the toilet bowl started to rise a second time instead of going down, and there was the sputtering M-80 turning fast little circles in the flushing water. I shouted to Pat, "What should we do, what should we do? It's going to blow before it goes down the pipes! Should I take it out?" But Pat was nowhere to be seen.

I stood, dumbfounded, over the toilet bowl. The water and the M-80 went down to the neck of the toilet bowl, and there it blew. I thought my eardrums had burst from the reverberating sound in that large empty room. White dust from the disintegrated toilet bowl lay everywhere. A small fountain of water at the jagged neck of the bowl gurgled about two feet off the floor.

Meanwhile, Pat was running into the bar, having pulled his pants down, shouting that someone had blown up the toilet right while he was using it.

Through the ringing in my ears, I heard a stampede rumbling down that narrow L-shaped hallway. The restroom filled with guys from the bar, including Pat, shouting and laughing. The bouncer sized up the situation using some obscure bouncer equation and carried me—me!—out of the restroom while perfect strangers yelled things like, "Break him in half!"

I was handcuffed and thrown in the backseat of a car by the bouncer. A friend of his sat in the back with me, alternately falling asleep and swearing at me. Pat, Karen, and Katie followed in Pat's car.

Waking the justice of the peace took a little time, but the wait was worth it. The door opened to reveal a little old man holding a flashlight and wearing a knee-length, red-and-white striped flannel nightshirt with matching slippers. (When we got to his office in the basement, there on his desk was a matching little pointed red-and-white striped flannel hat.)

In his tiny office—imaginatively furnished with large cages of dirty, noisy birds and World War II mementos including photos, medals, German handguns, and two grenades—the justice of the peace began searching for forms. His desk was piled so high with papers he couldn't find anything. He rustled through everything on his desk, the floor, and the bookshelves—pushing Pat and me and the two bouncers aside—and then did it all over again to find the next form. I was starting to sober up. And it struck me: I was not in Kansas anymore.

When asked to make a statement, the bouncer said, "He done it! I seen him!" He grabbed a hand grenade from the shelf and stuck it in the JP's face. "It was sumfin like this he throwed in the toilet! I seen it!" He was very convincing. I was very scared.

While the JP asked me for my name, age, and address, Pat kept interrupting him to say that he had no jurisdiction over me, that I was from Iowa, that the JP was only authorized to do business in this little Wisconsin county and had no authority over outsiders, that he, Pat, was in law school and knew my rights.

When the JP ignored him, Pat demanded a change of venue, repeating that he was a law student and knew that I had an absolute constitutional right to a change of venue. I had no idea what "venue" meant and didn't want to know. I just wanted Pat to shut up. The JP looked up over his glasses at Pat and shook his head with a smirk. "There's no such thing as a change of venue from a justice of the peace. So shut up!"

Pat, of course, has never stopped talking in his life, not even to breathe, so he kept yammering, and the JP kept getting madder. I was whispering sort of like a yell, begging Pat to shut up, but he wouldn't. Every time I tried to talk, Pat said, "Don't say anything to anyone. It could be used against you. Let me do all the talking." I was not comforted.

Finally, the JP gave the bouncer a handful of papers and said to take me over to the jail. Pat kept talking, talking, and didn't even stop as the JP closed the front door in our faces.

The police were waiting for me, and behind the booking counter were three holding cells holding at the moment several drunk and dangerous-looking guys. I imagined I would be joining them shortly. I was having trouble breathing.

The owner of the bar met us at the counter and said the toilet cost $50. He knew that because someone smashed it last week, so he still had the replacement receipt in his pocket. The fine would be $100.

As this was the last day of our visit in Minnesota, I had only $20 in my pocket. Pat shushed me. He clarified the situation for everyone. The bar owner could waive filing charges and accept $50 cash from Pat and me to replace his toilet, or he could refuse to waive the charges, and I would pay the police $100, and the owner would get nothing. The owner said the police had been very good to him over the years, and he would rather they have the $100 even if it meant he got nothing. Pat then pointed out how stupid it was to pass up getting paid for the toilet, and the police didn't need the fine anyway because they were supported by tax dollars. Again, the owner said no, and again, Pat argued and argued while I was, again, whispering in a frantic yell to Pat to shut up and pay somebody something to get me out of there.

By 4:00 a.m., Pat finally agreed I would pay the $100 fine.

And then Pat reached into his pocket and slowly, dramatically, pulled out a fat wad of bills (it amounted to $700, to be exact). He had collected January's rent from several apartments before he left Des Moines for Christmas break. As he painstakingly peeled off five twenties and deliberately laid them on the counter, he said, "Let's get out of this two-horse town."

I was so mad at him I swore I would never speak to him again in my life. I had thought his arguing and posturing with the JP and the police and the bar owner was due to us not having enough money to get me out of this mess. As we walked toward the car with our frozen dates in it, I cursed Pat with every creative expression in my lexicon. Pat? He was laughing so hard tears were freezing on his face. And that's the story. I have no idea what it means.

The great advantage of living in a large family is that early lesson of life's essential unfairness.—Nancy Mitford

The Exploding Toilet
Pat

I am going to give you one warning and one warning only. If you, collectively, do not categorically reject "The Exploding Toilet" piece submitted by Maggio, the erstwhile Kevin Michael Maggio, my compelling contributions to the book will never see the light of day. I've spent a lifetime trying to squeeze blood out of a turnip. That is to say, as a youth, seeing a consensus that I was the black sheep, the pinhead, the money-grubber, the opportunist, the doofus, I threw in the white towel and went to law school. Slightly ahead of selling used cars on the least-admired list, lawyering did nothing to dissuade the masses from the heretofore-mentioned consensus. But this last shot? Well, I can't take it. I don't have the strength to continue the fight with this dastardly rendition of "The Exploding Toilet" written with all the accuracy and recollection of a drunken sailor. I cannot withstand another stain on my escutcheon.

Now, to whet your whistle, a peek into the highlights of my stunning book contributions: A three-fourths chapter rebutting the charge that I don't have friends. I do have friends—at least one that I know of. I didn't end up in prison. I am actually in an office. I served my time and am out. Ha! I am not a pinhead. I had reverse lipo just above my ears, more on the left side than on the right.

Now, having laughed off my kisser at Maggio's version of events, I confess I was just kidding with all of the above and love Maggio's unique viewpoint (taken from a man so drunk that while he was pinned to the bar, he recalls hearing the crowd chant, "Crucify him! Crucify him!").

....

Mary's joke for two of the brothers, the laid-back oldest and the silver-tongued trial attorney:

Ciccio and Pat were captured by terrorists. The terrorist leader said, "Before we shoot you, you will be allowed last words. First, tell me what you wish to talk about."

Ciccio replied, "I wish to speak of my loyalty to my family and country."

Pat replied, "Since you are presupposing a question of national purpose, national identity, and possibly secession, I wish to talk about the history of the abiding and equitable constitutional process in the United States, special status, distinct extrinsic society, and uniqueness within diversity in both the congruous family unit and the historical context of esprit de corps herein."

Ciccio replied, "I'm changing my request. Just shoot me before Pat starts talking."

....

Smoking Is Bad for Your Teeth
Frank

In the summer between seventh and eighth grades, I worked as a farmhand for Harvey Scheerer. His real farmhand had a son about my age, and we often worked together on various projects. Bill, a nonfiltered Camel man, introduced me to cigarettes.

Usually, there would be only one time each day when we were left alone long enough to sit behind the barn and smoke. I got some sort of high from doing that and, unfortunately, liked it. In high school I started buying my own—twenty-five cents a pack.

At some point in my junior year, my detective mother figured out that I was smoking. In an earnest and loving attempt to get me to stop, she suggested that whenever I wanted a cigarette, I should chew a stick of gum. To please her, I did just that. When I wanted a cigarette, I first put the gum in and then smoked the cigarette. I tried to chew the greatest amount of gum possible, partially to cover the odor and partially to make her think her advice worked.

The strategy backfired on me in my senior year when I got my first cavity. I stopped the gum chewing and continued smoking. I should have done the reverse. Over the next five years, I developed five or six cavities, all of which were related to those gum-chewing days.

At this point in my life, I think it would be better to have no teeth than to be a smoker. I still smoke and have failed to quit many times over the years. I think this is the worst thing I've carried throughout my life. This habit will not have a good ending. If you have never smoked or if you have quit, you are both smart and lucky.

Small Beginnings
Rosalie

Dad had iron self-discipline. If he gained five pounds, he took note and promptly lost them. The weaker-willed among us hated that.

He used to smoke. As he tells it, he was working in the garden one day when he realized he was polluting both himself and the outdoors he loved so much.

"So I took that pack of cigarettes out of my pocket and threw them down right where I was working. I never touched another cigarette."

A few years later, Ciccio was caught smoking down by the basement door. Dad, with all the zeal of the former smoker, lit into him, you might say. "Whatever possessed you to start smoking?"

Ciccio said, "I don't know. One day I was working in the garden, and I found a pack of cigarettes."

E-mails

From: Mary
Subject: cell phone

Dang it. I lost my cell phone. Right now the only number for me is our land line. MMM

⊠⊠⊠

From: P.T.
Subject: cell phone

You lost your cell phone and all you can say is "dang it"?

⊠⊠⊠

From: Mark
Subject: cell phone

Mary, How come you can't just dial your own number, like in the movies, and your cell phone will ring, and the Mafia guy will pull it out of his pocket and say "This damn thing," and crush it with his heel? Then you would know where your cell phone is. I hope this helps.

⊠⊠⊠

From: Ciccio
Subject: cell phone

My cell phone didn't have the good sense to come in out of the rain and is thus no longer operative. Your advice won't work for me, Mark.

⊠⊠⊠⊠⊠⊠⊠⊠⊠⊠⊠⊠⊠

From: Mark
Subject: snake eats kangaroo

P.T., You have such a sweet, innocent, child-like appreciation of all nature's little animals.

That is probably the most reprehensible series of animal behavior photos I have ever seen. How do you find this stuff?

✉✉✉

From: P.T.
Subject: snake eats kangaroo

Dear Mark, It may be more palatable for you, with your background in economics, if you think of the snake as Sam Walton and the kangaroo as Bob's Five and Dime.

✉✉✉

From: Pat
Subject: snake eats kangaroo

In my business, fitting.

✉✉✉

From: Mark
Subject: snake eats kangaroo

Dear P.T., Lots of people must have these big snakes. I am always hearing ads on the radio and TV for "Reptile Dysfunction." No wonder! A reptile would naturally feel a little dysfunctional after eating a whole kangaroo.

One ad says, "Do you suffer the embarrassing consequences of reptile dysfunction?" If your reptile were to gag down a whole kangaroo and then get heartburn, boy, that would be embarrassing.

But I still don't believe the ad that says, "Eighty million suffer reptile dysfunction!" There just aren't that many kangaroos around. Mark

⊠⊠⊠⊠⊠⊠⊠⊠⊠⊠⊠⊠⊠⊠

From: Kevin
Subject: testing

Hola, mis amigos y amigas. Ciccio is not receiving any of my e-mails. I've called three support centers (all in India) and they think the problem is not at my end. Will you please reply to this when you receive it? If I don't hear from all of you in the next day or so, it may indicate the problem is mine. This high-tech stuff is all so mysterious.

⊠⊠⊠

From: Mark
Subject: testing

Kevin Michael, I did not get your latest e-mail. The problem must be on your end. Mark

⊠⊠⊠

From: P.T.
Subject: testing

Dear Mark, I did not receive this from you either, maybe it's on my end.

⊠⊠⊠

From: Mary
Subject: testing

I did not receive this e-mail either. That's what you get for asking a Maggio a simple question. MMM

⊠⊠⊠

From: P.T.
Subject: testing

What question?

⊠⊠⊠⊠⊠⊠⊠⊠⊠⊠⊠⊠⊠

From: Mary
Subject: ringy dingy dingy

Mom's missing rings were finally located at Kirkberg's Jewelry, being cleaned and having a couple of loose stones fixed. Yay. Love, MMM

⊠⊠⊠

From: Kevin
Subject: ringy dingy dingy

How did you locate the rings?

⊠⊠⊠

From: Mary
Subject: ringy dingy dingy

The rings were at Kirkberg's being cleaned.

⊠⊠⊠

From: Kevin
Subject: ringy dingy dingy

I know, but how did you find out? I thought nobody knew where they were. By what miracle did someone remember? Or did Kirkberg's call? I'm just curious.

⊠⊠⊠

From: Ciccio
Subject: ringy dingy dingy

Mrs. Kirkberg said that she called the house and spoke to a guy who went by "Maggio." She told him the rings were ready for pick-up. That is her story and she's sticking to it. So, Kevin, thanks for passing on the message.

⊠⊠⊠

From: P.T.
Subject: ringy dingy dingy

Kevin, the rings were at Kirkbergs.

⊠⊠⊠

From: P.T.
subject: ringy dingy dingy

Getting cleaned.

⊠⊠⊠

From: Matt
Subject: ringy dingy dingy

Kevin, they were right by the investment bonds that Mary and I found in the black trunk. By the way, Mary, did you take one of the bonds home with you? I have nine of them and cannot find the tenth.

⊠⊠⊠

From: Kevin
subject: ringy dingy dingy

Aren't those Dad's WWII bonds? FDR's special "invest in the war" bonds? Mary, I don't mind if you took one. K

⊠⊠⊠

From: Mary
subject: ringy dingy dingy

In addition to the gold, the bonds, and the jewels, there remains Dad's coin collection to be valued and sold. I've looked through it and determined it's not worth much so I will just cash it in and you can take 20 bucks off my share of the inheritance. Matt decided the bonds weren't worth much so he's keeping those. The gold was hardly worth mentioning and since you all voted that I should keep the jewels, I'll just thank you. That about ties it up.

⊠⊠⊠

From: Matt
Subject: ringy dingy dingy

Thanks for spilling the beans, Mary. I'm just glad you didn't mention the property in Florida. Matt

⊠⊠⊠

From: Mary
Subject: ringy dingy dingy

The beans? There were beans, too?

⊠⊠⊠

From: Mark
Subject: ringy dingy dingy

Kevin, There was a typo. It wasn't the bonds that Mary found at home, it was the bongs. And I think you are in a lot of trouble.

⊠⊠⊠

From: Kevin
Subject: ringy dingy dingy

Au contraire, it wasn't the bonds or the bongs, it was the bangs of our almost-beatified aunt, Margaret Mary Maggio, and they're worth a lot!

⊠⊠⊠

From: Mark
Subject: ringy dingy dingy

Where did you find the au contraire? Was it on top of the fridge?

⊠⊠⊠

From: Pat
Subject: ringy dingy dingy

Maggio, Since you brought it up, I would just parenthetically add that in the land where cheese grows in the wild, bongs are legal on any of the 10,000+ bodies of water. So if, for example, you were to visit, say P.T., and if, for example, you were to journey over water in a vessel, and if, for example, you were to discover a bong, with some stuff in it, hidden up under the newly created stereo cavity (said cavity personally enlarged, ostensibly, to make room for the new larger stereo), it probably would be legal. Love you.

⊠⊠⊠

From: P.T.
Subject: ringy dingy dingy

Dear Pat, That is a very well-written brief. It's no wonder you are a top-notch attorney. However, through no fault of your own, it no longer holds water. We have new information telling us the objects are bangs, not bongs.

⊠⊠⊠

From: Matt
Subject: ringy dingy dingy

Dear PeeTee, You betrayed my confidence. I thought us dentists were supposed to stick together!

⊠⊠⊠

From: P.T.
Subject: ringy dingy dingy

Sorry, Matt, it's a doc eat doc world out there.

⊠⊠⊠

From: Mary
Subject: ringy dingy dingy

Half a dozen of you be quiet.

⊠⊠⊠⊠⊠⊠⊠⊠⊠⊠⊠⊠

From: Mark
Subject: hairdryer

Dear Family, What a wonderful weekend we had! Such a nice diversion for me! I am enjoying my well-ordered barn and cleaned-up garage, thanks to the help of the brothers. I enjoyed everyone's sense of humor, the singing (with a bow to Mr. Pianoman KMM), and now the memories—seeing Margaret, the Nashes, and the house at Route 4. I got a little choked up remembering Dad when seeing the aspidistra plant from his funeral. But I still have a nice, warm feeling recalling the tale of how Beulah the horse bit Ciccio on the butt.

It is too bad that some people have to ruin it for everyone. We discovered that Terry was missing her (very expensive) hairdryer. Search though I might, I couldn't find here at the farmhouse. Those beyond suspicion include Mark (not enough hair) and P.T. (he can play with it anytime he wants since he actually lives with Terry).

Suspicion therefore immediately falls on Pat. Since we are kind of an anti-government community around here, I presented this to the militia guys up at the fake Army surplus store in Randall for adjudication. Pat, I am sorry to tell you that without notice to you or representation of you, the inquisition determined that you are the guilty party, based on (1) you have pretty nice hair, (2) your well-documented predilection to do shady things, and (3) the Black Sheep Thesis, which I was required to explain to the militia. They felt there were ample grounds to convict.

Terry, the victim, already has separation anxiety, and there is no way she can recover the precious time she has lost to this senseless act of wrongful removal.

Pat, if you are ever driving around here and a couple of guys in camo try to stop you, don't stop; just keep on driving. It would be best for all.

⊠⊠⊠

From: Pat
Subject: hairdryer

My Dear Mrs. Doc, Because of Pat's black-sheep personality traits, I want to step up and apologize sincerely to you for Pat not returning your hotshot Sharon Stone hairdryer. As politically incorrect as it may seem, I am going to come right out and condemn him. It was his responsibility to return that dryer to the gracious Mrs. Doc. Please accept this vicarious apology as though it were sent directly from Pat. Regards. Mary.

⊠⊠⊠

From: Terry
Subject: hairdryer

So it was Pat! That figures.

Mary, No need to apologize for Pat. I knew it was that klepto all along. I caught him rummaging through my suitcase earlier so I just assumed that was the prize he had decided upon. His hair did look damn good, though.

I'll write off the cost of the $112,398 hair dryer on my tax return. Love, Terry

P.S. Pat, since you have your grubby little hands on that contraption, you might as well hold on to it. Thanks to the stock market, it doesn't look as though we'll need a travel hairdryer anytime soon.

✉✉✉

From: Mark
Subject: hairdryer

Dear Terry, We now see that although guilty, and sheepish, or was it peevish—I always get them confused—Pat squealed and told us where your hairdryer is. After we put a little pressure on him, he sang like a chickadee.

It is indeed located in the corner bedroom, with the candlestick, by Colonel Mustard.

I have it in safekeeping and will see you get it, even though you failed to reclaim it. Under Maggio rules, which are Top Secret, you normally would not have the right to reclaim it at this time.

✉✉✉

From: Mary
Subject: hairdryer

Mark, she will never accrue enough points to reclaim it so just go ahead and sell it if you want. MMM

✉✉✉✉✉✉✉✉✉✉✉✉

From Kevin
Subject: Ciccio celebrates one year without cigarettes!

Wow, congratulations, Ciccio! Makes me want to sing, "To Dream the Impossible Dream" because that's about the hardest thing to do. Love, K

✉✉✉

From: Mary
Subject: Ciccio celebrates one year without cigarettes!

Yay, Leaver of the Pack!

Ciccio, I'm damb proud of you about the cigs. I never thought I'd see the day!

In your honor, a smoking joke:

A guy's walking down the street and sees little Ciccio smoking a cigarette. He says, "Kid, you're too young to smoke. How old are you?"

Ciccio says, "Six."

The guy says, "Six? When did you start smoking?"

Ciccio says, "Right after the first time I got laid."

The guy says, "Right after the first time you got laid? When was that?"

Ciccio says, "I don't remember. I was drunk."

✉✉✉

From: P.T.
Subject: Ciccio celebrates one year without cigarettes!

He has always been precocious.

✉✉✉

From: Pat
Subject: Ciccio celebrates today one year of not smoking!

Hmmm. I don't get it. Is the punch line missing? Ciccio never got laid. I know. I was with him both times he tried. He got slapped the first time but always the quick learner, he ducked the second time.

✉✉✉✉✉✉✉✉✉✉✉✉✉

CHAPTER 6

A Thought-Provoking Chapter in Which We Learn to Work and Work to Learn and Have Mixed Experiences, Not All of Them Productive or Instructive or Even Very Fun

When Asking for Money, Ask the Right Person
Frank

As far back as I can remember, one of my chores was to feed and water the ponies and horses each morning and evening. This was not just some days, this was every day, and was in addition to any other chores that Mom could think up while we were at school.

Because I was up early to get the barn business done, I also took it upon myself to awaken any school-age siblings on school days and either prepare or start the preparation for their breakfast. I liked this arrangement as I could get almost all of my morning stuff done before they arrived to create a circus atmosphere in the kitchen. By that time, I was outside having my morning cigarette and had ample time to get myself ready for school.

In my junior year, I started feeling sorry for myself, thinking that I was carrying more of a load than my siblings.

I approached Dad and told him I thought I should get $5 a week for my animal-feeding job.

Dad was quick-witted, so I shouldn't have been surprised by his speedy, shocking response. He kindly said that I had been reliable for years and he appreciated the daily feeding as well as the cleaning of the pens each weekend.

However, he said, I had done that long enough. He would tell my younger brother Pat that from now on those responsibilities were his.

I was speechless. No way was Pat going to do my job! With one simple conversation, Dad defeated my ploy to get an allowance. I should have gone to Mother.

My Catholic Education
Pat

There is something to be said for a good dose of discipline in the elementary and high school years. At least that is the way I legitimize my gauntlet-like plodding through grades 1-12. The nuns and priests were, as a group, both strict disciplinarians and top-drawer educators. However, when my disciplinary problems exceeded my educational progress, life rapidly lost its luster.

I learned, too late, that in my Catholic elementary school, as well as in my high school, the toughest nuns and priests were applied to the most difficult students. Duh! By the time I reached seventh grade, I was savvy enough to realize that Sister Mary Genevieve was wearing a flak jacket and had a bulge under her waistband about the same thickness as a MAC-10 machine gun.

My run-ins with various members of her tribe consisted largely of wicked tongue lashings that continued through high school and right up until I left the monastery—otherwise known as St. Benedict's College—after completing my first year of post-secondary education.

These combat nuns and priests had, and may I say it was not subtle, a psychological toughness matched only by their physical toughness. As she stood in front of the only door to my seventh-grade classroom, Sister Mary Genevieve, while dressing me down, said, "And we are not going to be able to call our mommy for help, are we, Mr. Madgio?" (Her deliberate mispronunciation of my surname was one of many strategies to keep me in my place.) To do that you'd have to get past me, and we are not going to be able to do that, are we, Mr. Madgio?"

During the school year, my knees usually started to rattle just after I finished breakfast each morning.

With keen twenty-twenty hindsight, it now seems that the high level of discipline, coupled with high expectations, drove me to study, to make an effort to meet expectations, and to generally obtain a respectable education. Nevertheless, the day finally arrived, in March of my junior year of high school, when I was a party to a parent-teacher conference designed to identify and select a college.

The discussion—and this is directly from my "Notes to Self"—went something like this:

Sister Mary Hermaneutica said, "Now, Dr. and Mrs. Maggio, Patrick is a very special student, and we need to place him where he will be challenged. I think Des Moines Tech would be perfect."

Parenthetically, the moment I heard these words, I had a vision of large horns on the head of a snorting bull, tearing through my cheesy red loincloth.

Sister Mary Hermaneutica continued, "He can learn to remove tires and wheels from garbage trucks. I can assure you he will be good at that. College isn't for everyone, you know."

Not that what I thought mattered, but I felt the conference went downhill from that point.

Santa Claus—or at least that is what he called himself after he climbed into the suit each Christmas—had a sweet tooth. Legally known as Chester Ratz, the nearly toothless tubby encountered Dad, practicing his trade as a dentist and do-gooder. Dad of course offered to make him a set of dentures. The jolly Mr. Ratz, it seemed, had no money but did have a commercial electric horse-racing parlor machine. You dropped in a nickel, and the thing lit up like the Las Vegas strip. He insisted Dad take the machine since he couldn't pay for his dental work.

Why are we talking about Ratz? In the late summer, after my high school graduation, I was in the basement playing the horse-racing machine. I had been "saved by the bell" in that it was a rainy Saturday morning, so I didn't have to pick four baskets of raspberries from our chigger patch. I mean, our raspberry field. So I was playing that machine like there was no tomorrow when Mom showed up and told me to grab my underwear and meet her in the garage.

"Excitement" was the word because I thought I was going to get to ride the train to some farm town farther away than Moorland. I didn't travel much. As I high-stepped into the garage, there was Dad in the driver's seat and Mom in the front passenger seat.

Mom said, "Hop in. You're going to college!"

Drat! I figured that my folks had been trying to find a meaningful way to punish me for joyriding in that "borrowed" tow truck last summer—and this was it.

Seven hours later, as we drove onto the campus, I noticed beautiful brown marble statues and monuments. I was surprised when I saw some of them moving. Turns out they were Benedictine monks strolling about. Turns out further that this was a prep school for becoming a monk. How blessed was I!

St. Benedict wasn't really a saint. He was given the benefit of the doubt because the Holy See was just plain tired of dealing with his surviving sisters who fancied themselves accomplished mystics. This monk-preparation institute had, as a direct and proximate consequence of the aforementioned "benefit of the doubt," a truckload of bad karma. Although Murphy hadn't been born yet, I read many forensic experts' reports, prepared by a scrivener on parchment, opining that at St. Benedict's College anything that could go wrong would go wrong.

Thinking college would be a place where a guy who had already had plenty of discipline could run around without much discipline, I was dismayed when the deacon advised that we were required to be in our dormitory rooms by 7:00 p.m. every night, seven nights per week. We were not allowed to leave our bathroomless rooms for any purpose, including for the purpose of going to the bathroom. One Saturday night per month we were allowed to be out of our room and off campus, until 11:00 p.m. Looking back, I marvel at the recklessness, the looseness, the gay abandon implicit in that one night a month. Clearly, not everyone at St. Benedict's was on the same page.

Although the deacon expressed complete confidence in the students' integrity, he assigned a prefect (a brown-robed elderly monk) to manage and supervise each dormitory floor. Prefects were trained to come down like a hammer on anyone found violating even the most insignificant regulation. The prefect issued to our dormitory floor was Father Conrad, who sternly advised that violating either the stay-in-your-room-after-seven or the do-not-leave-campus rules could result in being grounded.

My first thought was to wonder how being grounded differed from not being grounded. My next thought was to analyze the tensile strength of my bedsheets to determine the likelihood of their holding my body weight as I shimmied down from my dorm window to the ground. The thought after that was a constant one throughout that year: Oh, what a great calling, to be a monk and enter the monkhood for nothing less than a lifetime. And I had my parents to credit for this growth experience.

Even though I was unable to discern any demonstrable distinction between being grounded and not being grounded, there was a state known only as being grounded repeatedly, which state fell to your humble word slinger. What followed was brutal. The deacon calling my parents, additional bedsheet escapes, the deacon threatening to kick me out, numerous violations for peeing out my window, and additional—are you ready for this?—grounding. My one lousy night a month off campus was whisked away from me. Where is the ACLU when you need it?

My application for a transfer at the close of my freshman year, from St. Benedict's to the University of Iowa, was the finest, most complete, and most impressive application ever seen by the University of Iowa admissions secretary.

> You'll find that the things you learned in school will be vitally important to your success, provided that you are a contestant on "Jeopardy." Otherwise they're useless.—Dave Barry

Learning to Adapt
Frank

I was born with a fear of change and a desire to keep things as they are. At the end of World War II, my folks uprooted me, at the mellow age of nine months, from my birthplace (Victoria, Texas) to return to Fort Dodge, Iowa. I can't say the move bothered me much—I thought it was just a long car ride. But once we settled into our large, three-story home on Second Avenue South, I was there for the duration.

Five years later, Mom and Dad were building a new home in the country. Although I visited while it was under construction, I didn't plan to live there. I loved being on the site with all the big trucks, earthmovers, wet cement, and stacks of pristine lumber. To this day, almost sixty years later, I remember those visits.

On the day that we moved to the new house, I refused to get in the car. So here we had a five-year-old who wanted to forsake his family and stay in the old home. My wise father said, "Okay," and drove off. I had a rapid come-to-Jesus meeting with myself and readily hopped in the car when he returned five minutes later.

This probably makes you wonder how I handled going off to school. Not well. Mom and I had talked about kindergarten for a long time, and she thought I was prepared. But as we walked in the front door of the school that first day, I put a half nelson on the radiator pipe and wouldn't budge. But she was a real trooper and finally talked me into releasing myself. I think she threatened to bite my arm off, and I screamed like a fire alarm before we came to an agreement that she was the mother and I was the almost-dead child.

Until I graduated from high school, I'd never been outside the state of Iowa, and I kind of liked it that way. My first foreign travel was to the College of St. Thomas in St. Paul, Minnesota. Adjusting to college life was tricky enough, but the great adaptation came shortly after marriage.

I met my future wife at a mixer about three weeks into my first year. My older sister, Rosalie, student at the nearby College of St. Catherine, set me up on a blind date with a girl who found a better deal and canceled at the last minute. Her roommate filled in for her.

Mary's upbringing and mine could not have been more different. She was the only child of a career army physician. Born in Columbus, Georgia, she had lived in Minneapolis; Linz, Austria; Lowell, Massachusetts; White Sands, New Mexico; El Paso, Texas; San Antonio; Monterey, California; Caracas, Venezuela; Fort Belvoir, Virginia; Bangkok; Fort Sheridan, Illinois; and, finally, St. Paul.

After marrying, when I started looking for a real job, she informed me that we had to live somewhere else as she had been in St. Paul long enough. I didn't understand that reasoning. But after researching a number of cities around the country and not finding anything, she agreed that I could accept a local position, but it had to be with a company that would move us somewhere else. This was a little shocking, but I figured if I lived after the radiator incident, I could handle this. And so we have lived in Grand Rapids, Michigan; Fort Wayne, Indiana; San Juan, Puerto Rico; Midland, Texas; Houston; Manhattan; Westhampton Beach, New York; Houston again; and Manhattan, again. I think I'm outgrowing my fear of change.

The Triple "M" Poultry Farm
Matt

By necessity, our parents weren't able to coddle any of us. Neither were they able to police everyone's activities all the time. This arrangement afforded the older children some freedom in their behavior. I've heard hair-curling stories about their pranks and escapades, joy rides, and parties. However, while they were testing their limits and having fun, Mom and Dad were learning to be more intuitive and preemptive in their parenting. By the time I came along, there was little new territory to explore. They seemed to know if a dollar was missing from the change jar before I thought to take it. Economy of scale in raising children had played out in their favor.

One caper required a committee to formulate it, but I had the star role. One night the folks were happily entertaining friends in the living room when I—winsome and the youngest—was sent in to ask if we could have two cookies or three for dessert. Mother quickly replied, "Just two, of course." We were delighted to have two instead of the usual one. I remember feeling proud and accomplished.

We helped raise each other and fended for ourselves. A friend of Dad's once remarked that I surely had not been the last to the table. (I was bigger and taller than some of my siblings.) It wasn't until later that I realized his dry humor also spoke to the independence and drive we each had developed in the early years. Although we were never short on food and the essentials, there was a sense of survival of the fittest as the competition was pretty stiff. I remember even fighting over the better hand-me-downs.

Becoming responsible and self-reliant went with the territory. The usual childhood chores were strictly enforced along with a number of extras. Boys would cook, and girls would hoe the garden. It didn't matter as long as the jobs got done.

What began as a hobby for Mark and me turned into an educational although unfortunately nonprofit venture. The "Triple 'M' Poultry Farm" occupied almost all our time from ages nine to fifteen. We bought and sold equipment—incubators, laying boxes, and batteries (warming cages for chicks)—and we raised peacocks, several types of geese, ducks, chickens, pheasants, guinea hens, and quail. We built sheds and cages, pens and pastures, looking after more than three hundred fowl at a time. We bid at auctions for needed items and sold the chicks, ducklings, and goslings. Feed and medicine had to be kept in stock, and there were daily chores year-round. We even took a hunter's safety class to learn to shoot opossums, foxes, and raccoons, who from time to time would sweep down from the Gobi Desert like a great Mongol horde to ravage, plunder, and loot our poultry empire. Above all I learned how to work with a partner. In the required give-and-take, Mark and I disagreed often, but as in any partnership, two heads seemed to work better than one.

It wasn't much of a leap to apply the poultry farm strategies to schoolwork. When it came to homework, there was little in the way of parental hand-holding. As a parent of three, I'm already having trouble getting motivated to go to P.T.A meetings, Fun Nights, and spring programs. It's no wonder most of my teachers assumed I had no parents at all. By the time I began school, Mom and Dad had logged about sixty child-years of schooling with the older kids so when they did attend a school function, it was both meaningful and a source of pride to me.

The longest conversations we had about school usually came with report cards. I was so pleased to show them my grades, which might be four As, an

A-, and a B. The conversation would then consist of Mom or Dad saying, "Try to get all As next semester." That was it. At the time, it hurt and made me angry; but their nonchalant attitude nudged me, consciously or not, to work harder. I don't know to this day if they tailored their psychology to this effect or if they simply didn't have time to hash over every bit of grading minutia with each of the eight children.

As for vaccinations, a dental filling, or comfort after a fall, preparation and consolation were minimal. Their anxiety level didn't increase, and thus neither did mine. The day they dropped me off at college for the first time, they were gone within an hour. Given that I knew absolutely no one, I was shocked at how quickly they left. However, it caused me to buck up, and I made several lifelong friends in those first few days.

Mom and Dad made me spread my wings, which at the time is exactly what I didn't want to do. I was far too comfortable living at home, and they knew it. As a parent and as a dentist, I apply the same ho-hum attitude to what others consider "events." I advise parents not to overprepare a child for their first and subsequent visits to the dentist, and I try to ease adults' fears by downplaying the procedures and clearly explaining each step in a simple monotone voice.

I don't inform my children of activities, good or bad, more than a few hours ahead of time, so they won't obsess/agonize about them. I will, however, be honest within limits about what they might expect. I do not believe that the whole minutely detailed truth must be told about every issue. I certainly don't lie, but sometimes I don't tell the whole truth. As a dentist, when explaining an injection to a seven-year-old, I think it is preferable to say, "We are going to squirt some sleepy water by the tooth, and you may feel a pinch" than to say, "When I shove this cold, hard needle into your delicate cheek muscle and deposit therein a large amount of novocaine, you will feel pain."

For every one thing I learned about poultry running the Triple "M" Poultry Farm, I learned ten things about life, work, cooperation, and even death, which was common, resulting from harsh weather, varmints, disease, bad food, bad water, and our own inexperience. Mom and Dad had enough to do without supervising us, so it was a seat-of-the-pants learning curve all the way for Mark and me—a good way to learn (unless you're a pilot or brain surgeon).

The Value of a Dollar
Frank

Most of my memories center on either jobs that I have done or hell that I have raised.

During the summer between seventh and eighth grades, I worked on a farm owned by Harvey Scheerer. Harvey and Eva were wonderful people and good friends of my parents. I'm sure I got the job due to that relationship.

For the first day, Harvey had said he'd pick me up at 6:00 a.m. sharp—and that I should bring along a flask of water. He drove me, in his pink Cadillac, to a cheerless field in the middle of nowhere. Harvey bought a new Cadillac every year and drove it around the farm as if it were a four-wheel-drive truck.

When we reached the end of a narrow path between two cornfields, he gave me my instructions for the day. Lining this path on both sides was an electric fence. The stakes were of many different shapes and sizes. The wire was attached to a porcelain knob, which had been nailed into the stake. My charge was to unhook the wire from each knob and pull the stake from the ground. I was to leave each stake at the place of removal.

Well. I thought I'd be an old man by the time I finished this job although Harvey acted as if it was only a morning's work.

Time crawled. By 8:00 a.m., I had finished my water ration. Close to noon, when I thought I was about to expire, I saw a pink Cadillac flying across a plowed field toward me. I hoped he would stop and at least talk to me.

He and his hired man got out and teased me about how little I had done. Later, they told me that they were impressed with me. Why do people do that to kids?

When Harvey asked if I had ever driven a tractor, my immediate reply was yes—not the first little fib that had passed my lips. So he told me to go up to the farmyard and drive the Ford out to him.

As I hustled across that field, I hoped beyond hope that at least one of the two tractors had the word "Ford" printed on it—and that I could locate the key. When I finally got the gearshift knob turned right side up, I shifted into first gear and began a slow crawl to nowhere. At that speed, I would not have gotten the tractor to him until late fall. I started shifting up the gears, to second—not much difference—and to third, to fourth, and I was still crawling along. And I wasn't even out of the barnyard yet!

I decided to skip a few gears and took it up to sixth. That tractor took off like a racehorse out of the gate. In seconds I was in the plowed field. I bounced all over the seat and could not reach the clutch with enough pressure to disengage it.

I heard a lot of noise behind me, but I didn't dare turn around to see what was going on. As I got closer to Harvey, I could see that he and his hired man were bent double with laughter.

I finally got out of the field onto a smooth path where I could depress the foot clutch enough to disengage the tranny (not that kind of tranny) and slow down that excitable machine. Once the devil engine was stopped, I looked back across the plowed field to see hundreds of electric fence stakes spread out in my path. For the first time, I realized that the trailer behind this tractor was half full of stakes when I started and now was empty.

I spent a good deal of the afternoon picking up those stakes. But after that incident, I was a good tractor operator. I learned how to eat a ton of food at noon. I also learned about patience, hard work, personal accomplishment, and, best of all, how to judge the value of a dollar.

Once Was Not Enough
Matt

Because the poultry farm was not a profitable venture, Mark and I had to get outside jobs to subsidize it, and we ended up working together again at local restaurants in nearly every capacity. Although my savings account didn't grow a lot at the time, I was proud to have my own real income, spending every paycheck on my coin collection and propping up the poultry farm.

I got hired as a busboy and dishwasher at a nearby motel restaurant where Mark was already working. He broke the ice for me, and it was a great comfort to have him around even though we fought regularly. I suppose like many siblings we had an active love-hate relationship. We were four and six years younger than the next siblings, so we were like a second family for Mom and Dad.

The restaurant work itself was thankless, and we were teenagers at the bottom of the seniority list. But the boss, a short round man with a booming voice, quickly saw to it that we became committed to working hard and being punctual. "Work is work," he once shouted at the general staff. "That's why they don't call it fun." All right then.

The kitchen staff was a rough bunch. We called them lifers. They couldn't speak without swearing and had an assortment of addiction issues. Substance abuse was a very, very broad term in that kitchen. We took everything at face value and mostly tried to stay out of their way. I once was challenged to a swearing match with the cook. Thinking I'd heard just about everything, I agreed, only to be left in the dust by the breadth and depth of his imaginative vocabulary. I was glad I had Mark watching my back.

One night Fort Dodge was hit by a major winter storm, closing roads and shutting down power. Mark and I drove Mom and Dad to the motel on our snowmobiles and then picked up friends of theirs from their farm and brought them to the motel as well. With kitchen privileges, we were able to entertain the four of them with cocktail fare, shrimp, steak, and all the trimmings as they played bridge in their rooms.

Even though the job doesn't sound like much, I learned a great deal about human nature, finances, women with big hair, and the working world. I also learned that I didn't want to continue in this field much past my sophomore year in high school. The hard work had another effect on me. Although I didn't tell Mom and Dad, I was gaining more respect for them all the time. By law a teenager cannot tell his parents that they're great, so I didn't. But I knew.

··

To be rooted is perhaps the most important and least recognized need of the human soul.—Simone Weil

··

Try, Try Again
Frank

I didn't think much about college while in high school, mainly because the subject didn't come up until we had to take the SAT. The period between the SAT and my arrival as a new student at the College of St. Thomas in St. Paul is pretty much a blank.

My parents drove me there, and we were interviewed by a priest who was supposed to help with course selection. The first question he asked me was, "What do you want to be in your adult life?" What came to mind was "a guy who has a lot of fun."

I'd been around enough priests to suspect that wasn't what he had in mind. Because Dad, the dentist, was sitting right there, it came to me, "Yeah, that's right. A dentist." Then too, you know, the oldest son of an Italian father? I thought the son was supposed to want to follow in Dad's footsteps.

My answer set me off on a course of pure destruction. The priest slotted me into a premed track that included classes I couldn't even pronounce. My transcript read like a broken record: "Dropped for low scholarship," "Readmitted on probation," "Dropped for low scholarship," "Readmitted on probation," and so on for three and a half years. Many years later, I found out that I was dyslexic, but despite the ups and downs, I had a tremendously good time while I was failing in college.

I always held some sort of job during those years. I drove a fellow with quadriplegia to and from college, shoveled snow, raked lawns, washed windows, chauffeured a school bus, and did whatever I could to earn money. I worked full-time each summer and was able to pay all my college expenses.

Mary and I were married in the middle of her senior year. At the time I was working as a dispatcher for Univac, a division of Sperry Rand. I moved up the food chain there until I was told that I needed a college degree for the next promotion.

I started selling encyclopedias for Spencer International Press. I was good at this although I refused to make cold calls. A year into the job, the franchise manager was retiring and they planned to close the Minneapolis office, which serviced Minnesota, Iowa, Wisconsin, North and South Dakota. I flew to New York and talked them into giving the franchise to me. I got it, and I enjoyed building that business.

I was, however, plagued every day by one question from Mary, "When are you going back to college?" Yes, she asked every day.

After four years of trying to prove that a degree was not necessary to make it in the business world, I gave in and reentered college. I worked as the night auditor at the Saint Paul Hotel and attended classes in the daytime. We had two children, a house, a dog, and a car. I didn't have room for poor grades. As it turned out, I earned a truckload of high scores. Pressure does strange things to us.

College: Oops!
Matt

Academically, I floundered for a number of years but managed just well enough in high school to be accepted at Grinnell College. I didn't think I was ready for a huge university experience, and Grinnell, a highly rated small private school, was just two and a half hours from home.

Typically, I hadn't done my homework when choosing a college and had visited it—briefly—only once. After being dropped off there for my first semester, it came to me that I might as well have been on the moon.

The fear of a large university wasn't the problem. I simply feared leaving home, and it wouldn't have mattered where I went. In addition, there wasn't anyone there from Fort Dodge and, in fact, only 10 percent of the student body was even from Iowa. I had landed in an East Coast college mislocated by some cosmic error in the cornfields of Iowa.

Many of the other students had taken college prep courses that allowed them to pass out of just about their entire first year. These courses had been offered in their magnet schools in New York and Chicago, cities I'd never even visited. Nearly everyone had arrived at this fine liberal arts school with a rigid agenda, almost invariably prelaw or premed. I wasn't even sure what I was having for lunch, let alone what I might be doing for the rest of my life.

After spending a day or two getting acquainted with other students, my self-confidence dropped through the floor and pretty much stayed there for the rest of my Grinnell experience. I can only think my goat-like stubbornness kept me from sensibly transferring to a more amenable institution.

A grueling experience, my years there left me feeling as if I were at war. Competition was stiff. Socializing was rare. Intellectual loners crammed the library whenever they weren't in a structured classroom setting. No sororities or fraternities were allowed. There was no cohesiveness among the students, which went against my basic understanding of humans as social beings. If we had been antelope, we would have quickly perished for lack of herd protection.

On the positive side, I was inspired to start doing my homework although this wasn't the noble ideal of higher education that it might seem. By now I knew better than to try to be part of the herd as there were no herds. I remembered how I came to land at Grinnell in the first place: I hadn't done my homework. It took about a year to get a grip, and then it hit me: I would beat them at their own game—and it did seem to me to be just one big game.

Getting top grades wasn't as much about learning as it was about having the right answers and, in my opinion, those are two different things. Orchestrating the class lineup for a semester to get a delicate balance of the time and effort that each required was an art. Knowing which courses to take in the summer rather than during the school year and which professors to choose also played a part. I stopped thinking about playing when I was working, and when I did get to play, I didn't let myself worry about work. Such a simple concept, but I didn't catch on until my sophomore year.

By this time I had regained a bit of self-esteem, enough to know that I had to get out of Grinnell for a while. I will be forever thankful for the encouragement I got to take my junior year abroad, a move that might not have been an option at a large university at that time.

For the second time in my life, I embarked alone on a journey to an unexplored place, but this time I remembered to do my homework—and it paid off. That year was memorable partly because I was celebrating my sabbatical from Grinnell but primarily because the University of St. Andrews in Scotland was everything a twenty-year-old could ask for and then some.

Physiologically, I felt my sight was keener, and I could hear more clearly. All my senses were at peak performance for the entire year. For lack of anything more compelling, the registrar classified me as a second-year medical student. At Grinnell I had taken prerequisite and liberal arts classes and hadn't yet been exposed to upper-level coursework in biology, a major I chose from a simple need to choose something, anything. I had no idea until my year in Scotland just how keyed into this area I was.

Although the language barrier was a problem at first, I quickly picked up on the Scottish brogue. I took to my studies as never before and learned more in that one year than in all the previous years.

Each Sunday after church services the entire student body, dressed in red wool gowns, paraded out onto the pier. St. Andrews is a seaport town on the North Sea, and the pier walk was spectacular, complete with a ninth-century castle in the background. The eleventh-century Catholic cathedral had been dismantled bit by bit after the Reformation in order to build the rest of the town, and the ruins of its foundation were as picturesque as an Iowa boy could want.

The many Americans studying abroad there at the time all became good friends. I dated Sarah, a lovely young woman from Pennsylvania, and made a number of friends with whom I still keep in touch.

I joined the university swim team, which held practices in the sea. As the tide came in, a gate was lowered in a cement "pool" built on the shore to capture the water. Later in the day, the captured water warmed up even as the tide went out. The swim team allowed me to meet many fine people and to travel Scotland during the swim season. I wasn't their top man, but it didn't matter.

Not until my second semester did I feel truly comfortable with the whole picture. Mom and Dad came to visit that spring—their first trip abroad—and I was able to be a competent host as I knew the territory by then. I was old enough to relish a visit from my parents—probably the best single visit I ever had with them.

In addition to making friends for a lifetime that year, I also backpacked for a month at a time to Ireland (north and south), Spain, Portugal, and the British Isles. I remember reading that youth is wasted on the young. I felt I was the exception—nothing was wasted on me, and the events and sights of that year feed me to this day.

I'm still impressed that while raising and educating eight children, Dad managed to find a way for me to go abroad. For twenty-five years, Mom and Dad had children in college, often four or five at a time. I had, of course, done the groundwork of arranging financial aid, grants, and loans to get me there; but they still had to help. Once again I had the experiences of my siblings to show me the way. Rosalie had lived in France for a year, Kevin spent a year in Austria, and Mark attended the London School of Economics. Their accounts of years abroad sealed the deal for me. I knew I had to go.

Later, I was glad that going to Scotland was fun because returning from Scotland was not fun. Back at Grinnell, I was told that my advisor had been fired and that all my transcripts were suspect. I spent nearly my entire senior year sorting out the discrepancies, thereby missing the chance to enroll in medical school as I'd planned. By the time the dust settled, I was unable to continue my education uninterrupted.

I moved to St. Paul, Minnesota, where I roomed with Mark only a few blocks from Rosalie. For the next year, I worked in an emergency room at a large hospital while taking classes at the University of Minnesota.

At that time I applied to dental school rather than to medical school and was accepted. My practical experiences at the hospital seemed to tell me I didn't want to be an M.D. In addition, Dad tried to discourage me. I'm still trying to figure out if he was right. I chose not to go into medicine for a lame reason: I didn't think I could handle blood and surgery. However, after the first year of dental school, I realized they wouldn't have been a problem.

At the University of Iowa College of Dentistry, we not only had the somewhat unusual experience of dissecting a cadaver, but also for the first two years we were in classes and training with the medical students. As a result, I came away with a good understanding of the whole body, not just the mouth, which has been helpful to me in my practice as well as in my private life.

I was in hog heaven. Dentistry suited me to a T. My grades soared, and my friends multiplied. Best of all, I became engaged to the most wonderful woman on earth. She has tolerated me (and my goofball family) for twenty-some years now.

When I was growing up, Mom scolded me for having "busy fingers." I fidgeted and played with anything I could get my hands on. Little did we know that one day, those hands would be clever dentist hands, which must fidget and play with tiny tools and parts and burrs and pokers and scrapers and drills for a living. On the self-esteem thing, I am much better, thanks for asking.

....

When we talk of leaving our childhood behind us, we might as well say that the river flowing onward to the sea had left the fountain behind.—Anna Jameson

....

My Life With Cars
Frank

I wasn't entirely educated in the classroom. After I graduated from eighth grade, I had a summer job at Mills Dental Studio where dentures, crowns, and partials were made. You might guess that my father the dentist had something to do with that.

Lucky for me, I needed a car to get to and from that job. I was only thirteen, but I could get a license under some weird Iowa law.

We found a really cool 1949 Lincoln sedan for $200. Believe it or not, it had power windows and power seats. I didn't have $200 but, to my surprise, Dad marched me into the bank where he cosigned on a $200 loan.

I had a great time with the car that summer and didn't put a cent into it. I did reverse the shackles to make the back end higher. One day I was working under the car with Dad's drill. He happened by and asked what I was fixing. To his surprise and dismay, I explained that I was drilling holes in the muffler so it would "rumble." He didn't pass out, but he was incredibly not impressed.

I incorrectly assumed that I had my high school car firmly in my possession. Not. I had to sell it in the fall. I parked it on the side of the highway with a For Sale sign. With the $245 I got for it, I paid off the loan, plus the $5 interest charge, and that was the end of my first car. But I did learn about the "loan" thing. Dad always said that if you had good health, good friends, and good credit, you were the richest man in the world.

I bought a car or two each summer after that. During senior year in high school, I bought and sold so many cars that as a freshman in college, the State of Iowa sent me a notice indicating that if I registered one more car in my name that year, I had to apply for a dealer license. That was mostly caused by a 1951 Chevrolet that I bought for $65. I needed a lot of parts to get it into shape. One day I bought six 1951 Chevys for $5 to $10 each, just for the parts. I towed all of them to the house and parked them on the gravel road that led to the barn. When Dad got home that night, he asked who was visiting.

When he found out that all the cars were mine, he gave me a deadline to get them off the property.

The summer between my ninth and tenth grades, Mom accidentally bought a fire-engine red 1931 Ford Model A. She knew the auctioneer and was trying to help him get higher bids on the car. He knew her tricks, but he thought she really wanted it, so she got it for $205.

Not too long after we got it, I was driving into town and blew a rod right out the side of the motor. Horrified that I was the one to blow up the car, I bought it from her and set out to restore it.

I drove to junkyards all over the state to find parts and to get as many short blocks as I could find. I ordered parts from Warshawsky's in Chicago. I bought original mohair seat fabric from a place in Omaha. I had the car sandblasted and painted. At a time when most young people bought this vintage of car to "soup it up," I was restoring it to its original condition.

By the time I left for college, the work was complete. A good friend of Dad's collected old cars and had some real beauties stored in a Quonset hut on his property. He offered me $2,000 for the car, saying he wanted to show it. He added that whenever I wanted it back, I could have it for $2,000. What a deal!

When I came home for Easter vacation freshman year, Mom told me that the guy had given my car to his son for his sixteenth birthday, and two days later the son totaled it. So much for friends of the family.

At St. Thomas, having a car was a no-no. But I couldn't resist a 1950 Buick that an upperclassman was selling for $10. Being almost entirely brake deficient, the car could be stopped only if I downshifted and then found a curb.

In addition, the automatic gearshift didn't work. I pounded a hole through the floorboard with a pliers and a nail. Then I put metal rod through the hole and tied it on to the gearshift lever on the transmission. That way, I could actually shift gears.

After I had been driving this fun but dangerous car for a few weeks, I discovered two disturbing issues.

The first was that the city of St. Paul had impounded the car for parking tickets, and the former owner "stole" it out of the impoundment area. The second issue was that the dean of students, an unfriendly guy by the name of Father Vashro, had been looking for the car due to multiple on-campus parking violations.

As luck would have it, a student who lived on my floor in Ireland Hall asked if he could rent my car over Easter vacation so he could get home to see his family in Nebraska. Since I had planned to hitchhike home, I agreed to rent it for $45.

All of us were surprised when he didn't return from spring break. As he never picked up his belongings in the dorm, I began to think the car had taken him into the next life. Fortunately, one of his friends heard from him. The guy just hated college. I have mentally thanked him many times for taking that car off my hands—and at a profit.

After I was married, I bought a 1957 Nash Rambler station wagon. My dear friend Ken Stilling and I test-drove the heck out of this car: accelerate, brake hard, turn sharp, push the needle up, brake again. We felt we'd given it a good going-over.

I paid $75 for it and felt myself a fortunate man. When I drove up to our Ashland Avenue apartment in St. Paul, I knew it was my lucky day: there was a parking spot right in front of our apartment. That was, however, all the luck I was going to get that day. When I put the car in reverse to back into the parking space, there was no reverse. Cars. You gotta love 'em.

E-mails

From: Mark
Subject: weather

Matt, Little Bullet passed away this morning. I guess it is going to be one of those days. Did the monsoon hit you last night? We got three inches, roof damage, tree limbs down, the whole shootin match.

⊠⊠⊠

From: P.T.
Subject: weather

Dear Mark, I am sorry to hear about Little Bullet. I'm sure my grief would deepen if I knew who or what Little Bullet was.

⊠⊠⊠

From: Mark
Subject

Dear P.T., You are most sensitive.

Thank you for the sympathy message regarding the loss of Little Bullet. He was this spring's Orphan Lamb. He had a great first two months of life, but his last two months of life were marked with various health problems. He was a good boy, though; he never did nobody no harm.

You will not be surprised to know that you were the only one who sent a sympathy message.

✉✉✉

From: Pat
Subject: weather

Mark, I am glad you wrote, perhaps under-emphasizing the whole potentially traumatic event. It occurred to me that, given sheep herd mentality, if one sheep dies, the rest follow suit. Is anyone still standing?

✉✉✉

From: Ciccio
Subject: weather

If sheep are followers, how do you get behind them?

✉✉✉

From: P.T.
Subject: weather

Dear Mark, Still thinking about you and wondering how you are doing with the loss of Little Bullet. It sounds like he was a bit of a genetic misfire and maybe a name like Little Scud or Little Dud would have been more apt. Again, my condolences. Love, P.T.

✉✉✉

From: Mark
Subject: weather

Dear All Yous, Our scary rainstorms continue. It is a weird pattern. I blame the hurricanes in the Gulf and the lazy, shiftless bureaucrats and politicians in Washington. I blame them for everything anyway. Even if they didn't do this, they probably really screwed up something else that I don't know about, so it is only right and fair to blame them for these storms.

The sheep have politely but firmly asked for a few small watercraft.

Later. Well, the monsoons have abated. I am going to put on my chest waders and go see where the sheep are swimming.

⊠⊠⊠

From: Matt
Subject: weather

Were the sheep in the lap lanes, or the diving area?

⊠⊠⊠

From: P.T.
Subject: weather

Too funny, both of you! Kind of brings new meaning to the concept of sheep dip.

⊠⊠⊠

From: Mark
Subject: weather

Dear Kevin, Once again you have mis-read the weather forecast. What the 90% chance means is that 90% of the rain and hail will fall almost directly on my farm, and the other 10% will fall in Webster County near Fort Dodge.

Because of the nonstop rain, I've lost two hay crops and had damage to my tree crop. I think I'll go see the government today and ask them to put me up in a hotel for two-and-a-half years.

I'm trying to decide what to name the Sperm Whale that has been circling the house. He seems friendly—in a porno-shop-of-the-animal-kingdom kind of way.

And, Pat, your fish story does not impress us in Iowa. We have been flooded since March, with rain every other day from March to August. I've got minnows in my hayfield that are bigger than your fish. They eat alfalfa and corn. If you run into one of them with a tractor, you can do a lot of damage to the tractor. I am hoping to get some fresh water shrimp started in my orchard. It is swamped as well. Last night, I dreamed of 12-foot great white salt sturgeon breaching out by my mailbox.

The illegals are now running bootleg salmon for sale—by that I mean they have a salmon in each bootleg. I am thinking of trading the sheep in for salmon. I just hope I don't have to squeeze any salmon eggs out of those slimy she-devils. I will have to ask the guys at Roland who are already raising salmon in their soybean fields how many ram-salmons you need for so many girl-salmons. So many things to learn—and this after spending the last 40 years learning about sheep.

✉✉✉

From: Kevin
Subject: we're having harsh weather, too, and I'm just beside myself with anguish!

Pat, our high so far this week was 70 degrees, too. I feel so cheated. Most of our relatives are having snow and arctic temps but not us. Why me? Why me? Oh well, I guess the grass is always greener. K

✉✉✉

From: Matt
Subject: we're having harsh weather, too, and I'm just beside myself with anguish!

You dogs!

✉✉✉

From: P.T.
Subject: We're having harsh weather, too, and I'm just beside myself with anguish!

Kevin, I'm kind of new at this voodoo thing, but I'm wondering how your lower right second molar is feeling.

✉✉✉

From: Pat
Subject: Merry Christmas from Denver!

Drat, Kevin! Those pictures are great but you gave away too much. We had the sistas and bros believing we live in the banana belt. It is the only thing we have over them. Now the jig is up. They used to not know any better. But now they know we get snow and cold weather, too. How we gonna fix this, Maggio?

✉✉✉

From: Mark
Subject: Merry Christmas from Denver!

Pat, To fix this snow snafu, I think we could send them all boxes of those nice big red grapefruits (make sure they're Indian River grapefruits) and just say they grow in our window boxes and all over the place. That would do it for Mark, I am pretty sure. Love you, Priorly Kevin

As for you, Kevin, Merry Christmas and a Happy New Year to you too. May the joy and peace of the true Christmas bless you throughout the coming year. And if your damn white Christmas crosses the Nebraska state line, I'm taking the sheep and moving to New Orleans, the city where deviance is no big deal.

✉✉✉

From: Pat
Subject: Merry Christmas from Denver!

Mark, Thanks for the great humor. It reminds me of Pat's. Love you. P.T.

✉✉✉

From: Mark
Subject: Blizzard time! Double the rations! Sheep are now at 150 pounds corn + 500 pounds hay DAILY

Weather. Wether. Whether.

One freezes 'em off.
One cuts 'em off.
One can't tell if you've got 'em or not.

I made up that little spelling rule to help my college students who cannot spell, read, write, or do simple math, or in fact do any kind of thinking. I figure I can't help them much with the thinking, the learning to read, write, spell, or do simple math, but I can damn sure help them remember how to spell that one word. This is what my career has become.

✉✉✉

From: P.T.
Subject: blizzard time

Yes indeed, the forecasters were right this time. I guess even a blind dog stumbles onto a bone now and then. I just finished carving a path in our driveway so when I have my heart attack later today Terry can get me to the hospital.

✉✉✉

From: Mark
Subject: blizzard time

Dear Terry and P.T., I am glad you can still see your roof line. That way, when you get home in the evenings, you can climb in an upstairs bedroom window to get in. Just make sure you are at the right house.

✉✉✉

From: Pat
Subject: blizzard time

Mark, I heard from the grapevine that one of your little lambs nearly froze to death. But you brought him into the house and kept him in the oven at 350 degrees for two hours and he completely thawed. What happened after that?

⊠⊠⊠

From: P.T.
Subject: blizzard time

Marco, It sounds like a good day at your house for baking bread, then breaking said bread. Even in this blizzard, will you remain steadfast in your policy of denying house privileges to your beasts?

⊠⊠⊠

From: Mark
Subject: today's weather

P.T., You asked, "Will you remain steadfast in your policy of denying house privileges to your beasts?"

For guidance on this question, I go to the Ten Cat Commandments in the original Hebrew, as handed down to Moses on Mount Sinai, from God, who was in charge of all the cats at that time. I have given these to the cats to ensure they stay true to our religion.

I will provide a translation of the Ten Cat Commandments for you in case your ancient Hebrew is rusty:

ONE. I am the farmer, your boss, who brought you out of the land of confinement, out of the house of slavery and government-run animal shelters. Do not have any other farmers before me. And get the hell out of the way when I am carrying water buckets in the barn.

TWO. You shalt not make for yourself an idol, or a carved image, or in fact do anything else. Just sit there and try to catch mice.

THREE. You shall not curse the farmer, even though he may say unto you, verily, "Ye are a lazy and worthless cat."

FOUR. Remember the Sabbath day, to keep it holy, especially by catching a lot of mice on Sundays. This is not work, so it is OK to do it on the Sabbath.

FIVE. Honor your father, if you know who he was, and your mother, by catching mice in their memory.

SIX. Thou shalt not murder any chick or duckling or gosling or any other creature under the sun that might grow up and thenst could be eaten by thine farmer, or which canst lay fresh eggs which thine farmer might heartily enjoy. Killing sparrows and blackbirds and rabbits is permitted, since they do not have souls.

SEVEN. Thou shalt not commit adultery, and to mark you as a cat of honor, you shalt be fixed, if the farmer canst catch ye.

EIGHT. You shalt not steal any eggs or milk or little fish or anything else the farmer might want, even though you mightily crave such treats.

NINE. You shalt not bear false witness against your neighbor, whether he or she—or, if castrati, it—be any of the fluffy creatures that say "baaa" nor against any creature of the barn which has the cloven hoof regardless of whether it says "baaa" or makes some other noise, like "mooo," or against birds of the air or lo even against birds of the chickenhouse. You may bear false witness against the one who says "ruff ruff," but then run real fast right after you do.

TEN. Ye cats shalt not covet thine farmer's house, or thine farmer's neighbor's wife's lap. Do not sit unto thereon. You shalt not covet the farmer's male servant or female servant, or look up her skirt, or his ox or his ass or anthing else you can think of. Just stop coveting things. Concentrate on catching mice.

So, then, P.T., I think you can see that the Tenth Commandment clearly outlaws cats coveting my house, or coming in unto thereunder, and they greatly fear crossing my threshhold. So no, they can't come in.

✉✉✉✉✉✉✉✉✉✉✉✉✉

From: Frank
Subject: e-mail

It is not a good thing when your e-mail program says, "There are no new massages on the server." Just wanted you to know that. Maybe I should get a life.

✉✉✉

From: Mary
Subject: e-mail

I think it's against the law to have the massages actually right on the servers . . . in public anyway. By the way, is Pat getting our e-mails? MMM

✉✉✉

From: Mark
Subject: e-mails

Mary, Don't say anything to Pat about his e-mail being turned off. This is how they tell you, "Your services are no longer needed."

✉✉✉✉✉✉✉✉✉✉✉✉✉

From: Mark
Subject: tsunami

Brilliant analogy with the stock market, so now just tell me when. I don't like the look of the market in the intermediate future. The incredible national deficit, foreign competition for production of goods, gas prices, baby boomers, continental drift, and Rap music have combined to give me an uneasy feeling. I'd love to trade all my cars for rafts, but which raft and when? So, wise one, please let us all know when you see the tsunami heading for Wall Street and recommend a good raft shop.

⊠⊠⊠

From: Ciccio
Subject: tsunami

A good stockbroker would swap cars for rafts the day before. He would look stupid at the end of the first day, but what a hero the next day!

⊠⊠⊠

From: Pat
Subject: tsunami

Yes, not unlike the mugu patient in the hand of the dentist or the mouse in the hands of the cat or the client in the hands of the lawyer . . .

⊠⊠⊠⊠⊠⊠⊠⊠⊠⊠⊠⊠⊠

From: Kevin
Subject: plane landing in the Hudson

Hi, Ciccio. This story has been mesmerizing. I'm especially impressed with the quality of human nature in a crisis, even in the cold, even when the economy's in trouble, even when we're at war, even in NY ("Excuse me sir, could you please tell me what time it is or should I just go f—myself?"). The pilots, passengers, ferryboat operators—virtually everyone involved drew upon their highest selves to act, react, and help each other. It has been a testament to the best in people.

I'm wondering what it was like for you, being so close to it. Any comments from your NY point of view? Love, K

⊠⊠⊠

From: Ciccio
Subject: plane landing in the Hudson

It was a spectacular and miraculous event. A lesser pilot could not have done the deed as it was done. One wing in the water and it would have had a horrible ending. Lots of individual personal stories in the local papers. One guy took off his pants as he thought he'd have to swim, and then climbed out onto the wing. Another guy did swim to shore—one of those people who doesn't trust anyone (lots of them in NYC). Other passengers made new reservations for later that day while they were standing on the wing waiting to be rescued. They were a plucky bunch.

That's the plane AJ uses all the time to travel to Charlotte. Now, all of a sudden, they want to rid the airport grounds of Canadian geese. But the animal rights people are having a fit over the thought of the geese being displaced or, God forbid, killed. Well, skip the "God forbid" part as they don't believe in God.

⊠⊠⊠

From: P.T.
Subject: plane landing in the Hudson

I believe many of those geese already gave their lives to pull off this prank. We call them "Suicide Geesers." I admire the decision to "rid all airport grounds of Canadian geese." But don't you figure once they lose the Canadians, then the Snow geese will take up the cause? And you can never trust a pigeon. Bastards! But the most frightening thought would have to be Osama Bin Pelicans, them are MEAN cave-dwelling sons-a-beaches! What do you suppose would happen if they just put a screen-like structure over the air intake of those jet engines?

As an aside, did you see where engineers were trying to analyze exactly what happens when birds meet jet turbines? They were shooting chickens into running engines, seriously, and they weren't volunteers (the chickens, not the engineers).

⊠⊠⊠

From: Kevin
Subject: plane landing in the Hudson

Ciccio, thanks for the report. Seeing those people standing on the wings of a plane in the middle of a river was bizarre to say the least.

P.T., I didn't hear about the chickens, but I heard on one news channel that engineers threw turkey carcasses into the jet engines during training exercises to see what would happen to the plane and how the pilots would react. They also tried ducks but, as a practical matter, that created too much confusion in the cockpit when the pilot yelled, "Duck!" I also heard the NFCWGG (National Federation of Chinese Weeder Geese Goslings) has lodged a protest against banning geese at airports because much of their income is derived from weeding & "feeding" the grassy fairways in between the runways. The President of NFCWGG said, "Honk, honk, HOOOONK, honk-honk-honk, honk honk!" which was incendiary and has only strengthened the FAA's resolve to ban geese at airports. Domestic geese are furious that these undocumented aliens have incited the bureaucrats, and the situation is getting more fowl by the minute.

✉︎✉︎✉︎

From: Ciccio
Subject: plane landing in the Hudson

Kevin gets all the points for tonight except for 25% of the points that go to P.T.

✉︎✉︎✉︎

From: Mark
Subject: plane landing in the Hudson

This gives new meaning to the term "goose the engine!"

✉︎✉︎✉︎

From: Kevin
Subject: plane landing in the Hudson

Oh, ye of little pride!

⊠⊠⊠⊠⊠⊠⊠⊠⊠⊠⊠⊠⊠⊠

From: Ciccio
Subject: el mismo

Say, who is this "El Mismo" person? All I could find online was that the singular neuter form, lo mismo, typically means "the same thing."

⊠⊠⊠

From: Pat
Subject: el mismo

Ciccio, the *Post* had a relevant article and photo. The last person heard criticizing the great El Mismo was carried out of his home at three in the morning and taken to a little art colony in the highlands of central Mexico. He's never been heard from again. Perhaps he wanted to live in an art colony. But perhaps, too, he is taking a dirt nap. I'd caution you to refrain from any criticism of the great El Mismo.

⊠⊠⊠

From: P.T.
Subject: el mismo

The true story about El Mismo is this. One evening at dinner we were talking about our favorite Spanish words. After the usuals came up—*miercoles, biblioteca*, I offered *mismo* (same).

I thought it'd be a great name for a mediocre superhero. When the superhero who was the same as everybody else arrived on the scene announcing, "I am El Mismo!" the crowd would say, "So?" My sidekick would be *asi asi* (so so), and my butler would be *mas o menos* (more or less). I hope this clears things up, although you never know, I could be lying. Bwaahaahaahaaaaa.

✉✉✉

From: Mark
Subject: el mismo

Ciccio, I am deeply offended by your explanation of *mismo*. P.T. and I have been called a lot of things in our day, but "single neuter" might be one of the most hurtful. I am going to see if the government can give me something or do something for me after this incapacitating offense.

✉✉✉✉✉✉✉✉✉✉✉✉✉

From: Matt
Subject: office photo

Hi All, This is a picture of us at the office. I am experimenting as I have never sent a picture by e-mail. Hope it works.

✉✉✉

From: P.T.
Subject: office photo

Hope again, Mister. I couldn't open it.

By the way, have you had any trouble getting mepivicaine anesthetic, or don't you use it? There's a nationwide shortage and we can't get any until the middle of March. I guess I could turn it into a marketing ploy: "Needle-Free Dentistry! No Shots!"

Later, skaters. Love, P.T.

✉✉✉

From: Kevin
Subject: "More troubling news from the outside world about dentists and lawyers"

Did you see this article?

⊠⊠⊠

From: P.T.
Subject: "More troubling news from the outside world about dentists and lawyers"

You dog! I was in the process of sending that article out when your e-mail came in.

⊠⊠⊠

From: Mark
Subject: "More troubling news from the outside world about dentists and lawyers"

I saw it. Why can't you dentists and lawyers just get along?

This is the case of the woman who went to a dentist for a bridge and came away with what her lawyer claims are "horse teeth." A jury awarded her $197,000. For the life of me, I can't figure out what all the hoo-ha is about. I think her teeth look very natural.

⊠⊠⊠

From: P.T.
Subject: "Court sides with fun-loving dentist over tusk prank"

What about this one? Gol, this oral sturgeon is quite the rascal.

⊠⊠⊠

From: Kevin
Subject: "Court sides with fun-loving dentist over tusk prank"

Odd what stories go national. Two 19-year-olds on LSD were charging people a dollar to cross a footbridge in a popular Boulder park, threatening naysayers with a broken golf club. Lucky for them it made the newspapers because otherwise they would have no idea what they did with that time.

⊠⊠⊠

From: Pat
Subject: "Court sides with fun-loving dentist over tusk prank"

You talk about fun-loving . . . ! Bro Paul was seen giving a guest lecture entitled "Spittum" at the International Clown Museum just outside Milwaukee. It's over with. We missed it. So I don't know why I would even mention it. Some of his break-out discussion group topics were: Clownor/clownee, Goofor/goofy, and "How to laugh your way through excruciating pain and get paid for it."

⊠⊠⊠

From: Mark
Subject: fun-loving dentists

Dentists? Pain? Where'd you get such a damn fool idea?

BTW, you dentists, if you haven't gobbled up all the Vicodin yet, I think there's a pretty strong "secondary market" at college for them. I could probably move it fairly quickly.

FBI: I am just kidding. Really. I don't mean it. Time for your coffee now.

⊠⊠⊠

From: P.T.
Subject: fun-loving dentists

I swear to God. So this lady is telling me what a great dentist I am. I'm starting to blush and my head is perceptibly swollen.

Then she says "Of course old Doc Zimke had Parkinson's and was going blind."

Yeah, that horse is really fast compared to my dead mule.

On another note, I had an elderly man in the other day. When I asked him how he was doing he said, "Well, I got out of bed this morning and I got erect, so I knew it was going to be a good day." And I said to myself, "Please, God, strike me mute."

⊠⊠⊠

From: Matt
Subject: responding in summary

Thanks!, You're right, that's so cool, I never knew that, yes he is, maybe Wednesday, what a milestone, glaciers? those crazy California politicians, okay, not until they're older, now I see.

⊠⊠⊠

From: P.T.
Subject: responding in summary

Dear Mr. Cliff's Notes,

Nice job. I was wondering if I could start having my e-mails sent directly to you for processing. Every Thursday I would like you to send me a synopsis of the pertinent facts.

My inbox has been eating me alive. Whereas I feel blessed that so many people send jokes, pictures, films, and newsy e-mails—not to mention those who think I need to lose weight, get a bigger man unit, or find Jesus (I didn't realize he was lost)—I have become overwhelmed. Your summary is swift and economical, and deserves a big ditto!

Sincerely,
Mr. Looking for More Free Time

⊠⊠⊠⊠⊠⊠⊠⊠⊠⊠⊠⊠⊠

CHAPTER 7

A Hair-Raising Chapter on Travel in Which We Reveal Our Sicilian Roots But Fail to Say Much About Our Irish Roots, Mostly From Ignorance, and Also in Which We Wrongly, So Wrongly, Cast Doubts on Someone's Driving Skills

Passports and Grasshoppers
Rosalie

In the spring of 1994, Mother called. "Your father wants to go to Sicily. Will you plan the trip and go with us?"

Dad's parents had emigrated from Sicily in the early 1900s. As a boy growing up in the United States, with its riches for those who worked hard and its Saturday movie matinees, Dad couldn't understand anyone trading it for impoverished, hardscrabble, Mafia-dominated Sicily. He watched his father—who made a dollar a day working at the Chicago and North Western roundhouse in Boone, Iowa—set aside part of every week's earnings against the day when he could return home.

And Dad couldn't figure out why.

I'd rarely had a more exciting request from Mother. Over the next months, I spent happy hours researching Sicily, learning Italian, planning our itinerary, renting a car and hotel rooms, and shopping for a travel mate among the sibs. What with schedules, budgets, and druthers, the winner was Kevin. (The travel mate was a necessity. It took two of us at any time to, um, work with Mom.)

The Friday night before our Tuesday departure, I called Mother to chat. By and by, she said, "You know this trip we're taking next week?"

Yes, yes, I know that trip.

"Well, do we need passports?"

"WHAT! What do you mean, do we need passports?"

"Well, I mean, do we need passports? Because if we do, we don't have any."

"Mom! What do you mean, you don't have passports? Omigod. What could you possibly mean? You and Dad travel all the time!"

"But we go to Mexico and the Caribbean where we don't need passports."

"You guys went to Rome a few years ago. You had to have passports for that."

"No, I think your father used his voter registration card."

"HE DID NOT USE HIS VOTER REGISTRATION CARD! Aarrrrrrghgh."

Hours later, after ascertaining that no embassies or consulates were open until Monday and after repeated phone calls among Mom and Kevin and me, it finally occurred to me to ask, "Mom, did you want to go on this trip?"

"Not really," she said. "I haven't been feeling very good."

Oh.

Mother suffered from multiple and serious medical problems, although none of us ever heard her complain. She had such a ferocious appetite for life—for going and doing and playing—that she didn't give her medical problems an ounce more air than they needed.

Years later, when I organized Mother's files after her death, I found two perfectly good passports, valid for 1994. We never did figure out if she knew they were there, or if she was just playing the foxy and crafty Mother cards she had been dealt. But the foxy and crafty part got a lot of votes.

The upshot was that Kevin said if they weren't going, he wasn't going. Lawyering in Colorado at the time, he had a schedule that had recently gone into overdrive, and he was just as glad to jump ship.

I sat with a broken flush—four consolidator tickets, the kind you can never redeem. (Because of Mother's health, we had travel insurance and eventually Mother and Dad were reimbursed, but it took both lawyer brothers over six months to get the refund.)

Late Friday night, I called daughter Katie. "You want to go to Sicily Tuesday?"

She did. Working in the film industry, she was able to juggle a few things, and a genial travel agent converted Kevin's ticket to one for Katie. The first move after that was to downgrade everything: instead of the comfortable sedan, a shoe box of a car with no air-conditioning and a number of eccentricities; instead of hotels with balconies and elevators, hotels with cockroaches and towels the size of pot holders.

I see in my travel journal: "Note that my bedroom has one 40 W bulb for the entire room. I can hardly see. There's a little lamp but (a) it has no shade so it's painfully bright and (b) to plug it in I have to unplug the fan. Not on your life! The fan is all that stands between me and a raving lunatic (also me)."

That trip is a story in itself, involving relatives who loved us too much, a forty-year-record heat wave, an overly attentive policeman named Rizzo, a fall into a grave, a little old woman—a stranger to us—who played sick to entice us into her house for couscous, a happy older fellow who followed us about on his bicycle, and more. Notice the theme: in Sicily, the biggest danger is being killed by kindness.

In the spring of 1997, Mother called me. "Your father still wants to go to Sicily. Will you plan the trip and go with us?"

One guess as to my next question.

After I'd seen the color of their passports, I learned more Italian, rented more hotel rooms, planned another trip, and shopped for another travel mate. Kevin, gun-shy by now, was out of the running. The winner this time was Pat.

The four of us had a glorious two weeks together in Sicily. We went, saw, and were conquered by the island and the people—and amassed a painted Sicilian cartload of memories. Dad was able to appreciate the incredible beauty and richness and loving kindness that was Sicily, the heartfelt places and people that had pulled at his father. At intervals, Dad said, "I see. I understand now."

Mother and Dad talked about the trip for years afterward. As for Pat and me, we had adjoining rooms and, as this was one of the periods in which Mother and I were chalk and cheese, Pat was Mother's pal while I got to spend time with Dad (always considered a treat in our family). I still remember Pat saying, as he headed off shopping once again with Mother, "You owe me big-time!"

Pat and I used to pass notes under our adjoining doors. One day after I'd slid a scrap of paper under his door referring to Mother in terms that I wouldn't have cared to share with her, I realized that she could walk in his room and pick up that note, and my ass was grass. So there I was, fifty-five years old, down on my hands and knees, trying to retrieve my note with a nail file.

One afternoon, I came into the tiny hotel lobby to see Mother sitting on one of the four bar stools not far from the main desk. A handsome young man worked both, but as he came through the swinging door from the kitchen with an armload of bottles, he looked more harried than usual.

"Hey, Mom. What's going on?"

"I'm trying to get him to make me a Grasshopper, but he doesn't seem to understand. I'm having him bring out everything and then I'll show him how to make one."

Mother had no Italian. The young man had no English. I couldn't imagine how they had gotten this far.

"Mom, you're probably not going to be able to get a Grasshopper here."

"Sure I am. They have Grasshoppers all over the world."

"Mom, this is a tiny town in an isolated part of Sicily. Why don't you have a nice glass of red wine? You like red wine."

We palavered for a while, to no good end. After he'd brought out everything he had, also to no good end, Mother finally said, "Oh, for heaven's sake then. Have him bring me a Brandy Alexander."

That was Mom. It was hard for her not to make anything happen that she wanted to happen.

Three years later, I was sitting with Dad at the kitchen table in Fort Dodge, telling him about my upcoming trip to Sicily with my children. He was pleased to know some of his grandchildren would see Sicily.

"I'd sure like to go back."

"You would? Dad, really?"

"I'd love to go back."

Dad had just turned eighty-six, and although Mom was only seventy-six, her health was still precarious. But they wanted to go. Their enthusiasm and innocence and toughness impress me to this day.

Same drill, except that this time, the travel mate and godsend was Mary. And since she is a photographer, we have stunning proof of a sun-filled trip visiting the relatives, enjoying the comfort of the same hotel, and appreciating the Greek and Roman ruins in more depth the second time around.

One photo shows Mother from the back, walking up the ancient cobblestoned lanes in the mountaintop village of Erice. Her perfect posture and curly auburn hair are those of a woman fifty years younger. Eight months later, she was dead. When we were told how diseased and ineffective her heart was—and had been for some time—it was clear that she had traveled through Sicily on a combination of willpower, chutzpah, and moxie. And she did it without a single Grasshopper.

And so now, this fall, we're renting a villa in Sicily for a month, planning for all eight of us and our families to get there at some point during the month. Pat and Mary and I will no doubt have our sad times as we walk the places we walked with Mom and Dad, and the others may be sad that circumstances didn't make that possible for them. But no one visits Sicily without smiling and feasting and loving and rejoicing and remembering. And that's what we'll do.

Toad's Wild Ride in Sicily
Pat

I traveled to Sicily with Mom, Dad, and Punky in November 1997—an extraordinarily courageous and adventuresome trip for my parents given their health and ages.

With the exception of Palermo, where one had to wear earplugs, everything we saw in Sicily was remarkably quiet and peaceful. Things started to get noisy, however, when the rambunctious, free-spirited Sicilians ("Coming through! Coming through!") were joined by the Americans in their rental cars. My older sister was one of those scary rental-car Americans.

I never thought of her as a multitasker until I noticed that she was driving very fast in a foreign country, while looking at the road map, pointing out landmarks, shouting "Bruto!" out the window to other drivers, honking (oh, wait, that was part of driving), and discussing where we should stop for lunch. I was horrified when I read the speedometer (on the autostradas she seemed to stabilize at around 160), but she explained that those were only kilometers and not to worry because there was a good exchange rate that fall.

I satisfied myself that my seat belt would actually restrain me in the event of a crash, and then I moved my head carefully to the left and asked her politely to slow down. She mumbled something, so I said, "Eh?" quite loudly. Mom and Dad were mummified and unable to utter a word. I was all that stood between us and wheelchairs—or worse.

As we tore down the narrow winding mountain roads—sheer cliffs to the right, sheer cliffs to the left, roads obviously designed by first-year engineering students—Punky repeatedly honked her horn. Yet there were no sheep in the roadway. Why was she honking the horn? Was it her way to dissipate the tension? Her way to distract us from this wild ride? No. She said she was honking as a safety measure. Safety measure? I was thinking a double-thick seat belt might be a wise safety measure. Or good bulletproof glass. Maybe industrial-strength air bags. Rubber baby buggy bumpers.

We will never know what Mom and Dad were thinking or if they were scared because they appeared unable to move their lips.

Talking while driving, for my sister, was not a good idea. I learned that late in the trip when she tried to turn the new rental car around in front of a centuries-old church, with her imagination. I say "with her imagination" because it was a physical impossibility to get that particular car to make that particular turn. Her thinking, as near I could determine, was "to solve this dilemma I just need to give it more gas." My thinking was to back up. I decided it might be dangerous to share my thinking with someone who was operating in another dimension. She blamed the subsequent conflict (the car lost to the church in the third round) onto losing her concentration because she was talking.

One of the things she talked about or attempted to convince us of was that she drove like that because everyone else did. Frankly, it was such a blur out my window that I have no idea what anyone else was doing. She brought up the old chestnut, "When in Rome, do as the Romans do." She said our survival depended on driving as insanely as everyone else did. Sounded weak to me.

Meanwhile, I was still mystified at the horn honking. I waited until we came to the only stoplight in Taormina and asked her if she knew why she was constantly honking the horn. She said the honking was a safety measure that warned oncoming traffic to get out of the way. That certainly made sense.

I looked in the backseat at the white faces of my parents to see if I could detect any degree of understanding of this explanation, but they were deer caught in the headlights. Oddly—and this may have no connection with anything—each time Mom and Dad scrambled out of the car after our automobile excursions, they beelined for the nearest glass of vino.

When we returned the car, we all feigned shock (three of us were possibly still in shock from the trip to the airport) as the rental agent pointed out a number of new dents in the car. My sister apologized. The agent smiled and waved us on. Punky explained later that he was just making conversation. "In Sicily," she said, "they're happy if they get the car back in one piece."

My Two Cents' Worth
Mary

From my own personal experience, there is only one thing more frightening than the hellacious drivers in Sicily, and that would be my sister driving us around in the hellacious traffic conditions in Sicily.

Stop signs are bad jokes (because some drivers—oh, not many—actually think the other car is going to stop). Yield signs are like old-fashioned punctuation marks—a semicolon, say—that everyone ignores. And speed limits are viewed as laughable roadside art.

There are lanes marked *Veicoli Veloci* (fast cars), but there are no signs for *Veicoli Lenti* (slow cars). Implying that any Sicilian is driving slowly is probably as dangerous as telling them their babies look like sea otters.

Before Punky and I went with Mom and Dad to Castellammare del Golfo, I had picked up a sense of dark foreboding from Pat, a survivor of the last trip. Rendered twitchy and incoherent trying to describe the chaos they call driving, he warned me that Punky showed signs of demonic possession behind the wheel. He tried to reassure me by saying she could hold her own with the absolutely worst—or would that be the best?—Sicilian driver. I was not comforted.

Because Mom had a panic attack on the last trip during a particularly perilous skirmish with scores of cars all attempting to take ownership of the same lane, I planned ahead for my term of service in the backseat. (Dad sat in the front seat because he had nerves of steel. Also, because he was the only one who would.)

I hunted through magazines until I found some attractive cat and dog faces of the right size, cut out the top halves of their faces, pasted them on cardboard, and ran string through them so we could tie them around our heads. The resulting masks had no eye holes, so Mom and I could sit in the backseat never knowing how close we came to destruction each time the car swerved or jerked.

Of course, when Punky looked in the rearview mirror, she saw a cat and a dog in the backseat, adding to her already-erratic driving. I don't think she should have complained though. It was self-defense.

Dad probably taught Punky how to drive. He was the sort who hated those cars that followed so closely in front of him.

In a loosely related story, one day Mom bought a cheap alarm clock from a street vendor in Castellammare del Golfo for about five bucks. Almost immediately she lost the back plate that held the battery in place.

The next time we saw the vendor, she conveniently had the clock with her. "Get out and tell him this one is broken and you want another one," she said to me.

"Um, no, I can't do that. You lost the back."

"Well, he doesn't know I lost it. Just get me another one."

"Um, no, I think not."

So she huffed out of the car and tried to tell this man in perfect English why he needed to give her a replacement clock. He pointed to the back and said in perfect Sicilian something like, "You crazy lady, you lost the back."

Back and forth they went, in parallel universes. Finally, Mom turned to me and said, "Just take a new one and leave the old one on his table."

"Mom, I can't do that. You broke it. He shouldn't have to give you a new one."

But I was talking to her back as she headed to the car. I gave the man five bucks for another little clock worth about five cents. When I got in the car, Mom said, "I'm not talking to you anymore. I'm mad at you. And I'm never going to use that alarm clock."

Her threat to ostracize me never materialized because barely had I shut the car door than we sped off at a dizzying rate through twisted, cobbled streets, narrowly missing pedestrians, other vehicles, and stray cats. Mom and I were united in a fear greater than our alarm clock discord. The incident was never mentioned again. Except by me. Here.

Wanderlust
Kevin

By the age of eighteen, having grown up in the Iowa countryside a few miles south of Fort Dodge, a town of twenty-two thousand people, I had been outside the state only four times: Minnesota for the state fair, Nebraska for the state fair held at Aksarben (guess what that spells backward), Illinois to attend the national Key Club convention, and Missouri for about five minutes to buy fireworks with Mom—but that's another story. And yet, every one of my siblings and I have traveled extensively. Four of us received part of our college education in Europe.

What possessed us, the landlocked, to hunger for foreign parts? I can only think that a little influence goes a long way with a child. Searching my formative years for clues to my wanderlust, I found a few seeds planted early on that inspired my love of travel.

The town of Manson is about twenty miles from Fort Dodge. Every year during the first week of June, merchants on Manson's quaint little main street displayed their sale-priced wares on the sidewalk for Crazy Dayz. Mom bought us clothes for the next school year at Crazy Dayz bargain prices.

Manson was located on the same railroad line as Fort Dodge, and for fifty cents, a child could ride from Fort Dodge to Manson. Mom and Dad took us down to the Fort Dodge Depot, a real, live funky depot with pews in the waiting room, teller windows with bars, a dock, dollies of various shapes and sizes, passengers carrying strange trunks and suitcases, and goods and commodities waiting to be shipped.

We piled out of the Pontiac station wagon and rushed to explore the depot. As I recall, there weren't the usual parental rules of conduct, and we were allowed to roam freely around the depot. Mom and Dad put us on the train and waved good-bye to us as fervently as if we were heading off to college in New York. In the beginning, I used to wonder if I would ever see them again.

When we chugged into the depot in Manson, there were Mom and Dad, waving to us as though we were long-lost relatives newly arrived from California.

In actual fact, we had traversed twenty miles in some forty minutes. But what an experience. For one thing, we weren't supervised, not by Mom and Dad, not by any other adults. We went from car to car, seat to seat, opening and closing windows and hooting out of them, hanging out on the "back porch" of every car, and saying to each other, "Come look at this!" "No, come here and look at that!"

For another thing, the terrain didn't look like Iowa. There were few roads to be seen. We traveled through fields, along drainage ditches, over rivers on iron bridges, through woods. We might have seen it before while riding in cars or on foot, but it seemed like a foreign country to us.

Once in Manson, we were treated to ice cream and new clothes—although we didn't see the clothes again until fall—but it was a perfect ending to a perfect journey.

By now you know that Dad was Sicilian. His parents immigrated in 1904 and 1906 to the United States, passing through the Ellis Island Immigrant Station in New York Harbor. In 1914, Dad was born in a railroad cabin in the woods near Lehigh, Iowa. Sicilian was his first language, and his mother—whom we called Nonna—died in Fort Dodge at the age of ninety having never learned to speak English.

Every year for Christmas, Dad ordered several large boxes of edibles from an Italian warehouse in Chicago that shipped in the goods fresh from Italy and

Sicily. He always chose the same treats of his childhood, things that we could not get in Iowa: two balls of provolone cheese covered in wax (it's common to see these today in Italian delis, but they were a novelty in the 1950s in Fort Dodge); dried figs on a rope; Greek and Italian olives that tasted like nothing we knew; and the best, torrone—nougat candy in three flavors, each piece foil-wrapped inside its own elegant little box with a picture of a famous Renaissance Italian on the cover, eighteen little boxes inside a larger gift box. Mom and Dad gave these as Christmas gifts to family, friends, and business associates and saved some for us so they could put one of the little boxes in each Christmas stocking.

We were raised as Americans but with enough Sicilian grace notes to make me wonder what life was like in other countries.

One of the best things Mom and Dad did for us was to invest in a brand-new set of *World Book Encyclopedia*. I was then in fourth grade and watched with great interest as the sales rep gave us a little tour through the volumes and explained how to find information. I especially liked the transparencies of the human body. Mom and Dad said they'd bought the set on a two-year payment plan, so we'd better make good use of them. They turned a bedroom into a study complete with a large homemade desk that could seat several of us and a bookcase for the encyclopedias.

At about the same time, I saw our female dog Sport doing strange acrobatics in the driveway with a stray male dog. I was just old enough to think it had something to do with sex. Turning to the encyclopedia, I figured out that the making of puppies might be involved. According to volume 4, the pups would be born after sixty-three days of "gestation." I marked the calendar, and sixty-one days later Sport had five pups. This all had nothing to do with foreign countries, but it convinced me that the encyclopedias really worked, that the information therein was true and reliable. After that, I was like a kid in a candy shop. I dug into articles about countries and unusual cultures (and the sex thing) all over the world.

When I was in grade school, Dad did a couple things that seemed odd to me. First, he hired a man who had escaped the Hungarian Revolution of 1956 with his life and was working for money to bring his family to the United States. I can't remember his name; but he had a red face, greasy hair, bad teeth, couldn't speak English, and was extremely polite. I was puzzled because we sure didn't need any help around the place what with all of us doing chores inside and out. But Dad was doing a good turn for a man in need, and it planted a seed in me about a strange and faraway place called Hungary.

Second, when I was ten, Dad hired a fourteen-year-old boy from Mexico named Manuel to do little jobs around the house and grounds for which he got paid. Again, I didn't understand why because we didn't need the help. Again, it turned out Dad was doing a favor for a person in need. For me, it was strange and fascinating to hear a kid speaking Spanish. I read all about Mexico in the encyclopedias and tried to ask Manuel questions, but we couldn't understand each other.

In my high school years, Dad found a newly arrived hardworking Lebanese carpenter named Fouad. We kids picked up on these hints of a greater global community.

Mom belonged to a ring-of-the-month club for a while. She paid a monthly membership fee and received an inexpensive ring from a different country every month. I remember the one from India. India? We had something in the house from India? It seemed so strange that I had to find India on a map in the encyclopedia. The ring was copper with a red glass stone, and it turned Mom's finger green. Each month I looked forward to seeing the next ring and thinking about how it actually came across the ocean on a boat or in a plane all the way to our house in Iowa.

But it wasn't only the immigrant helpers or the cheap foreign rings or the encyclopedia. Mother visited Mexico when she was only nineteen. This sounds ordinary because today it's easy to go to Mexico, but in the 1950s not many kids at school had a mother who had been outside the country. Mom and Dad were married in 1943, and the U.S. Army Air Corps stationed them on Matagorda Island in southern Texas. Dad's commanding officer and landlord was Dr. Rodriguez. His wife, Juanita, realized Mom was a lonely young woman out of Iowa for the first time, far away from her family, her husband on base without her for two weeks at a time, and in need of companionship. Juanita put Mom in her car, and they spent a month driving around Mexico. Mom had pictures and stories of Acapulco and its cliff divers, this at a time when only the richest Hollywood stars vacationed there. She saw ruins, museums, mountains, oceans, and more than a poor young woman from Iowa could even imagine. It opened her up to the big wide world, and she passed this enthusiasm on to us by her interest in Mexico and other countries.

When I was in sixth grade, Mom shocked me by saying the two of us were flying to Dubuque that Friday to visit her younger sister, Sister Thoma, who was a brown Franciscan nun. This would be my first flight, and I was excited and scared. We flew a prop plane on Ozark Air Lines out of Fort Dodge with several stops along the way. It was the most fun thing I'd ever done. As if that weren't enough, once in Dubuque, we went to the really, really big Ringling Brothers Circus with Sister Thoma. In those days it was unusual for a nun to do something so worldly. When we visited the convent, I played ping-pong with several nuns, which also surprised me. My only experience with nuns was at my grade school where they were stern disciplinarians. I couldn't imagine a nun playing ping-pong or going to the circus, but that's what happens when you travel.

The kicker to my emerging interest in travel was Punky's summer in France in 1964 when she was twenty and I was fifteen. She worked in a summer program for American French teachers, and she wrote often to tell us about unusual places, people, and customs. I was fascinated that someone so closely connected to me was actually living across a huge ocean thousands of miles away.

The day she returned to Fort Dodge, Mom prepared a big meal, and we ate in the dining room with fancy china dishes and sterling silverware. Punky produced several items from France. There were perfectly carved crystal knife rests. Who ever heard of such a thing? She put them on the table and we used them. There were tiny salt and pepper bowls made of clear glass with tiny glass spoons for each. You would take a spoonful and spread it on your food by tapping the spoon with your index finger until you got just the right amount. We all tried to use them. It was difficult. I thought "they" should just use a saltshaker. She brought out a can of water she was served on the airplane. It was the size of a tuna fish can and had to be opened with an old-fashioned can opener. We thought this was costly and impractical. If you wanted a drink of water, you simply got a glass, filled it with water, and drank it. We knew the funny-looking can idea with Evian written on it would not last.

Then Punky brought out her photos. There were the usual tourist subjects like the Eiffel Tower, Versailles, the Louvre, and so forth, all spectacular despite their overpopularity and even more spectacular because the person sitting at the table, my very own sister, had actually been to these places and took these pictures herself. Then she showed pictures of places in France I didn't even know existed—magnificent Roman aqueducts, feats of long-ago engineering, elegant centuries-old châteaux, villages with cobblestoned streets. I was mesmerized.

Lastly, she said we could all understand French if we wanted to give it a try. She spoke simple words about simple topics, like food and dishes on the table. She gesticulated with her hands and eyebrows, and pretty soon we all understood a little French. It was amazing. I knew I had to go to France.

And I did. With the push of my childhood curiosity and the imperative of our family's openness to the world, I have traveled and studied in some thirty countries and, yes, they include France and Italy and Mexico and Hungary.

E-mails

From: Punky
Subject: Sicily

I thought you guys might like to know that our cousin Vincenzo Maggio was not only the editor of *L'Osservatore Romano*, but also of *Sindacato*, the journal of the Italian Confederation of Workers. We come from good union stock!

I also found a telegram Dad sent to Bad Cousin Paul (Dad being Good Cousin Paul). You remember how Nonna's sister Francesca married Nonno's brother Giuseppe? Francesca and Giuseppe had two kids, Paolo (he was even a bad kid, I guess) and Serafina. When their parents died young, Nonna and Nonno felt bad about their orphaned niece and nephew so they let them live on *our* land. By and by, Paul "forgot" who owned the land, and he wouldn't give it back. I think he killed an attorney who came to the house to talk about it—spent seven or eight days in jail for it (remember this was Sicily).

He also fired at a nun who came to see him when Nonna tried to donate the land and house to an orphanage. So that's where things stood when Dad sent this telegram, but in Italian, to Bad Cousin Paul:

DO NOT sell my property in Camporeale. According to the magistrate, to the Consul General of Italy, and to my attorney, you will be thrown back in prison if you do. Paul Maggio, son of Francesco.

Dad had a reply from the telegram company:

We are sorry your telegram to Paolo di Maggio, widower in Camporeale, Palermo, Sicily, Italy is undelivered for the following reason: refused by addressee.

Well, duh.

⊠⊠⊠

From: Ciccio
Subject: Sicily

So which attorney was murdered? You left out that important fact. When we are there this fall, should we reclaim the property? Punky could be our front man since she speaks a little Italian and does not look like an attorney. Well, okay, she could be our front woman.

⊠⊠⊠

From: Mark
Subject: Sicily

If Punky gets to be the Front Person, can I be "The Beard"? Isn't there usually "a beard" in these situations? Also, who will be the mouthpiece? Could Pat do that? If we have a mouthpiece, should we have a Cod Piece? P.T., does your Cod Piece still work? How large is it? That just leaves the pigeon. Who do we have who can be the pigeon?

⊠⊠⊠

From: Ciccio
Subject: Sicily

Mark, I am worried about you. Do they have shrinks in the Ames area who would be willing to have a few sessions with you?

✉✉✉

From: Pat
Subject: Sicily

Mark, It perhaps was an oversight on your part, but did you notice that your e-mail went to the two sisters (women)? That question to P.T., about the size of his Cod, is probably the type of subject that should be discussed only among us men. Love you.

✉✉✉

From: P.T.
Subject: Sicily

Dear Mark, I have long been aware of the affliction of dyslexia suffred by Ciccio and openly amdit to being mildly affected by it mesylf. Howvere, I worked vrey hard to earn the tilte of Doctor and still prefre being Doc as opposede to Cod. By the way, my Codpiece is porbably the same size as yuors, about 8 x 11 and in a balck frame. Love, T.P.

✉✉✉

From: Mark
Subject: Sicily

Dear Poor P.T., I think it is wonderful how you used your dyslexia to get through dental school. You told me that in organic chemistry class, you were able to speak in pig Latin, but dyslexic, and it turned out to be chemical compounds and phrases, earning you about a B-. It's a good thing you had a firm grasp of Pig Latin before entering dental school. Who taught you pig Latin? Was it Evin-Kay?

By the way, I would not use the term "pig Latin" because it is deeply offensive to quite a few groups (pigs, farm animals generally, those pig-dogs on TV, Latin majors in college, dental students who failed chemistry, people whose middle name really is "-Kay," and Hispanics). Ors-yay uly-tray, Ark-May

⊠⊠⊠

From: Pat
Subject: Sicily

Mark, You've really got a handle on El Mismo! A genuine dyslexic always sees the last part of the sentence before he sees the first. Thus, his ability to predict the future while being confused about the present.

The boy wonder not only was Lex Luther dyslexic, he was a teacher of the fruits of dyslexia. Why, when I was in law school, P.T. taught me a number of new words, but I later learned he didn't mean to. For example, he wrote from college that he had gone out with a young woman named Meg who was already a mother (not his doing). Typical for his level of wit, he intended to refer to her as Ma Meg but in his letter it came out as Smegma. It sent me racing to the dictionary. In the same letter, he referred to a personal body part (which I won't clarify here) as the gliftle. From that day on he liked to think of himself as a smithword. Regards.

⊠⊠⊠

From: Punky
Subject: Sicily

Paddy, tell the truth—are you laughing when you write that stuff? You better be or I'll think you don't have a very good sense of humor.

⊠⊠⊠

From: Pat
Subject: Sicily

wes, jes, yes I am laughing so hard I can hardly see the keys . . .

⊠⊠⊠

From: P.T.
Subject: no news

Dear Punky, You shouldn't send e-mails with the subject line "No News." Consider your brother Padraigh who, in his self-claimed throes of dyslexia, must be seeing "On Swen." What is the poor lad to think but that it is a cheer for a Viking rowing team? You could use a topic like "Tap si a muddyhead."

⊠⊠⊠

From: Pat
Subject: no news

I'm feeling the love . . .

⊠⊠⊠

From: Mark
Subject: keep me in the loop, okay?

Pat, In your deposition, you said, "Dyslexia is an affliction affecting only society's brightest and most honorable members (typically left-handed people who say 'baaahhaaaabaaaaa')."

I have several sheep that say "baaahhaaaabaaaaa" and I am wondering if there might be such a thing as "dyssheepsia." For example, one will start to eat at the north end of the feeder, and then run wildly to the south end of the feeder, thinking there might be better feed there. This lack of focus sounds like what you mentioned. Has this ever happened to you?

⊠⊠⊠

From: P.T.
Subject: keep me in the loop, okay?

Dear Mark, There are several dyslexics in this bunch who may be wondering why you'd want to stay in the pool. Especially in Iowa, in February. Love, Tap

⊠⊠⊠

From: Punky
Subject: keep me in the loop, okay?

They say I have ADD but they just don't understand. Oh, look! A chicken!

✉✉✉

From: Matt
Subject: keep me in the loop

It's not a chicken, it's the Easter Bunny. Happy Easter, one and all. My thumb really hurts.

✉✉✉

From: Ciccio
Subject: viel Schnee!

Paul, I know you're not dyslexic. Still, I'm impresed at how close you came to the corecct spelling of "God bless you" in French! The second "e" should be a "u," but that's realy close. Suprissed you don't use spell check. The only one of us who knows how to spell is Rosalie and that is a good thing because Juno does not offer spel check. I never use it myself as I have been in sort of a speling schol trainining programme for the paste there years.

✉✉✉

From: P.T.
Subject: viel Schnee!

Gud luque wit you're spelling classes. every since I tuk sum classes I dont need spellcjheck enny more.

✉✉✉

From: Ciccio
Subject: viel Schnee!

Paal, I'ts obvus thatt uoo have tacen the same lessons that iv'e tacen. Alltho
the cost is hei, the benafets are gud. I have nevr speld bter. Chico

⊠⊠⊠

From: Mary
Subject: viel Schnee!

meneeder

⊠⊠⊠

From: Mark
Subject: AADD

Pat, It is not politically correct anymore (since last week) to call the condition
ADD, as you did. You now are supposed to call it AADD, to wit and
heretofore:

AADD (Airman Against Drunk Driving work to eliminate the alarming
number of DUIs on Air Force bases)

AADD (Artistic Attention Deficit Disorder explains the "artistic
temperament" including moodiness, quick temper, chronic forgetfulness,
disorganization, jumping from one project to another, and obsession with
one's work)

AADD (Autonomic Adaptive Distributed Deployment is used in
component-based services).

You folks in ADD/ADHD/AADD have a varied and busy life.

⊠⊠⊠

From: Mary
Subject: AADD

Let us all continue to encourage Pat.

⊠⊠⊠

From: Pat
Subject: AADD

Mary, At the break of day I checked my e-mail and now write to advise that none of the sibs, overnight, provided any "encouragement" to me. Love you.

⊠⊠⊠⊠⊠⊠⊠⊠⊠⊠⊠⊠

From: Mark
Subject: brush up on your Italian

I will now translate Mary's Italian e-mail. I am pretty good at this.

Here's her Italian: "Grazie molto per tutto il vostro lavoro su questo progetto. Siete amavate da tutti!"

Translation: "Thanks so much for all your hand washing, your questions, I'm pregnant. Sit and I'll make love to you all!"

⊠⊠⊠

From: Ciccio
Subject: brush up on your Italian

Mark, outstanding!

⊠⊠⊠

From: Kevin
Subject: brush up on your Italian

I like this Sicilian proverb: "Faith is salvation, not the wood of a ship." I always used to get those mixed up—faith/wood, wood/faith—but now I know they're not the same. Those Sicilians are so smart! K

✉✉✉✉✉✉✉✉✉✉✉✉✉

From: Mary
Subject: Guthrie

Last night I auditioned at the Guthrie Theatre for a bit part. It ranks right up there with one of the least-thought-out things I've ever done.

I had nestled in my pocket one of those little holy packets that Nonna made to ward off evil. If I get a call, I can thank that little cotton bag with the medal and the hair in it. Love, MMM

✉✉✉

From: Pat
Subject: Guthrie

Well, aren't we special. And you have the advantage of that little cotton bag. Send that thing out here, quickly. I'll ask for ten unfettered, limitless wishes. (The tenth will be for ten more of the same.) I am so glad for (euphemism for "jealous of") the great experience you're having with the Guthrie. Perhaps one day I'll be elbowing folks in the airport lines and pointing to the monitor: "Eh. That's me sister!"

✉✉✉

From: Mary
Subject: Guthrie

I hope you're all sitting down. The little cotton bag worked! Pat, if you want it, what are you willing to pay for it?

I got a part in *A View From the Bridge* by Arthur Miller at the Guthrie! Is that crazy, or what?

Here's what I know so far. It will be performed on the main thrust stage. It will be performed about a million times in October and November. I don't think I have any lines, but they will use the lines on my face. I will see Mike sometime around Thanksgiving.

Then the stage manager called! I'm going to the read-through! She said the Essentials (what those of us with no lines are called to keep us coming back) don't usually come to the read-through but if I want I can. I told her I'd have to move mountains, but that I'd be there. She thinks I might be playing an old grandma! Would that I could channel Nonna . . . ! Too many exclamation points! Oh boy! The read-through is Tuesday around noon and oh boy! I get to go!

✉✉✉

From: Matt
Subject: Guthrie

Mary, that's fantastic, way to go, break an arm. Let us know when the performances are so we can attend. Is it air conditioned? I might refuse to do pretty much anything that would involve no air-conditioning.

✉✉✉

From: Mark
Subject: Guthrie

Wow, Mary, congratulations on getting the part at the Guthrie. You are a real go-getter! I didn't realize they had moved into the "million performances on the thrusting stage" displays. I never pictured you getting involved in that kind of thing. But I suppose you know what you're doing.

✉✉✉

From: P.T.
Subject: Guthrie

Holy Shiite, This is huge. Think of what this means to the rest of us Italo-Americans. We can make it too! I know how much energy and enthusiasm you have given to the thespian world and to have this chance to be totally immersed, to see behind the scenes, and in a play by a bone fide bigwig is beyond compare (in Italian, that would be "beyondi compari," unless, of course, you are using the first-person imperfect past-tense participle in which case it would be "si, Maria, you rock"). Buona fortuna! Paolo

⊠⊠⊠

From: Pat
Subject: Guthrie

Dearest Triple M (I use this moniker because it saves me typing three Ms), I am so happy for you I am at a loss for words. Suffice it to say that I agree with everything that has been said except that P.T. can't use bona fide. Only lawyers can use that expression. If we let regular people use it, we will no longer be able to charge $200 per word.

On a minor note, if you are successful at channeling Nonna, if you have a few extra seconds with her, would you ask her for next week's winning Colorado lottery number? I would pay you $25.00—not bad for a few seconds' work. With the proceeds I could be a much more loving, engaged, sensitive brother. Love you.

⊠⊠⊠

From: Mary
Subject: Guthrie

Yes, Pat, I will ask her and if she gives it to me, I will definitely give you $25! Love, MMM

⊠⊠⊠

From: Pat
Subject: Guthrie

I'll be taking all Mary's e-mails from now on. I am officially her agent for all purposes as we ramp up to the opening night at the Guthrie. I'll thank you for that courtesy.

⊠⊠⊠

From: Mary
Subject: Guthrie

Update on the Guthrie . . . But first, Maggio, how the hell are you? Quit it. If you stay in the hospital any longer I'm going to have to take away some points. The sooner you get out, the more points you get. And if that isn't a worthy goal, well, then saddle my junebug.

Back to the important stuff. I got to go to the Guthrie yesterday and I still don't know who I am. (I have never had a clear idea who I was since the age of reason so I was looking forward to hearing it from an authority.) I got to do improv and movement exercises with the other Non-Entities. I mean, Essentials. And then we watched *On the Waterfront* for "color" to add to our characters. What characters? I tried to sneak that question in but the AD (the director's right hand) didn't fall for it.

Speaking of Eth (director Ethan McSweeny to those of you who haven't had e-mail correspondence with him like some of us), he did drop in on us to share some of the sunshine. We bantered and laughed and traded old stories. That was before he came in. Then when he arrived, we Essentials huddled and waited for signs that we could talk or nod in his presence. The sign never came and when he left, the sunshine went with him.

Eventually, a classy woman named Marcella the Movement Coach came in and pretended we were important by telling us we were doing the exact same exercises as the real actors! Well, didn't we just preen.

I have an appointment today with the costume department. I am hoping that will give me a clue as to the character I'm playing. Wouldn't that be great since the first dress rehearsal is in three weeks?

But don't worry about me. I'll be okay even if I don't find out today what part I'm playing. I can handle it. We middle children are good at that. Not knowing shit, I mean. Love, MMM

✉✉✉

From: Matt
Subject: Guthrie

Mary, that is so cool. So far anyway. Please keep the updates coming. Really enjoy reading about this slice of your life.

✉✉✉

From: Mary
Subject: Guthrie

Yesterday I was honored to attend rehearsals with the full cast, minus the Essential children. Evidently there is someone even less essential than us. But we Essentials stuck close to each other and tried to catch a ray or two deflecting off a boot buckle of the cognoscenti. One of their slaves gave us water, which was nice. But we huddled immediately and did not know the protocol with water. We watched our betters until they drank theirs and then felt we could drink ours.

We Essentials are so not on the charts. It's like being invited to dinner except you are still at your own house and everyone else is at the castle. Being an Essential keeps one humble. I treat the lesser beings (stage crew) with great consideration. I never look directly into any of the real actors' eyes. I look at about their belly button. It's a sign of respect. And I never speak, even when spoken to.

The only acting I get to do: I get to give a lawyer a suspicious look. In my mind, I'm thinking the stink-eye look. I'm going to play that look for all I can get. I may even take a bow right after it.

One of the Essentials committed a huge faux pas by stepping over the threshold into the actual dressing room of one of the real actors. The rest of us were mortified and felt it reflected so poorly on us that we tarred and feathered her ourselves.

$\boxtimes\boxtimes\boxtimes$

From: Mary
Subject: Guthrie

Hi Cats! It's looking as though we've moved into Fall and it couldn't be nicer. I always miss Dad when the seasons change. (And when they don't.)

I've gathered you together to update you on My Life In the Theater. My role underwhelms me. I have less to do than the door, which at least opens and closes twice.

Regarding my role, it's a non-speaking, non-equity role and at one point I thought the director had forgotten he cast me as I've had no direction whatsoever. I wandered around in the shadows. Then, when he did turn his light on me, he gave me a nod. That is, in my role as the Italian grandmother, I got to nod at someone. I loved it. I was good at it. Yesterday, the nod hit the cutting room floor and I no longer get to nod.

You will know me because I'm the oldest person on stage. I wear thick black stockings, a black dress, a black sweater, a black scarf, and black nun shoes. At one point, I have a costume change where I trade my black sweater for a dark gray one. I hope everyone still recognizes me.

Gotta go dust off my invisibility cloak. Love, MMM

$\boxtimes\boxtimes\boxtimes$

From: Ciccio
Subject: Guthrie

Haven't heard from MMM for about an hour. This bothers me. She's probably learning a new move for the stage, rehearsing 12 to 13 hours per day. Poor Mike.

$\boxtimes\boxtimes\boxtimes$

From: Mary
Subject: breaking legs

Hi All! We had our first preview performance last night with a paying audience and got a standing ovation! Hah! I knew I was good! I knew they'd love me!

Oh wait, that might have been for the main character, John Carroll Lynch. Oh yeah, now I remember. They stood when he came out. Oh, well, that's different. Never mind.

I think I'll be hearing from the director today about my mistakes. "Mary, why were you in your house during the fight scene?" I might say I was checking on my supply of Depends. But maybe I'll just admit that I missed a cue. "Ethan, Can I buy a cue?"

After the standing O, I got dressed in street clothes and got my wig off. My hair had been pinned down and a wig cap stretched over it, with a wig over that for about eight hours so when I left the Guthrie, my hair looked like Bebe's, Liz's former dog. So what? Mike's in Fort Dodge. I'm going directly home.

I open the back stage door and there are a hundred people waiting for the star to come out. I pretended I had just finished cleaning the toilets and was headed back to my wife-beating husband and his meth lab.

⊠⊠⊠

From: Mary
Subject: sustenance

How could I leave you all in the lurch for so long? No news about the Guthrie? No news about me? So sorry!

Mark, Laura, and Matt are coming to see the play. They'll give you "A View From the Seats," but in the meantime, I can tell you we are getting standing ovations every night. Of course, historically in Minnesota, a standing ovation is given to anyone who walks on stage, talks, and doesn't fall over. More important than the standing O is that you can hear a pin drop during the performance. And every night is a little different—the actors have different energies. Some nights the audience is rolling in the aisles, and other nights they are quiet and restrained like good Lutherans. Tonight they were restrained but being glad it was over, they stood and clapped for a long time.

We've had three reviews. Two praising ones and one by a pathetic child abuser. I overheard people talking tonight as I waited in the lobby and it was very interesting. No one said anything about our show but it was interesting conversation nonetheless and I just thought I'd share that with you.

I got home at 11:30 the other night after two hours in traffic and sat my angry ass down to write to MN Dept. of Transportation just to ask if the planner went to Transportation School or Gridlock School. Or was he just a sick twisted bastard who enjoyed torturing people? I haven't heard back yet.

Hope you are all fat and sassy! Write! I love sibling e-mails! Love, MMM

✉✉✉

From: Mary
Subject: Guthrie News Release

"Welcome to Arthur Miller's Greek Tragedy, American style, the 53-year-old *A View From the Bridge*, currently being given a wonderfully full-bodied revival at the Guthrie Theater in Minneapolis. Director Ethan McSweeny has assembled an excellent cast for this production. The eight main players, supported by an ensemble of six actors, make the stage, and at times the orchestra aisles, teem with the hustle and bustle of life in 'the shadow of the Bridge' that faces New York.

"All the actors did a good job but the most remarkable was Mary Maggio in her utterly convincing role as the Sicilian nonna. Her heart is totally exposed as she struggles to make a living by renting her rooms to illegal immigrants. She has captured not only Miller's rich intentions, but all the nuances in the pauses between her actions at the window and in her rocker. Although seen mostly behind a scrim, her excellence extends right through the entire play. She portrays all the power and substance of the aged wise elder seen in a Greek tragedy. Perplexity was deftly conveyed in her portrayal of the beleaguered, emotionally full yet inherently spellbindingly holy woman. Despite the important role, Maggio was tender and put forth a superbly realized and real character. We shall miss her as she intends to resign from the theater after this brilliant perfomance.

"In an interview, Maggio said, 'I've had many difficult roles, but this one takes the cake. It took three people—the director, assistant director, and intern director—to keep track of my cues. And the costume changes in this production, well, let's just say they were excessive. The window didn't always open smoothly. Sometimes I'd come in and my rocker would be moved over a couple of inches. It was a nightmare. I can't do it anymore.' Her performance will go down in history as one the most heart-rending portrayals of an Arthur Miller character ever performed."

⊠⊠⊠

From: Mark
Subject: Guthrie

Okay, everybody, Matt and Laura and famiglia and I are booked for the matinee Saturday. Join us if you can get away. At the end of the show, we will throw roses at the stage toward Mary, raise our hand-lettered signs, toss confetti, and shout, "Brava! Brava!"

⊠⊠⊠

From: Mary
Subject: Guthrie

I am tickled you are coming but, please, don't trouble yourselves with the unwieldy signage and cumbersome confetti. You can throw things at me when I get home.

As for the standing ovation, you won't be alone. Unless, of course, you stand up at my first appearance. Then the ushers may come and have a chat with you.

By the way, it is customary at each performance that family members press folded one-hundred-dollar bills into the hands of "their" actor. The more the better. This whimsical custom holds true whether or not the actor nodded at the right time.

Can't wait to see you. Love, MMM

✉✉✉

From: Mark
Subject: Guthrie

Mary's invitation to the Guthrie allowed me to suck up quite a bit of culture in a fairly short period of time. This is important, since my excursions off the farm are few and far between. The best part was spending a little time with family who, for some reason were particularly enjoyable this time around. Pat was not there.

We saw the theater production, which was very good. It had some perversion in it, but nothing more than you would see at the average middle school in Berkeley. Mary was not required to demonstrate any perversion, which was gratifying. It's better to keep some parts of your personality private. The only unrealistic part was that as an Italian grandmother, she did very little cooking or force-feeding of others. It was hard to see into her apartment, so maybe she was up there cooking and making people eat, but I couldn't see it. The leading actor dressed up her ankles to look just like the 1930s-1940s. They were very appealing, as ankles go. Either it was a really great make-up job, or her ankles really do look like that. We don't know which.

Aprŝs theatre (translation: Theatre of the Apes) we had a wonderful lunch at a very "avant-garde cafe" (translation: the guard wants coffee). Many of the people in the cafe were trŜs chic (translation: three chickens or, out in the provinces, it would be "three gizzards"). Some of the men were dressed as men. Trying to fit in, Matt kept saying "oui oui!" and it was not until much later that we realized he was actually saying "wee wee" because it was a large booth and difficult to get out. Poor Laura. Laura ordered a dish called Julienne d'le Stinkpeu. Punky told her it translated as "Cutlet of Wiener Schnitzel." As it turns out, there seems to have been some problem with the translation. It was actually something like "Big Plate of Sliced Winter Garlic" and, not wanting to be rude, Laura ate it all. Poor Matt.

Mike is doing very interesting wood carving. On some of the pieces, he does not use sharp chisels, but rather his teeth. He has built a nice little dam in the backyard out of sticks and small trees. I guess it all seems harmless.

✉✉✉

From: Matt
Subject: Guthrie

Dear Mary, Hope you're basking in the feeling of an event well done! And thanks for picking up our hotel bill. You really didn't need to do that.

✉✉✉

From: Ciccio
Subject: Guthrie

Punky, Sorry you aren't here. We miss you. According to Mary, we are having a much more fulfilling visit than your group had. Sorry. We even had better seats at the theater than you did. We met the whole cast, not just a few of them. And everyone agreed that last night's performance was the best so far.

✉✉✉

From: Mark
Subject: Guthrie

What? She paid your hotel bill?

✉✉✉

From: Ciccio
Subject: Guthrie

Where was I when the hotel-bill-paying was going on?

✉✉✉

From: Mary
Subject: Guthrie

The big news is that Dustin Hoffman was in the lobby yesterday. We are all excited about our proximity to a Name. None of us actually saw him so it might not have been Dustin Hoffman. He may not have been there at all or he may not have been there to see *A View From the Bridge* (although, if I were him, that's what I'd see). He may have been there to see *Little House on the Prairie* and that would make me sad if that's true because it's a trifle for girls who like bonnets.

On another note, I'm pretty sure there's a ghost on the set. It knocks. I knock back, but am afraid to knock too much in case I'm swearing or something. I usually just reiterate what the ghost has said. I'm trying to befriend it. Love, MMM

⊠⊠⊠

From: Mark
Subject: Guthrie

Actually, Mary, for ghosts, repeating things symbolizes passing gas (repeating) and so they do not like your implication. I know this is an unpleasant topic, but I felt compelled to mention it.

What ghosts really like are cookies, as you know. It works okay to send cookies to your brothers, and then when you are at the theater, be sure to tell the ghost (loudly, because they are often hard-of-hearing) that you sent cookies to us. They will like that.

⊠⊠⊠

From: Pat
Subject: Guthrie

Ciccio, Just a note, confidentially, about triple M. Mike and the kids have now attended her last 112 performances and are catching two today. No end in sight. It is theoretically possible they go because they enjoy it.

⊠⊠⊠⊠⊠⊠⊠⊠⊠⊠⊠⊠

From: Mary
Subject: yo, Irish girl cousins!

So far here's what I know. We're going to get together the weekend of July 25-27 in Minneapolis.

(The only reason we didn't invite the boys is because, generally, they have cooties and we will already have our hands full with mosquitoes. But if you have any brothers who want to attend, we could take a vote.)

I'll find a hotel that's cheapish and nearish to the airport and to the Mall of America. I will have a cookout at my house in Bloomington on Saturday. I have not received confirmation from the tap dancing men in shorts but will let you know as soon as I do.

What I'd like to know by oh, say, May, is whether you plan to come. (I don't know why I need to know this. It's just something people do. Please keep it to yourself if it makes you feel better.) Hope you can come! Mary Maggio

⊠⊠⊠

From: Mary
Subject:

Okay, pals, here's the new deal. Quite a few of you can't come. I guess we shouldn't have invited Punky in the first place. But what's done is done. I hate to cancel the dancing men in shorts. I suggest we go ahead with whoever can make it.

⊠⊠⊠

From: Mary
Subject: yo, Irish girl cousins!

Okay, cats, on Saturday, July 26, as many of us as can will gather at my house and discuss concerns such as water rights in the Southwest, the power of the judiciary, and acceptable levels of lead in Cheerios.

Oh wait, that's another gathering I'm thinking of . . .

Ours will consist of reunion, warm fuzzies, and laughs. Diane, you said you'd bring all the food, right? (Ha. Just kidding.) We'll eat and lounge and talk. You will bring nothing but your own selves and any photos making fun of Margee. (Ha. Not kidding.)

I checked events in the Twin Cities for that weekend and here's what I have lined up for us: On Friday, the Vikings training camp opens in Mankato OR we could go to Lumberjack Days in Stillwater. Saturday is the MN River Challenge in which I have entered all of you for the bike/canoe/kayak event. Sunday Hootie and the Blowfish are playing and who would miss that?

What I need to know is this: Who needs reservations and for what nights? (I think Mary Kay said she'd pick up the tab.)

⊠⊠⊠

From: Mary
Subject: yo, Irish girl cousins!

Some of us Nash cousins gathered in Bloomington this past weekend and tried our hardest not to have any fun but we were soundly defeated in our efforts.

Uncle Kevin (our only boy) seemed embarrassed by the way Mary Kay and Margee were acting with the ten-dollar bills and the tap-dancing men in shorts. I wish you all could have been here, though, as Uncle Kevin gave us each $1,000. (We were going to uninvite him unless he ponied up, so he gave us the money but he wasn't very cheerful about it.)

Perhaps Connie, Margee, or Mary Kay will e-mail you with details about the gathering but don't believe a word they say! Love, Mary

⊠⊠⊠⊠⊠⊠⊠⊠⊠⊠⊠⊠⊠

CHAPTER 8

A Poignant Chapter in Which We Tell a Few Stories About Those Powerful, Enigmatic, and Unforgettable People We Called Mom and Dad

Reunions
Frank

D ad was always in attendance at our family reunions, but I think it was Mom who insisted that we have them. She was big on all of us spending time together, and she actually expected us to like each other. We had so many reunions that they're all jumbled up in my mind, but two stand out.

Mom had trouble balancing her medications after an operation, a few kinks from menopause, raising eight kids, and I don't know what else. The fact was that she sometimes got a little off base.

In 1977, we rented a whole resort—an old-fashioned, family-style place—in Branson, Missouri. I sure wish we had bought some old-fashioned property there that summer. Anyway, Mom was having one of those bad days, and I noticed that from her cabin, she was calling in each of her children, one by one, to counsel with her.

On exit interviews, I found that she was telling everyone that she was going to leave Dad. Everyone felt disheartened by this turn of events. Sure enough, when she got me in there, she explained that she had had it and was leaving him.

I asked her if she had a place to stay and if she had money. She said no to both. I explained that no sane person runs away from home while on vacation. I also told her that she should go home with him, move money into her account, and get living quarters. Then she could give him the slip. She liked the idea and thanked me for being such a good son.

All this blew over by the time they got home, of course. They remained married and devoted to each other until their deaths.

One year, one of us thought it would be a good idea to have the annual reunion at Mom and Dad's. We could do some necessary repairs and general fixing up of the old homestead. They had over four acres that needed a lot of care. They did all the work themselves, and they were aging, so some help was in order.

For a whole week, the eight of us and most of our spouses as well as many of the grandchildren worked like immigrants. Interestingly enough, most of us are handy and resourceful. Two buildings and the barn were scraped, primed, and painted. The interior of the garage was completely rebuilt. The interior of the house was cleaned with a toothbrush. Wallpaper was hung. New white gravel was brought in for the road to the barn. Small children stained the picnic tables and yard furniture. Older children trimmed bushes, planted flowers, and weeded rose beds. We were beavers.

The part that sticks in my mind, however, was the plot to take me out of the picture. I don't know which sibling's fine Italian hand was behind the plot, nor do I know the reason. I've come to think it had something to do with the fact that I was the favorite child.

Part of the refurbishing involved a tree-removal project. A 150-foot-long row of honeysuckle bushes had been planted in 1952 and never trimmed. The bushes were now 25 feet wide and 15 feet tall, studded with wild trees that had seeded themselves in the hedge and needed to be removed.

Mark (who was obviously part of the plot) brought his Bobcat to help with this project. A Bobcat is not a small dangerous animal. It is a small dangerous earthmoving machine. Instead of cutting down the trees with a chain saw, which would allow them to grow back, we wanted to uproot them. The smaller trees weren't a problem, so we were feeling pretty confident when we set to work on a 20-foot-tall tree with a 10-inch diameter.

When everything was in place—Bobcat chained to tree, roots cut with chain saw, ropes attached to direct the fall—the signal to begin was given. Then things went south.

This enormous tree—by now 50 feet tall and 6 feet around—groaned, creaked, swayed, and fell right on top of me. There I was, face smashed into the lawn, a ton of tree limb across my back, another across my legs.

Immediately the killers went into action. Mark threw the Bobcat into reverse and started pulling. When he did that, my Italian nose became a plow, leaving a great furrow in the grass. My "stop!" was not loud enough to be heard over the louder roar of the damn Bobcat, but Mark stopped anyway just to see if I was still alive.

Next thing I heard was Pat yelling that he was going to cut me out of there. Before I could object, the chain saw was attempting to separate me from several of my limbs. Terror lent me enough volume so that some repentant, or possibly wavering, soul heard me and had Pat turn off the chain saw. I was so unnerved by then that I don't remember the part about getting out. I think either Mom or Dad saw them trying to do away with me and stopped the nonsense. Needless to say, since then, I watch my back at family reunions—especially when heavy machinery is involved.

....

Letter in Mom's handwriting, in Dad's words, following their fiftieth wedding anniversary celebration:

Dear Family,

Words to describe the feelings in our hearts, in the celebration of the event of the past weekend, have not been invented. We are indeed so thankful that you, our children, gave us the gift of a memory that will last as long as we do. Little did we realize that when God in His goodness bestowed upon us eight little ones that He was blessing us with a life filled with so much love. We are indeed proud and ever thankful that you belong to us. Your presentation of this event in our lives was the greatest moment we have ever experienced. Thank you for the efforts you expended and the thoughts and love you shared to make the evening so memorable. In a rating of 1 to 10 it deserves a 10+++++.

Many plaudits have come our way from those who attended this glorious evening. It is "the talk of the town." Enclosed are a few testaments that seem to sum up the feelings from 180 cards and more arriving every day.

Love always, Dad and Mom

....

They Shoot Horses, Don't They?
Paul

I'm not a big fan of the concept of "midlife crisis." We all sometimes do things that are perceived as outlandish or out of character, but when these activities occur during a certain age range, the doers are said to be having a midlife crisis.

An example that comes to mind is the man in his fifties who goes out and buys a flashy sports car. This could be a vain attempt to regain one's youth, a bit of tonic for an aging ego. It could also be that this car has always been on his mind but would not have been practical for a family of ten. Now that many of the kids have left the nest, he may have more discretionary income, and he isn't bound to spend it on a hearse-like station wagon. Dad always seemed well grounded, so I am not sure if he went through a midlife crisis. But certain events raised our little eyebrows.

One early fall day in 1964, he and Pat left the house in a shroud of secrecy driving our white circa-1960 Pontiac station wagon with its pastel pink interior and baby blue accents. They returned later that evening in a 1964 fire-engine red Ford Mustang. They had driven to the small town of Goldfield, Iowa, and brought back the first Ford Mustang sold in the state.

At the age of eleven, I was just developing an interest in cars, and this was probably the coolest thing I had ever seen. In fact, the entire family was agog at this beautiful little car with its chrome mustang, tail and mane flowing, adorning the front grille. It turned out to be such a fun and reliable car that Dad traded it in for a 1967 model three years later. The 1964 Mustang's career was abbreviated when Pat ran it into a bridge abutment and totaled it. Fortunately, he was not seriously injured, and we soon had a new white 1968 Mustang. This was the car in which I learned to drive.

Dad and I did a lot of pheasant hunting in those days. We headed out into the Iowa farmlands, laid out amid a grid work of gravel roads forming square miles. When we found a ditch that showed promise of harboring pheasants, we parked the car and walked the ditch, hoping to scare something up. Oftentimes, to my delight, Dad sent me back to retrieve the car, so I got in a lot of driving practice without the nuisance of traffic signals or traffic.

One winter morning, I headed to the garage where I met Dad for my ride to school. I noticed small black flecks covering the white hood of our Mustang. When Dad came out, I asked him about this. He said he'd driven through some fresh roadwork and had gotten tar on the hood. Seemed plausible to me. It didn't occur to me that they don't do much tar work in the winter in Iowa.

That evening after dinner I thought I'd be a good son and see if I could clean the tar off. What I found was not tar, but hundreds of tiny chips in the paint. It was with trepidation that I proceeded to bring this information to my father's attention.

The truth came out. While pheasant hunting, he parked the car so he could walk a ditch. He walked down one side, crossed over, and headed back up the other side. Suddenly a rooster flushed in a ruckus of feathers and cackles. Dad ran two steps up the side of the steep ditch, brought up his gun, drew a bead on his quarry, and pulled the trigger just before noticing the Mustang behind the bird. He shot the car.

Midlife crisis? I still don't think so. Dad had a zest for life that wouldn't quit, and the Mustang—and the later shooting of it—was characteristic of a man who was quick to seize the moment (and who had busy, quick hands).

Dad's handwritten will:

Being of sound mind and health, I this date make my last will and testament. I hereby bequeath all my monetary and earthly possessions to all eight of my children, disposition of which shall be decided by and for themselves peacefully and with the love that Mother and I instilled in them. For this love is priceless and is the only possession you may take with you into eternity.

Waiting for Godeer: Not an Absurdist Play
Mark

Initially, it was Mom's idea. "Why don't you go deer hunting with your father on your farm? You've seen a lot of deer. And he doesn't have a hunting buddy anymore."

Dad began hunting with his father in the Des Moines River Valley near Boone in the 1920s and early 1930s. There they collected walnuts and hickory nuts, and also hunted the wily and elusive morel mushroom. With a borrowed single-shot musket, they did a little rabbit and duck and, later, deer hunting.

The small railroad towns of the century before the last century are now remote railroad junctions or rights-of-way. One day, we'll be hard-pressed to find anyone who will even remember that these towns once worked hard, and studied, and built, and danced, and drank, and laughed, and drove buggies, and rode the interurban electric railway for a nickel.

That area was also the site of the C&NW's Kate Shelley High Bridge, the longest double-track open-span railroad bridge in the United States. My grandfather once shot a duck across the river, and Dad was expected to somehow make his way across the High Bridge (2,685 feet long), slide down the other bank, and fetch the duck, which he did with appropriate trepidation. It's easy to understand why, in later life, Dad always appreciated a good German shorthaired pointer. Those early days established for Dad the code of conduct, the rules of the road, in all affairs of the hunt.

Because many of the Italian families in that locale were coal miners and railroad workers—some freezing and starving in the winter—the deer hunting tradition with him was based on finding food for the family.

Dad rarely missed deer hunting in the fall, and he bagged his share. His best "catch"—a huge buck—came to live with us afterward. Okay, it was dead, and it was only the head part of the deer, but it evoked for him a memory of seasons past and a promise of seasons to come.

Dad's ancient method of deer hunting, handed down from his dad, involved hiding and waiting for the deer to come to him—the use-one-bullet-and-drop-it method. That was pretty much the whole banana. No chasing, no driving, no drinking, no hordes of noisy townsfolk stirring up the woods. No banging on garbage can lids, no firing lines. No baiting, no salting, no deer urine, no coyote pee. No camouflage makeup or doe-scented underwear.

Like the Samuel Beckett play, where Vladimir and Estragon are waiting for Godot, we often found ourselves looking like tramps, complaining of our ill-fitting boots, and maybe a private-region medical problem. But still we waited for the deer. After Vladimir and Estragon wait for Godot for two days, the play ends like our deer-hunting days did:

VLADIMIR: Well, shall we go?
ESTRAGON: Yes, let's go.
They do not move.

Every year, we set aside the day before hunting season opened to scout deer trails, tracks, beds, and scraping or destruction of young trees for antler velvet scratching. Laboring under Dad's one-bullet rule, I also usually needed target practice. Dad hit the target dead center the first couple of times, so I'd leave him alone. He hated wasting bullets.

I tried to follow the rule, but it is a tough taskmaster. Once or twice I got carried away amidst a herd of a dozen or more deer, and I used more than the one-bullet rule allows. Later, when Dad and I met up, he'd say—as charitably as he could and knowing that I was empty-handed—"It sounded like a shooting gallery over there! Did you get a deer?"

One day I was lying on my belly like a beached sea lion up in an open tree stand, taking advantage of the hospitality of some unknown bow hunter. I'd asked Dad earlier if he wanted one of the tree platforms. Because Dad was so energetic, it didn't occur to me that a man in his early eighties might not want to shimmy up a tree. He said he had a good hiding place against a stump in the fence row.

Directly beneath my bow stand were three deer highways meeting in a cloverleaf interchange. I wasn't surprised when late that forenoon a herd of eleven deer came sauntering toward me. Remembering Dad's rule, I waited until the end of the procession when I dispatched a nice big buck. I got a second deer as well—legal under Iowa's "party hunting" laws. I went to find Dad and waited to tell my news until he'd asked the obligatory shooting gallery question. He was as pleased as if he'd gotten one of the two deer himself. There would be dancing and singing in the camp that night.

Actually, we never camped. We always stayed at the farm—primitive, but we both could cook; so homemade spaghetti or chili con carne or marinated lamb steaks or meatloaf or beef from my own Angus, fresh biscuits or garlic toast, maybe some roasted sweet potatoes, were soon forthcoming. We always had a big green salad, and the dinner conversation was as enjoyable as it can be. No radio, no television, no newspaper.

After dinner, Dad would partake with me of strong drink (he required coaxing). Only one or two, in those little pony glasses that waited for just such an hour. I usually kept only one selection from which to choose, and Dad never demanded anything in particular. I knew Drambuie would do it. Another year it was sherry. I think we had Canadian whiskey another year. We were alone on the darkened Iowa prairie, enjoying the company and the conversation until 9:00 p.m. bedtime.

Saints Peter and Paul country church north of Gilbert offered us spiritual nourishment on Sunday mornings during deer-hunting season. Once we found ourselves at the Gilbert Corner, stopped by a deputy sheriff on patrol. It's possible that I was exceeding the fifty-five-mile-per-hour speed limit on that deserted rural highway. I don't say that I was, but it's possible.

We were, of course, armed to the teeth, though following the law, we believed. Both guns were unloaded and sheathed; our deer licenses and driver's licenses were in order, although our pockets and pants bulged with ammunition. The great buck knife was safely in Dad's ammo box. But even though we were following all the rules, as Dad always insisted, one can be a little nervous in these circumstances.

"This is my boy, Mark," Dad said. "We're on our way to church over at Gilbert."

"You are father and son?" the deputy asked.

"Uh-huh."

The deputy, an astute observer of human nature, could see that we were both dressed in four layers of heavy peasant-type clothing, topped with blaze orange double mittens for us both, Dad with his yellow stocking cap mask, me with a Russian rabbit hat. I could see that he was trying to process this information in regard to our religious affiliation, as there are several churches in the Gilbert vicinity.

We casually mentioned that we might have been deer hunting, but did not admit to anything about the speeding. He took our licenses, checked to see if we were wanted, came back, and politely told us, "You're father and son." Right. He was sharp. We were waiting for a ticket, or worse, but he just admonished us to slow down and let us go, free to practice our religion, or our shooting, or whatever.

A couple of years we hunted a Lehigh farm where the cornfields abruptly met the edges of dramatic riverine valleys and what could only be called

Iowa gorges. The deep timber—oak, walnut, hickory, cottonwood—covered thousands of acres, and the cornfields thrust and parried into the timber when geography and geology allowed.

This farm also had a herd of free-ranging horses who suspected we might have feed hidden on or about our persons. They always liked Dad best and would cluster around him as though he were a horse whisperer. This was comical for me since I knew the general area where Dad was supposed to be hiding, and in that vicinity I'd see a circle of horse rears, and I knew they had found Dad and were frustrating his hunt. But the way we hunted, there was no such thing as a wasted day or any real frustration.

The score wasn't the most important thing to Dad. As for me, long after the venison was eaten and the days swallowed up by time, I still have the best part of those outings: my treasured memories.

....

E-mail from Dad after his ninetieth birthday:

I will have you know this tardy "THANK YOU" note is not intentional, but is due to unforeseen circumstances, which shall remain secret.

You all made it a most perfect and unforgettable day. Am at a loss as to what to say, but I know that if I had another 90 years to live I would fill the days with thanks and blessings for the love you have showered on me all these years. Even though you are now adults, I still and always will think of you as my "children."

Mother and I were certainly blessed with such a lovely family and I daily thank the good Lord for His goodness, blessings, and mercy—

Thanks!!!!!!!!!!—
God bless—

Love—dad

....

4

Dad's Bread
Kevin

I loved Saturdays. No school. I couldn't wait to get outside. I got up early, ate a hasty breakfast, did my chores, and got out the door as fast as I could. There were tree houses to build, ponies to ride, baseball to play, places to explore, and an underlying anticipation of the unexpected. I never kept track of which Saturday was the first one of the month. But when I stumbled into the kitchen with sleep in my eyes, thinking of breakfast, and saw Dad's bread dough, I knew it was the first Saturday of the month. Bread day.

Dad was never preachy about his faith: he led by example. So it was typical of him to explain cryptically that the first Saturday of the month is dedicated to the Blessed Virgin Mary just as the first Friday of the month is dedicated to Christ. I didn't know any more than that until I started to write this and did a little research. Apparently, the Blessed Virgin Mary told Lucia at Fatima that she would confer special blessings on anyone who honored the Immaculate Heart of Mary on five consecutive first Saturdays of the month. Dad made bread for the family and went to Mass every first Saturday of the month, so there was a spiritual aspect to his bread making that I didn't appreciate as a child.

Dad's routine was to start the bread early, putting the dough in two huge pots. He covered the pots with dish towels to keep the top of the dough from drying out as it rose out of the pots like big white chef hats. Dad attended 6:30 a.m. Mass in town and returned a little after seven. That gave me a window of opportunity to pinch off some raw dough and work the dough ball so he couldn't see that I had been there. I loved raw dough—a taste like nothing else I knew.

Dad kneaded the dough every two hours throughout the day, except that his idea of kneading was more like boxing. He threw flour on the counter so the dough wouldn't stick, took the dough out of the pots and flung it on top of the floured counters, rolled up his fists and punched the daylights out of those big dough balls. Not understanding how yeast worked, I was fascinated to see the dough balls cower back into their original small shapes as Dad punched them silly.

All of us were excited and never strayed far from home because there would be bread at noon, bread at dinner, and bread before bedtime. I don't know if it's genetic with Sicilians, but every one of us loved bread. For lunch, Dad stood at the stove making two or three pieces of fry bread at a time in a cast-iron skillet while we sat around the kitchen table waiting for our serving. We each enjoyed several pieces of fry bread hot off the skillet, which meant Dad stood at the stove for about an hour frying bread and bringing it piece by piece on a spatula to the table. With butter and syrup, it was a sublime lunch.

All day Dad's pots of dough kept rising and getting punched, rising and getting punched. By dinner there was still enough dough to make pizza despite all of us kids secretly pinching off snacks all afternoon.

Dad made Sicilian pizza on rectangular cookie sheets—before round American pizza was "invented," before pizza parlors, and before pizza delivery. Sicilian pizza consisted of only four ingredients: thin crust, tomato sauce, cheese, and anchovies. Even those of us who didn't like anchovies loved Dad's pizza. And even as we ate pizza, we knew this wasn't the end of bread day. We chewed and chewed, and eyed those tireless dough balls still rising over on the countertop.

About two hours after dinner, Dad made three or four large loaves of bread, the crowning glory of bread day. Before sliding them into the oven, Dad carved diagonal slits in the top that made them look fancy although the slits probably had more to do with helping the bread bake properly. The smell of baking bread permeated the house, and we could hardly wait to be called for a slice of bread before bedtime. Sometimes I'd stand next to Dad when he removed the loaves of bread from the oven, basking in the rush of heat and bread smell that whooshed over my face the moment he opened the oven door. The bread cooled on a rack for about half an hour, an unbearable half hour as far as I was concerned. We each got one thick slice of bread with fresh butter—sometimes, if we were lucky, two slices—but Dad said we had to save some for breakfast after Mass the next day. By morning, the crust was hard as a rock, but the inside was light and fluffy and full of air pockets. This was traditional Sicilian bread.

Fast-forward about fifty years. One cold, gray, leafless November day, I flew back to Iowa to visit Dad. This was about a year and a half after his stroke.

The weather was sad, I was sad, and Dad was sad, wounded physically by his stroke and emotionally by the loss of Mother. His brain-stem stroke affected his equilibrium, so he had to steady himself with a walker. When he puttered in the kitchen, he set his walker to one side and braced himself against the counter with his stomach so he could use both hands to prepare a meal or do dishes without falling. It was quite an effort but he told us he didn't want help unless he asked for it.

I called from the Des Moines airport to tell Dad I had arrived in Iowa, had a rental car, and would be home in about an hour and a half. He said nephew Tom was at work, so he'd be alone when I arrived. This was unusual because either Tom or my siblings were with Dad as much as possible. I was looking forward to having some rare time alone with Dad and he told me he couldn't wait to see me.

As I walked up the steps of the back porch, I was churning with mixed emotions—happy to be "home," scared to be walking into such sadness with Dad hurt and Mother gone, with memories of the ten of us in that house for over fifty years, the site of so much of my personal history.

When I opened the door, I was bowled over by the smell of Dad's bread. I started to cry. This frail old man had used what little energy he had to bake bread for me. I tried to tell him how much it meant to me. He said he was happy I came to visit but he didn't have anything to give me except bread.

....

> My dear father! When I remember him, it is always with his arms open wide to love and comfort me.—Isobel Field

....

Tight Ship
Frank

Mom ran a tight ship. Coming from a family of eight children herself, there wasn't much she didn't know about running a household. Her father had been the successful owner of a new-car dealership and for years the family lived high. But during the Great Depression, his dealership burned to the ground, and he had no insurance. Gone were the big house, servants, and cars. The family of ten moved into a small three-bedroom house. Grandpa never recovered financially, and Grandma worked for Social Services for thirty-some years.

Married at eighteen, Mom had six children on the ground by the time she was twenty-nine, and all eight were out when she was only thirty-four years old. In addition to caring for us, she had social obligations as the wife of a popular practicing dentist.

In order to keep this machine above water, she had to be a disciplinarian. There was zero tolerance for children fighting in church or running through a department store. We had to behave *all* the time. No exceptions. Can you imagine getting two, five, or eight children dressed and in the car and off to church, on time, every Sunday? Then can you imagine that all those children actually behaved themselves throughout the whole service?

If an agreement exists on the most appropriate way to raise a child, it is surely not between two people married to each other. I think Mom and Dad worked this out by dividing the responsibility. Dad was in charge of all important family issues that arose between the toolshed and the creek. Mom was in charge of everything else.

Her boot camp might have appeared a little over-the-top to some people. And maybe it was. But how could you manage a family of that size without some vigorous organization and discipline?

The way I view this portion of my upbringing is that Mom and Dad did the best they could at the time. With what they were given, they did a much better job than I could have done, and for that I love and respect them very much.

··
Why should I be reasonable? I'm your mother.—Lynne Alpern and Esther Blumenfeld
··

The Redemption of Louie Mortellaro:
A Morality Play in Three Acts
Mark

Act 1: Here begins the story of the redemption of Louie Mortellaro, one of the many morality tales Dad loved to tell us kids to deepen our faith, to develop godly devotion, or just to get us to keep quiet in church. Many of his stories seemed to start with, "Once there was a man with no shoes." Or sometimes, "There was a beggar man sitting beside the road."

During the Great Depression, Louie Mortellaro had money. An Italian immigrant shopkeeper in the seedy part of town, he was at once a grocer, delicatessen chef, purveyor of liquor, and wholesale supplier of all things Italian and delicious.

According to Dad, Louie was not a paragon of virtue. When the little short widow lady came in for some freshly sliced cappicola or maybe a little mortadella or prosciutto, Louie's thumb rested on the edge of the scale, invisible to Mrs. Giardelli. When Dad bought his salami, he always asked for "just plain salami, Louie, no thumb." Louie was also prone to using what we were told was six feet of white butcher paper to wrap eight ounces of provolone cheese. "I gotta make a livin'," Louie told Dad.

Louie did indeed make a living. He was a wholesale liquor distributor when America was not supposed to have any wholesale liquor distributors. He also owned real estate, some of it nice and some of it in the ghetto. And he was a successful loan shark—as successful as they got in small Midwestern towns in the 1930s—nicknamed Kingfish, since he lived like a king and was a loan shark. Get it?

Act 2: After college and dental school, Dad went to the local bank to get a $500 loan to buy a car. The banker informed him that Dad was (1) young, (2) broke, and (3) Italian.

"Tell me something I don't already know," said Dad.

The banker said, "How about this? No."

Dad went to see Louie, a distant relative, about borrowing the money. Louie launched into a diatribe about the uselessness of Dad's prayer life, Mass attendance, priest friends, and belief in God.

"Paul, why're you asking me for a car loan? Ask your god for the money. If he's so big, he'll give you the money. You don't have to ask Louie for the money! You know what, Paul? I'll tell you about my god."

Louie pulled a wad of large bills from his pocket and waved them in front of Dad's face. "Money is my god. That's what got me my new car, that's what got me everything in my store. Money got me the best salami, cheese, wine, whiskey, everything! Your god is no good, Paul. He can't get you a new car. Only Louie can get you a new car."

Dad shrugged and said mildly that he couldn't agree with Louie.

Act 3: A few months later, when Dad was in the store, Louie came out from the back room, looking pale and thin. "Paul, you gotta help me. Something's wrong with my stomach. I've got terrible ulcers. Maybe I'm dying."

Louie grabbed Dad's arm. "Paul, you're a medical man, you've been to college, help me find out what's wrong with my stomach."

Dad asked him if he had been to the doctor. Yes, Louie had been seen at the Mayo Clinic and was told there was little they could do for him.

"You've had good doctors, Louie. Follow their advice. I hope you get better."

"No, Paul. I can't do that. The doctors, they told me to stop drinking and to eat baby food, like oatmeal. Look around you, Paul." He waved his arms broadly.

"I've got the best spiced ham and salami, right from Italy, hanging on that wall. And over there, I got cases of Canadian whiskey and Cuban rum—better than what they have in Omaha. My wife makes spaghetti sauce like you never had before. I've got aged provolone cheese and fine cheese from Parma. It's like heaven. But I can't touch any of it. I can't eat anything! I can't drink anything. When I do, I feel like I'm gonna die. I got no strength left. What am I gonna do?"

Dad again said he was sorry that Louie was ill and that he'd keep Louie in his prayers. "But, Louie," said Dad, "what about your god, money? Couldn't you do something with money?"

"Paul, I've been crazy for money all my life," Louie said. "And I've never cared about religion or God." He shook his head. "It's too late. I'm too old to start now."

Dad said, "You're never too old, Louie."

Epilogue: Before Louie died, he lent money to Dad (at a high interest rate—what did you expect?) to buy two houses for Dad and his sister and mother.

> The death of any loved parent is an incalculable lasting blow. Because no one ever loves you again like that.—Brenda Ueland

A Death in the Family
Mary

I don't remember exactly the order in which things happened, who called whom and when, but when Dad suffered a severe brain-stem stroke early one Monday morning, we all came home. Mom had alerted us to the situation on her car phone while she was following the ambulance that took Dad to the hospital.

The prognosis, especially for an eighty-seven-year-old, was bleak. Mom was distraught. The man who was always there for her, the man who put her on a pedestal in 1943 and wouldn't let her get off, the man she had lived with for fifty-eight years was as good as dead.

Some hours after being admitted, Dad came out of his stupor in a never-seen rage. Hallucinating from his stroke, Dad was profoundly convinced that he had been kidnapped, especially after seeing the restraints on his arms. He begged Mom to get him from a tray "that fork and that *knife*." The knife! He needed a knife.

Baffled, she didn't give it to him. He then demanded she get him the clock on the wall. "But that belongs to the hospital," she said.

"But I *need* it," he said through his teeth. He told us later his plan was to throw it through the hospital window and escape, naked as a jaybird. That ought to get someone's attention, he thought. The stroke had temporarily rewired his head.

Speaking of his teeth, he gnawed off most of his restraints before being caught. Days later, he was still black and blue from shoulder to fingertips as a result of struggling against the restraints. Dad was a tiger when he had to be.

Meanwhile, Ciccio and Pat, men with a mission, had been driving to Iowa from Texas. We had all seen that the house and grounds were getting to be too much for Mom and Dad, to say nothing of housekeeping and meals. Ciccio and Pat were coming to talk things over with Mom and Dad and, we all hoped, get some help for them.

Halfway to Iowa when the news broke, they drove like maniacs (oh, what am I saying, they were already driving like maniacs), got in the next day, and went straight to the hospital. When Ciccio walked into Dad's room, Dad was able to say, "Hi!" and then quickly, "Have you got your lawyer with you?"

Ciccio allowed as how he did, and Pat came in. Dad immediately asked Pat to file a complaint, to report the kidnapping and abuse to the sheriff's office. Pat said he'd do that, and Dad rested more easily for the first time since his admission.

We were completely focused on Dad, so it wasn't until Friday that we realized Mom wasn't doing too well. Heading to the hospital to visit Dad Saturday morning, she couldn't even walk around the car to get in the passenger side but had to be helped into the backseat.

Outside Dad's room, she asked for help to get to her feet. "I don't want him to see me in a wheelchair."

She took four steps into his room and collapsed on top of his bed. Several hours later, she was ensconced in a room four doors from Dad with congestive heart failure.

Mom had had two open-heart surgeries, a hysterectomy, partial stomach removal, ninety-eight stitches from a snowmobile accident, two defibrillators (including an experimental model early in the history of defibrillators), and was on nineteen different meds when she was admitted that morning. Despite years of surgeries, tests, hospital admissions, and drugs, she never complained about her health.

She'd rather talk about sky sailing in Mexico (just months after one of her heart surgeries), or the week she and I spent in Seattle, or the unforgettable trip to Scotland and Ireland or to Italy or to the Cayman Islands. She wanted to talk about living. The other didn't interest her.

But now, she was in a room down the hall from Dad. ("Mom, do you have any messages for Dad?" "Tell him I love him and I miss him.") She faced either Dad's death or years of caring for an invalid while she herself was, as her doctor of many years put it, "a very sick cookie," certainly not capable of caring for anyone. Mom loved casinos and gambling, but she never lost more than she could afford to. She knew when to quit. My impression was that she took a look at what was on the table and decided she didn't have good cards.

Mark, who we all thought was Mom's favorite child, arrived at 3:00 a.m. on the red-eye from Washington, D.C. We didn't want him coming into a dark house, so Punky set her alarm and got up to greet him. He was exhausted and wanted to go straight to bed. Punky suggested he should go to the hospital. So in the middle of the night, Mom (who was delighted) and Mark had a good visit.

Early Tuesday morning, Dad said he wanted to see Mom. When told, she said, "If he wants to see me, he'd better see me now."

Dad was still curled up and as limp as his blanket, but he was so determined to see Mom that he was gotten into a wheelchair and taken to her room.

They spent fifteen minutes together with the door shut. Dad never told us what they said during that time. When someone checked on them, Mom signaled that she was utterly exhausted and that Dad should be taken back to his room.

She died within minutes, less than seventy-two hours after being admitted. Until the day he died, Dad claimed that she sat up on the edge of her hospital bed and waved to him as he left. We know that couldn't have been true. Then again, it was his truth, and it comforted him during the years that followed.

Mark, who'd gotten up after a few hours of sleep to get back to the hospital, arrived after Mom died. The middle-of-the-night visit turned out to be priceless. Kevin didn't get in from Denver until that afternoon, but he had said his good-byes on his last visit.

Matt and Laura were the ones we worried about. They were in Ukraine, in the process of adopting Kate. How should we tell them, thousands of miles away, that the day they left, Dad had a stroke and now Mom was dead? All we could do was hold up the funeral for six days until they got home. We all still grieve a little that Mom never saw her new granddaughter Kate, although she knew Kate was coming and that Kate would carry Mom's middle name.

The morning of Mom's funeral, I helped Dad get dressed in his handsome black suit. Each arm had to be lifted and directed, the shirt pulled up and buttoned. He could do nothing for himself, but he declared he would crawl out of there if we didn't help.

The hospital bureaucrats put up a big fuss. They didn't want to release Dad to attend Mom's funeral because they feared liability—they said it could kill him. He said, "Okay!" He was not afraid or concerned in the least about his death. He had long ago made his peace with God, and now his wife was gone, and he was infirm. We sent several of our best serial debaters to the camp of the hospital bureaucrats to demand his release, and ultimately we won his freedom that morning.

Punky and I wore white, the brothers were in black. Dad didn't go to the church, fearing to distract people from Mom—it was her day. But I rode with him in a limousine to the grave site. There, a hunched, proud man watched from the automobile window as his beloved was buried. Some of the immediate family members came to the car to touch his hand, but we soon returned to the hospital. That night I lay beside him in his hospital bed out of a spiritual calling to be by his side, to hold him on this unbearable day.

MARY: Can I get you anything, Dad?
DAD: I want Mother back.

In the next four years, before he died, Dad overcame many of the consequences of the brain-stem stroke, a severe mastoid condition, a broken hip, and the indignities of old age. We rallied around him, and he rallied around us. He became mother and father. He and we grew to know each other in ways we'd never imagined.

He wanted to live in the family home that was so much a part of him. In the beginning, we each spent a month there with him, overlapping our times so that he would never be without one of us. Coming from California, New York, Colorado, Virginia, Iowa, Minnesota, Wisconsin, we took our vacations with him and scheduled our visits around his doctor appointments. We did this without thinking, without discussion. It was simply what you did.

As for Dad, he regained all his wits (and he'd always had more than anyone we knew) and learned to adapt his days to his physical abilities. Despite his terrible but silent grief for Mom, which remained unabated until the end, despite pain, discomfort, and physical woes, he was kind, good-humored, and intensely alive to current events, to the pile of books he was reading, and to the smallest events in our lives.

The month before he died, I overheard this:

NURSE: Dr. Paul, do you have any pain?
DAD: Well, only when I see Bush on television.
NURSE (later): Dr. Paul, are you nauseated?
DAD: Not really, except when I think about this war.
CICCIO: Dad, next they're probably going to want you to say your ABCs.
DAD: You want them frontwards or backwards?

And so there at the end, I held his hand for hours, for days. I whistled and sang "Ave Maria" and "'O Sole Mio" to him. I found out at his wake that he had chosen those songs for his funeral. The coincidence was heartwarming.

No one could have told you beforehand what Dad's favorite songs were or even if he had any.

And I urged him on, "Go, Dad, you're almost there! Are you leaving now, Dad? Good job! Finally. Go, Dad, go."

My Favorite Dad Story
Kevin

In 1974, Dad was flown to the Mayo Clinic to have a cancerous vocal cord removed. Afterward his voice was low, weak, and raspy. Although he participated in some experimental procedures for recreating vocal chords from injections of collagen, he never regained his normal speaking voice.

Up to that time, he often took center stage at Toastmasters or to emcee or to tell long, outrageously funny stories. (He and Punky were emcees at her college father-daughter banquet, one of many invitations for this funny, well-spoken man.) Now he could barely be heard. We tried to accommodate him by being quiet when he talked, but I never thought we did a very good job of it. We're all too chatty.

His stroke left him with impaired hearing (during some periods he was completely deaf, so we communicated with a dry-erase board), damaged nerves in one eye, which produced a crippling dizziness (partially modified by his wearing an eye patch, cataract surgery, and special prism glasses), and damaged equilibrium so that riding in a car nauseated him. The first year or two after his stroke, he gamely agreed to ride into town to Matt's house for a holiday meal. Once there he always seemed to enjoy himself, but the rides became increasingly onerous, so eventually he stopped going into town except for doctor appointments.

In addition, Dad was nearly annihilated by Mother's death. She was never out of his mind or heart. He didn't talk about her much because he said it was too painful; but when he did mention her, always tearfully, it was obvious he was irreparably heartbroken.

One spring day, Dad had two doctor appointments in town. Getting out of the house and into the car was a lengthy undertaking involving painstakingly bathing and dressing, the use of hand railings, a walker, and a wheelchair, followed by a delicate struggle to get him into the car without falling. This process was repeated to go into the first doctor's office, then again to leave it, then again to go into the second doctor's office, and then again to leave it, and finally to go home and reverse the exit procedure to get into the house, all the while feeling dizzy and nauseated.

Mary was Dad's driver on this trip. They drove home through a gorgeous Iowa spring day, blue skies overhead, blooming flowers carpeting the earth. Halfway home, Dad touched Mary's arm to be sure she would hear him. He looked up at her from his crumpled little body, patch over one eye, voice low and raspy, Mother on his mind as always, and said, "I . . . have . . . so much . . . to be . . . thankful for!"

> We are never done with thinking about our parents, I suppose, and come to know them better long after they are dead than we ever did when they were alive.—May Sarton

E-mails

From: Matt
Subject: grieving

Dear Family, Sister Jane Rogers was in the office today talking about death. She does this a lot because she is the grief coordinator for the whole county. She told me, in a somber way, to watch out for the 2«-month anniversary of Dad's death. She said that is when grieving gets most profound. I was glad she apprised me of the upcoming tumult, and wanted to do the same for you all. Why should I be the only one in despair on April 12?

Mark and I made off with most of whatever was left at Route 4 today! Just kidding. Good to be there with Mark, as it's hard for me to be in the house alone—and hard to see life in the house coming to an end, but it must. All for now.

✉✉✉

From: Ciccio
Subject: grieving

Matt, That's okay as most of us are unable to figure out the exact date that is 2« months after Dad's holy ascension. I know Pat can't do it as he is a lawyer and that also puts Kevin out. Mary and Punky can't do it because they are girls, Mark can't do it as he has a Ph.D., P.T. can't do it because he lives in the cheese state, I can't do it because I want to be fair, and you can't do it because you brought up the whole thing. So tell Jane that she should talk to some other family about death and the 2«-month thing.

✉✉✉

From: Kevin
Subject: grieving

When I was in Fort Dodge, Jamie from Fort Dodge Hospice called one day and we talked for about 15 minutes. She also told me to watch for the 2« month mark as a potential dark time; I didn't think much of it at the time but now I'm getting worried.

✉✉✉

From: Mark
Subject: grieving

Dear Family, You guys are all off.

2« months in people-time is only three weeks in Dad-time, so that's already gone, and you've already grieved through the worst part. We passed that mark over three weeks ago, and you all missed it.

It's like getting dental work done by Dad. He was so fast, you never knew what hit you. Then it was over. And you still had your tongue, but you weren't sure if you wanted it.

Because of his rabbit-like speed, Dad even managed to violate the time-space continuum. I know this, because Mom would call me from Fort Dodge and say they were leaving for Story City, and they would make it in 42 minutes, which is a physical impossibility if all four rubber tires remain on earth-mounted pavement. The time-space continuum seemed easier for him to violate if: (1) he was driving a big Lincoln or Mercury and, most important, (2) Mom was cat-napping.

So when those professional grieving people tell you to "Watch out!" you can tell them for Dad, "Watch out!" as he continues to violate the time-space continuum. Mark

⊠⊠⊠⊠⊠⊠⊠⊠⊠⊠⊠⊠⊠⊠

From: Matt
Subject: headstone

Dear Family, I'd like to have us get two matching granite vases for Mother's gravestone, one on each side and mounted on the granite base. Any comments?

⊠⊠⊠

From: Pat
Subject: headstone

Great idea about the urns—I'll chip in. And thanks!

⊠⊠⊠

From: Kevin
Subject: headstone

Hi, Matt. I always felt the headstone begged for flowers—this is a great idea. Mary said she'll pay my share so please invoice her.

My feelings about Mom's absence are just as perplexing today as they have been for nearly four years in that I feel at peace with her death and yet still miss her. Happy Mother's Day to Mom!

⊠⊠⊠

From: P.T.
Subject: headstone

Dear Matt, In the jargon of attorneys, when one says he would like to "chip in," it is generally accepted to mean that he would like to foot the bill. For example, if he says "I'll chip in for lunch," that means he would like to take you out for lunch. That being said, I wholeheartedly support the purchase of vases for said headstone. Might I suggest that we buy the larger ones and, I wonder, do they come in platinum or gold?

⊠⊠⊠

From: Pat
Subject: headstone

In his youth, rejected from nearly every CC (College of Comedy), the one-time baby of the family, Paul Thomas, took the path of least resistance and entered the sobering world of IP (Inducing Pain) by attending dental school.

Nearly five weeks after the onset of the dental school experience, at a time when his appetite for inducing pain was plenty whetted, he received notice that the Jerry Seinfield School of Laughs had an opening. Seems a cordial, pleasant but overweight student had laughed himself to death, thus leaving a seat.

It was way too late. The addictive qualities of inducing pain had totally overwhelmed the erstwhile comedian. As a direct and proximate result of his ship leaving without him on it, Paul Thomas, aka El Mismo, spends the remainder of his years fighting the "approach-avoidance" demons of comedy. For example, when he shorts a patient on Novocaine and yanks a tooth, and the patient bellows: "God dammit, that hurt!" the repressed comedian in him causes El Mismo to laugh so hard that he is forced to lay down his instruments of pain and take a seat.

⊠⊠⊠

From: Kevin
Subject: headstone

And then?

✉✉✉

From: Mary
Subject: headstone

Great idea, Men. And thanks, Pat. I looked up "chipped in" and found: "chip in: to contribute money or labor." As you probably won't be available to do the heavy work, I think it was so nice of you to offer to pay for the gold vases.

✉✉✉

From: P.T.
Subject: headstone

Dear Matt and Laura, You have certainly urned my gratitude, thanks so much!

✉✉✉

From: Kevin
Subject: headstone

P.T., oh ye of shameless humor!

✉✉✉

From: Mary
Subject: headstone

I think we are all aware that P.T. has no shame.

✉✉✉

From: P.T.
Subject: headstone

Yes I do, I have shame about the time I called Pat and Kevin buttholes. Or wait a minute, maybe it's remorse. Yes, it is remorse, my mistake Any time you spend an hour with a bar of soap in your mouth, well, I guess you could call that remorse.

⊠⊠⊠⊠⊠⊠⊠⊠⊠⊠⊠⊠⊠⊠

From: Matt
Subject: Mom's birthday

Dear Family, Memorializing Mom on what would have been her birthday, we took wintergreen ivy (she wasn't much for fall colors) to the gravesite and put it in the urns.

Sad, cold, dark, and rainy today. Still, I remember how she loved her birthday—much more willing to command and expect attention than I have ever been for my birthday. Always glad to give it to her as she didn't want or expect it so many other times. The gravesite looks nice, and she and Dad are together again. I'm glad they chose to list the names of their children on the reverse of their headstone. It hit me today how impressive that is, eight kids, not to mention eight great kids! So there you have it.

Hope you all had a wonderful time in Sicily. We are still licking our wounds over not being invited, but we understand, you just had to be exclusive.

Actually, yesterday we booked our family on a Disney Cruise for Jan. 5-13. Sort of boring by comparison to Italy, still, it suits us at this point in our life and maturity level.

⊠⊠⊠

From: Kevin
Subject: Mom's birthday

Matt, Thanks for tending the gravesite. Mom would like that. She never missed visiting the cemetery and decorating all the graves.

⊠⊠⊠

From: Mark
Subject: Boone cemetery

Dear Everyone, Last evening as I was coming home from work, I decided to stop at the Sacred Heart cemetery in Boone for a private visit—Nonna's and

Nonno's graves, Margaret Mary's grave, the little angel, and the mysterious Paul Maggio resting there since 1912.

I would not describe myself as mystical, but I certainly believe in things I cannot know or see. Anyway, as I was wandering around, I heard footsteps in the forest that edges the cemetery. About 50 yards away a beautiful deer, probably a doe, was stepping through the trees there, not at all alarmed by my presence. You can imagine that it reminded me of Dad—he liked to think himself into the minds of the deer—where they were, what they were doing at the moment, when they might show up. It seemed oddly coincidental to me, or maybe a spiritual moment.

Then, as I turned to go back to el carro, I heard the whoosh and low vibrating roar of the locomotive on approach to Boone, perhaps an eastbound Union Pacific. I figured it was a coal train hauling Powder River Basin low-sulfur to the big-city people in the East, to keep their lights lit for the winter to come.

The tracks are not near the cemetery, and the wind and conditions had to be just right for me to hear it like that. But then I heard another, more distinct musical sound. Ding, ding-ling, dinggg dingggg. It was the brass bell of the ancient steam locomotive, mounted high and up front, to indicate that the train was pulling into the station or passing across a switch. That locomotive is from the Boone and Scenic Valley RR, the tourist line that operates on the old Fort Dodge-Des Moines-and-Southern tracks through Boone. Someone must have taken her out for a spin on a Thursday evening.

Immediately my mind was drawn to how many times Dad and his parents must have heard that sound. Boone had 70 trains a day in its heyday. That was the line Dad would have taken for a nickel or a dime from Boone to Des Moines and on to Iowa City, or from Boone to Fort Dodge when it was the Interurban (overhead electric) passenger line.

I will tell you what was my prayer, which I had decided in the car, long before the deer or the train or the bell. I was praying for the eight of us, not for us, but for help in our assignments with those who have been entrusted to us by fate or by God. We all have a daughter or a son or a grandchild or a college student or a neighbor or an English language learner, or an extended family, or a beginning writer, or a co-worker or a spouse, or a troubled soul whose wellbeing and future somehow hinges on each of us.

And I was praying that maybe Nonna or Margaret Mary, and Dad and Mom of course, would help us in our responsibilities. Not for our own good, but in our lovingly assigned tasks.

Well I think somebody was around there anyway.

☒☒☒

From: P.T.
Subject: Boone cemetery

Dear Mark, That is one of the most inspiring things I have read in a long time. Your prayer was answered, in part, by the very act of sharing it. Love, P.T.

☒☒☒

From: Kevin
Subject: Boone cemetery

What a beautiful experience, Mark, made special by your awareness. Thank you for your prayer which has enriched my day already. Love, Kevin

☒☒☒

From: Pat
Subject: Boone

Mark, Thanks for telling us about your Boone experience. Very thought provoking. I agree with darn near everything all of the sibs have said in response. Especially MMM's "I love you."

☒☒☒

From: Mark
Subject: Boone cemetery

Dear Siblings, Being at the cemetery got me thinking about making arrangements for end-of-life stuff, like a will and a gravesite.

At the time of Nonno Frank's death in 1937, Nonna and Dad purchased four gravesites in Boone. Nonna and Frank are using only two of them. Presumably the other two were for Dad and Margaret who were the only living children (and both single) at that time.

Since they're not going to use them, I think I'd like to be buried there. Are any of you interested in the other plot? I know you all have an aversion to taking the last of anything and, it's true, you would have to answer the awkward question, "Did you take the last grave? Well, did you?"

Let me know your feelings on this. For those of you who are tempted to say "ditto," please try to suppress the urge. I often do not understand the true meaning of your various "dittoes." Thanks.

✉✉✉

From: Mary
Subject: Boone cemetery

Mark, I think it's a super idea to get that gravesite. Mike and I are going to be fried so we don't need a plot.

But if you die before I do, I will come and play the harmonica over your grave. It would be nice if you could respond somehow.

Love, MMM

✉✉✉✉✉✉✉✉✉✉✉✉✉

From: Mark
Subject: a hunting we did go

All: I'll not soon forget the sight of nephew Sam, on the other side of the small river, jumping up and down inside his boots, yelling, "Two deer! Two deer!"

Sneaking through the woods in his direction, I motion, hands signaling wildly in my best Dad impression, and hiss, "Quiet, Sam! You'll scare them away! Where are they?"

But Sam keeps saying, "Two deer! Two deer, right there!"

He cannot cross to my side—the river is too high and frigid (I mean, no offense by that term)—but his whole body and personality appear poised to jump down the steep bank and join me on my side.

My gun in the serious business position, I scan the woods, seeking the two deer he wants me to shoot.

I almost trip over them. They are lying on my side of the bank, a pretty part of an Iowa wooded timber valley, undisturbed by modern idiots, surrounded by brush and trees and grassy areas, with cornfields further out. One bullet. Two deer.

What a sight to see Shmuel . . . ! It was his first day ever of deer hunting, and it was the first shot out of his gun. A true double, a clean kill.

Actually, in an ironic deer prologue, Matt took a shot at those same deer first, out on the ice field. He missed; it was a long shot. But what the old man cannot do, now the son can do. Maybe there's a made-for-TV movie in that.

As for me, now I am a man. When you have to gut three deer (I got one, too) on a solid ice field in 30 mph winds, and 12-degree temperatures, you know you are a man. No more saying to Dad, "Gee, Dad, if you really want to, you can gut the deer" as I used to. There is no more Dad; I am the unwilling adult now. It is one of those confirmations we all get, from time to time, that Dad and Mom—their generation in fact—are really gone, and now we are the adults, we are the big people, we are left to take up the gauntlet, or in this case, the deer liver.

⊠⊠⊠

From: P.T.
Subject: a hunting we did go

What a yarn! Can you imagine Dad's face if you were able to tell him about Sam getting a double? Congratulations on a most successful hunt and give Samwell my props.

Mark, you are sort of a history buff, not to be confused with a buff historian, and I wonder if you are well read in matters of Native Americans and their use of the common house deer. When they were finished with a deer, there was nothing left but the snort and maybe some ear wax. What do you guys plan to do with your deer?

⊠⊠⊠

From: Ciccio
Subject: a hunting we did go

Mark and Matt, Dad would have so enjoyed telling that story, to say nothing of how many times he would have told it. What's nice is that Sam knew Dad and he knows that Dad would have gone nuts over a double kill. Mark, your discussion on being a man was moving. Thank you.

⊠⊠⊠

From: Mary
Subject: Sam's Story

In one deer and out the other.

⊠⊠⊠⊠⊠⊠⊠⊠⊠⊠⊠⊠

From: Mark
Subject: Route 4

Dear Ciccio, Thanks for the work on Dad's estate.

By the way, did Dad finally include Pat in his will, or not? Just wondering.

I think what you sent is probably sufficient for the others but, as you know, I was his favorite. I must inform you that he wrote a DaVinci Code type of codicil leaving me the balance of whatever money you have left. In *Black's Law Dictionary*, this is called the "filio favorito codcillo." I don't think he would have wanted the others to know about it, so maybe you had better keep this under your hat. Dad would especially not have wanted Pat to know, considering how sensitive he is, and all.

⊠⊠⊠

From: Pat
Subject: Route 4

Dearest Sibs (especially my favorite ones), Having perused bro Mark's missive, I am compelled to write that I too was included in that grant by the Padre (I think he liked it when I called him the Padre). He actually, right after visiting lawyer Perkins, said that Mark and I were going to get the "overflow" proceeds. That is to say, everything. Hope this sit okay with you all. Love you. Get the hell out of here.

⊠⊠⊠

From: P.T.
Subject: Route 4

Dear Mattrick, Thanks for being our agent in the sale of the house; tell T.J. if she isn't going to buy the house, that yellow leather couch she wants is $175,000 and we'll throw in the house for free. Love, P.T.

⊠⊠⊠

From: Punky
Subject: Route 4

Ciccio dear, I am SO pleased you're buying the house. It's a grand idea and we, your brethren and sistren, are lucky sons-of-guns (Mom being a pistol and Dad a short revolver).

You've been a wonderful executor. I can't imagine anyone else being able to do what you've done so quietly, efficiently, and effectively. I know others helped with this and that but in the end, the buck stopped with you. You da best, mon!

⊠⊠⊠

From: Pat
Subject: Route 4

Dear Brethern and Sistern, I rise to ditto Rosalie's comments.

✉✉✉

From: Kevin
Subject: Route 4

Yes, Ciccio, I ditto Punky's comments (except for her weaponry metaphors) as well as P.T.'s (except for his semi-colon) and Pat's (except for his spelling of brethren and sistren, which did not ditto Punky's spellings so he lied); otherwise, I feel exactly the same. You've been a cool cucumber as the estate executor, and I appreciate your steadfast dedication to completing it quietly, thoroughly and quickly.

Mom and Dad would have been impressed with how you've handled everything and how us kids haven't killed each other yet (although, come to think of it, Mom always liked a good fight). It also warms my heart to think that the house will remain in the family.

✉✉✉

From: Mary
Subject: Route 4

I wrote a really nice letter to Ciccio, too, but I didn't show anybody. MMM

✉✉✉

From: P.T.
Subject: Route 4

Liar, liar, pants on fire.

✉✉✉

From: Mark
Subject: Route 4

All my checks were larger than your figures. I guess Dad had his favorites, and I was one of them. I haven't said anything, though, because I didn't want the others to feel small. Good boy, Ciccio. Thanks for all your efforts.

⊠⊠⊠

From: Matt
Subject: Route 4

No one responded to my request about Dad's antique post office except five of you. Therefore, I am going to sell it.

⊠⊠⊠

From: Mark
Subject: Route 4

Matt, Do you have a check for me?
Did Dad mention me anywhere in his will?
Signed, Pat

Pat Maggio
Attorney-at-All

⊠⊠⊠

From: Pat
Subject: Route 4

Matt, Thanks for all the work you've put in. I have received your mailings and really appreciate your special efforts as your time, while not as valuable as mine, is worth something.

Finally, now that I am dredging up enough courage to initiate an original thought (no dittoing), I'd like to say that the lawyer did nothing but get fat off the estate. We should not pay him.

⊠⊠⊠

From: P.T.
Subject: Route 4

Dear Ciccio, Yes, I received the check and thank you very much. I was talking to Mary and she only got $22,000. What is that all about?

⊠⊠⊠

From: Mark
Subject: Route 4

Ciccio, You are right once again. Dad's butcher knife collection would have brought considerably more money if we had auctioned it off at the men's prison in Fort Dodge. I imagine some of the larger cleavers and meat hooks would have seen some pretty intense bidding as well. You should have spoken up earlier.

⊠⊠⊠

From: P.T.
Subject: Route 4

Take what you will from the house, but I have learned a lot through this inheritance business. My original game plan was to go with "The meek shall inherit the earth." I would dream about how envious everyone would be when it was time to read God's will. "I, God, being of sound mind and good moral character, hereby bequeath the entire Earth to Peeeetey, the meekest of the meek." However, the earth has become a festering boil of strife and disaster and who needs one of those. So I have decided to be happy that I got good-doggie Sheba's bust and leave it at that. It's a nice little bust.

⊠⊠⊠

From: Punky
Subject: Route 4

You're fortunate. I have always wanted a nice little bust, but, oh well . . .

✉✉✉

From: Mary
Subject: Route 4

Confidential: Matt Only

Matt, did you ever get the total weight on that gold we found at the house? Let me know as I am planning my next trip to the Giggling Marlin.

✉✉✉

From: Ciccio
Subject: Route 4

Matt, Good to hear that the estate account is finally closed. Now you can divide what is left and send half to me and keep half for you.

✉✉✉

From: Ciccio
Subject: Route 4

Matt, I didn't realize I hit the "reply to all." Go ahead and divide the account balance by eight and mail checks. Thank you.

✉✉✉✉✉✉✉✉✉✉✉✉

CHAPTER 9

A Kind of Hodgepodge Chapter in Which We Come to Some Conclusions About Growing Up Together, Including Discussions of the Birth Disorder Factor

My Perspective
Mary

From my perspective, and that's all I have, the family was divided into three "generations": Punky and Ciccio were World War II babies with Pat on the cusp; Kevin, P.T., and I were baby boomers; and Mark and Matt were, well, babies.

Some things I learned from my siblings:

> You will share.
> You can love anyone, even Republicans.
> People are basically good.
> Closed doors won't keep them out of your head.
> The oldest of any group gets to be president of whatever club you've just made up.
> A show of strength can prevent a fight, but offering a steely look works too.
> You can blame the younger one, but you're still going to get it.
> Compassion is de rigueur because we are all in the same boat.

I once heard that there are 1,100 possible combinations in a family of ten. That's a lot of conversations—which may be why we are so loquacious. To get a leg into the nonstop but entertaining talk flying around the dinner table, you had to be a verbal acrobat. Words were our solace, our tools when constructing a bit of chicanery, our trays when we were serving up horse pucky, the raw material of jokes, and our way of playing with each other.

For example, Pat was upstairs in the back bedroom. Ciccio was downstairs. Mom was in her easy chair in the living room. Ciccio taught three-year-old P.T. a phrase and then told him to go upstairs and repeat it to Pat. "Tell only Pat. It's a secret."

So P.T. went skipping through the living room on his way to see Pat. Ciccio was downstairs with his ear to the ceiling, listening to P.T.'s progress. Ciccio heard Mom.

"P.T., where are you going?"

P.T. stopped. "I have a secret to tell Pat."

"Oh? What is it?"

"It's a secret. Ciccio said I'm supposed to tell Pat. Only Pat."

"You can tell me the secret because I'm the mom."

"Oh. Okay. I'm supposed to tell Pat, 'F—you, Pat.'"

Ciccio's eyes bugged out of his head. Mayday! Mayday! He ran out to the barn to hide. Mom went back to the bedroom and gave Pat a spanking. Pat had no idea what was going on.

Ciccio hid in the barn for hours, but she simply waited until the next time she saw him, and then he got a spanking.

I got a spanking once. That's sort of a joke because I got a lot of spankings.

We went roller-skating on the occasional Sunday, and it was an activity we all liked. So one Sunday we were at the table eating the noon meal after the obligatory Mass attendance, and Mom got out a package of doughnuts. Whoa. This was not the usual thing.

There's one missing. "Who ate it?" she asked nonchalantly.

"Not me," we all answered chalantly. But we knew someone was going down. She asked again. Hmmm. Still no takers. The steam was beginning to leak out of her ears, but we all swore we didn't take it.

I believe she decided not to ruin her Sunday ritual of reading the *Des Moines Register*, so before she retired to the living room, she said nicely, "I'll be reading the paper. Whoever did it can come in and tell me. There will be no reprisals. We will go skating. I just need to know who did it."

We conferenced at the table. The little ones were too little to have done it, leaving me as the youngest possible thief. The others talked me into confessing. They said I would never get punished because (1) she said she wouldn't and (2) I was little and cute. Then we could all go skating.

I opened the door and walked up to her chair. "I took the doughnut." Bam. She flew out of the chair, and I was getting a spanking.

We never did get to go skating. My siblings all swear to this day that they did not take the doughnut. Years later, we wondered if it hadn't been Dad. He wasn't in the room to fess up when Mom asked who ate it. There is a lesson here about taking it on the chin for the other guy, but I'm not sure what it is.

···

Children of the same family, the same blood, with the same first associations and habits, have some means of enjoyment in their power, which no subsequent connections can supply.—Jane Austen

···

Feathers and Forks
Paul

I am a relatively simple man, especially compared to most of my siblings whom I consider to be rather introspective and analytical. They've all done a lot of serious reading on intelligent topics by world-renowned authors and thinkers. As for me, murder mysteries, technical journals, and sports pages comprise the bulk of my reading. Thus my life's journey has been guided by a few simple tenets and beliefs. One of them is fate. I attribute my affinity for that concept to Dad who often said, "It's God's will" or "God's will, not mine, be done." Minus the religious connotations, it boils down to my version, "It's fate."

In the movie *Forrest Gump*, we see in the opening and closing scenes a feather drifting randomly to earth. That simple feather represents the haphazardness of the path to success. Throughout the movie, Forrest stumbles and bumbles his way through life with incredible coincidence and happenstance leading the way. He has enough amazing experiences and achievements to represent the lives of ten people. In the end, you can't help but consider him to have led a successful life to that point.

Was it all fate? I think not. Was it because Forrest sat down at a young age and wrote a mission statement, complete with a list of goals and the necessary steps to attain each? Certainly not. I'm a big believer in goal setting, but we can all think of times when the desired end was not realized despite astute forethought.

Each NASA space shuttle mission is planned right down to the gnat's ass. Hundreds of scientists and engineers with years of experience and highly technical equipment spend countless hours computing and planning the exact sequence leading up to the countdown. The big day approaches, the excitement in the control center builds. Now it's "T minus two and counting . . ." The intensity could be matched only by a Vince Lombardi halftime speech. Then it happens. An alarm sounds, or a red light flashes, or someone hears voices in their head. The launch is aborted.

Being the intelligent and resourceful reader that you are, I'm sure you can readily see the point I'm trying to make. And I wish you were here as I write this so you could tell me what it is. I guess the point is that there is an undeniable, imprecise, and ever-changing fate influencing one's path. This doesn't mean you can just lay back, become a feather, and go where the wind takes you. It does mean, however, that following your plan will require flexibility and resiliency.

In 1971, I graduated from high school where I was a mediocre student. The first three years of high school were hell, and then came sophomore year. By circumstances still a bit hazy to me, I ended up going to the University of Iowa in Iowa City, Iowa. Yes, I know, you thought it was the University of Ohio in Idaho City, Iowa.

I had precisely no idea of what I wanted to study or what kind of degree I was chasing. At any rate, I was assigned room number 5424 in Kate Daum Residence Hall, and I had two roommates. Both were sophomores and neither came from this planet.

The doors of the rooms across the hall were staggered from mine, one fifteen paces to the left and one fifteen paces to the right. I guess they call that equidistant. I felt like a contestant on a game show, not knowing what was behind doors number 2 or 3. I knew what was behind door number 1 (my room), and I didn't like it. As time went on, the secrets behind each door were revealed to me.

Door number 2 was a challenge because those people were never seen outside their room—apparently some shy and photophobic species. Their room was not equipped with lights, although there were lava lamps and lighters. The walls and windows were covered with cheap tapestries, and the inhabitants always squinted if they were obliged to open the door to visitors.

To this day, I don't know how many of them were in there, but I managed to befriend the one who could speak. I did this because he had a motorcycle and, rumor had it, if you talked nice to him ("That's the coolest bong I've ever seen, man"), he would let you use it. The motorcycle, not the bong. I was young and naive and knew nothing about drugs. In high school, the worst I can remember is some guys smuggling vodka in squirt guns into a dance. I was also curious and in need of friends. Despite the shortcomings that hung about the life-forms behind door number 2, they were a likable lot.

The occupants of the space behind door number 3 were regular people. They woke up and showered in the mornings, went to breakfast, went to classes, knew where the library was. They even had lights in their room and thus could study right there in the room. All three of them were in premed, and they were the most hardworking and intelligent students I had ever encountered. I found them to be likable as well, and we had a lot of good, clean fun. However, it was clear that the books came first. I actually began to develop "study habits," a phrase I vaguely remembered from high school. To make a long story boring, I ended up spending a lot of time with these guys. They helped me focus on school. I was able to settle on a field of study, became a good student, and ultimately received a graduate degree.

Here's where the fork comes in. I mean, that's a true "fork in the road" if I ever saw one. I see how easily I could have opted for door number 2. If I'd fallen in with those den mates, I'd be sleeping under a railroad trestle right now. Something made me choose door number 3. I'm not saying it's all fate, but there seems to be an enigmatic force in action here. As an eighteen-year-old, I could have had a lot of fun with the door number 2 guys. What a surprise to find that, with the door number 3 guys, a lot of hard work and boring study turned out to be inexplicably satisfying.

....

> Like all cultures, one of the family's first jobs is to persuade its members they're special, more wonderful than the neighboring barbarians. The persuasion consists of stories showing family members demonstrating admirable traits, which it claims are family traits. Attention to the stories' actual truth is never the family's most compelling consideration. Encouraging belief is.—Elizabeth Stone

....

My Take on Birth Order
Matt

Growing up in a family of eight children, I had to share nearly everything. "Youngest child" was mine alone.

My pride in this position has on occasion been shaken. Some years ago, I came across, and read closely, a study related to birth order, "Dumber by the Dozens." The gist of it was that intelligence is distributed from the oldest child to the youngest. Eight children and I am the youngest. Great! I am also the smartest! What luck. But how terribly sad for the oldest child, Punky, and the second oldest for that matter. And how curious that it was she who originally brought the study to my attention. Such humility.

Only after a tactful discussion with her did the true meaning of the study become apparent. What a crushing blow, one might think. However, being seven times dumber than such a bright individual is not so bad. And to include this information in the "youngest child" position certainly garnered me lots of assistance, sympathy, and attention. I made certain that everyone in the family saw this study, notably my parents. Lowered parental expectations are not to be sneezed at.

On the other hand, as one of eight children, I was obliged to come up with exceptional activities and to be high achieving so as to stand apart from the herd (with my apologies to the rest of the cattle).

Recollections of my childhood are sparse as I have never had a good long-term memory. I am only good at remembering people's teeth and faces. Still, I can rely on the family to accurately flesh out my past. I simply collate all the stories and edit them to my liking. This rose-colored glasses approach works for me. In the meantime, I use a repetitive incantation to work on my memory lapses. I can't think of it right now, but it has helped.

Punky was nearly sixteen when I was born, and she claimed me as her own. I suspect no one really noticed or cared except for Mother who was undoubtedly relieved. I was an adorable child, the most handsome in Webster County. Given that there is no photographic proof of this, there are few detractors.

Dad was the family photographer and a real gadget man with a huge collection of cameras. He and I share the distinction of being all but absent in the family albums and films—he because of his role as photographer and I because, by the arrival of the eighth child, he had run out of patience, interest, film, storage, and wall space. I heard that one of the relatives had a photo of me as a five-year-old. But when I went to collect it, I saw that I had only half of a head, the rest of the photo depicting our family dog, Sport. It was a pretty good photo of Sport, so I kept it. My being a nonevent photographically is yet another proof of my unique place in the family as youngest child. The birth-order phenomenon lives!

> Some people find out much too late in life that they are
> not the center of the universe. This must come as a real
> blow at age twenty-one or forty-one or sixty-one. Luckily,
> in a big family you know this from birth.—Liz Dolan

Large Families
Frank

Being the oldest male of two-female and six-male siblings has its positives and negatives. I have not figured out either.

Everyone from a large family has something to say about how they were affected by that environment. I didn't think about my position in the family until about ten years ago when a business situation caused me to do a little analysis.

About two months after I arrived in New York City for my new position as regional director of Manhattan for Smith Barney, one of my branch managers, Dennis McCrary, asked if I would meet with one of his higher-producing financial consultants.

Smith Barney had an employee benefit called the Capital Accumulation Plan (CAP), which allowed certain employees to buy Smith Barney stock at a 25 percent discount with pretax dollars. Basically, it was a good plan, and many employees had built impressive nest eggs with it. When McCrary had asked this particular financial consultant why he wasn't enrolled in the plan, the FC became quite upset and asked to speak with a higher-level muckety-muck, me.

The three of us met in McCrary's office at midmorning. After we were seated, the FC pulled his chair around toward me so that when he sat, our knees were almost touching. I asked what he wanted to talk about.

Well. He launched into a fifteen-minute screaming dissertation on all the things that were wrong with Smith Barney, all the things he was not allowed to do, what a terrible benefits plan we had, and on and on. His voice continued to get louder, his face redder, and the vein in his neck grew to the size of a garden hose. I sat silently, waiting for his head to shoot skyward like the cork out of a champagne bottle.

Now this FC was in partnership with another FC, and together they produced somewhere between $3 and $4 million each year, so McCrary didn't want to lose them from his branch.

When the vibrations in the room stopped, I asked if he felt okay.

"Yes."

Then I asked how on earth he was able to make his commute into the office every day with the knowledge that he was working for such a screwed-up company. He said it was extremely difficult.

I said, "Look, even though there is absolutely not an ounce of validity in anything that you have told me this morning, you obviously believe it. That being the case, you should get a job at Merrill Lynch. They'd hire you today. I will personally transfer all your clients to you so that your business will not be affected. What you feel inside will kill you, and no amount of money is worth that, so just change firms and get your life back on track."

By that time, all McCrary's blood had left the perimeter of his body and was rushing to his important organs in an attempt to keep him alive. I felt bad for him.

The FC then asked what I meant when I said he was off base on all his assumptions. Without going into too much detail, I spent half an hour going over his issues, or at least the ones I could remember.

The FC was relaxed and friendly when the meeting ended. McCrary had trouble rising from his chair but seemed to be breathing.

About three weeks later, I received another call from McCrary about the same FC, who was having a temper tantrum in the office and needed to speak with me immediately.

He had decided after all to invest the maximum in the benefits plan, but the deadline for signing up had passed. He wanted an exception for himself. We spoke, and he finally understood that when exceptions are made for the person who yells loudly enough, a firm is surely headed for disaster.

As time went on, the FC invested the maximum in the plan on each sign-up date, and he attended every annual meeting at Carnegie Hall as a happy shareholder.

Mary and I became friends with Dennis and Eugenia McCrary, but we were surprised when they made the trip to our daughter's wedding in Charleston. He said he came because he just had to know what kind of a family could have produced someone like me. He was talking about my people skills, okay? At any rate, he spoke at length to my parents and to each of my siblings. That's when I began to examine my upbringing and placement in the family.

It's obvious that one child needs to be concerned only with herself or himself. Two children would have one other person to focus on. With eight children, almost every action that one child makes has some effect on several, if not all, of the other children. This environment would make anyone more empathetic and aware of the results of their actions on others.

Being one of the older ones, I tended to stand back and let the others get their needs met before I took care of my own. That seemed only fair as my age could put the others at a disadvantage. At the same time, I felt I had to be successful in ways that would force my parents to notice me more.

The more children in a family, the less attention each one gets. A parent has only so much to go around before they're running on empty. Because of this, it is more than likely true that with each additional child, each child gets less. Yet with each additional child there are more of them to teach the younger ones.

The eight of us are close as adults. This may be the result of our banding together as children—not necessarily against our parents, although that happened on occasion, but to feed ourselves with companionship, conversation, projects, and complaints that we were missing from parents who had only so much energy and time to go around.

I've known people who've done well in life and people who've done poorly—and they came from all kinds of families. I don't think it's where you were in the pecking order or the amount of affluence or love that you received that determines your success in life. Once you start blaming others for your failures, you're in trouble. At some point, you have to tell yourself that everything that happens in your life from today forward is totally up to you and no one else. What matters is what you do with what you were given. And that's solely up to you, not your parents or your birth order.

> The family. We were a strange little band of characters trudging through life sharing diseases and toothpaste, coveting one another's desserts, hiding shampoo, borrowing money, locking each other out of our rooms, inflicting pain and kissing to heal it in the same instant, loving, laughing, defending, and trying to figure out the common thread that bound us all together.—Erma Bombeck

The Oldest Child
Rosalie

Is being the oldest of eight siblings any different from being one of eight? I've never been able to see the difference.

Certainly, being the oldest has a few distinguishing features. The first is that I was responsible for, that is to say, guilty of, anything that happened within a six-county area of the house. The second is that I saw more diapers than any of my sibs. You know how many diapers a family of eight needs? The short answer is "way too many." The third hallmark of being the oldest is a certain nervousness, a free-floating anxiety, a leaping about at sudden noises. I can't pinpoint the origins of these miasmas, but I've always thought it had something to do with being the oldest.

I don't ever remember feeling I was smarter or swifter or superior to or even, for that matter, older than my brothers and sister. This may be due to the fact that Ciccio and Pat terrorized me from their earliest days. Ciccio is fifteen months younger than I, true, but he's at least four times as energetic and ten times as tricky. What he and Pat didn't think of would hardly be worth mentioning, except that Kevin, Mary, P.T., Mark, and Matt came along and thought of it.

Properly cowed, I was in no position to lord it over anyone. Most of their plots involving me have been thankfully lost to a mind full of more elevating thoughts, but I do remember the crayfish.

I think it is accurate to say that in those days the creek writhed and bulged and seethed with crayfish, horrors with fiendish-looking, sinisterly waving appendages and beady, possibly evil, eyes.

One night, someone (you know who you are, both of you) sneaked into my bedroom with a coffee can full of creek water and crayfish and, with a judicious eye, placed it precisely where I was bound to put my feet when getting out of bed in the morning.

So I'm only half awake, I'm standing in freezing cold water, and yipping about my feet and ankles is the entire cast and crew of *Creatures From Hell*.

I had my revenge. No, no, not on my brothers. But every time I go to France, I order a bottle of dry white wine, a basket of fresh bread, a salad, and the *grand plat* of *écrevisses*. Crayfish to you. And I eat them. Slowly.

Over the years, it became apparent to me that every one of my siblings could do things I couldn't do. We had cooks, tree house engineers, escape artists, eccentrics, piano players, sneaks, athletes, storytellers, a kid who wore a different hat every day, and Teflon kids (Mother never got mad at them).

A language in a remote area of South America has no comparatives. A person is rich, poor, tall, smart, or crazy, but not richer, poorer, taller, smarter, or crazier. That's the way I feel about us. Multiple talents and personalities seem to even us all out. As adults, we inhabit a level playing field. The others can do things I could never do. And how do you compare a dentist with a lawyer with a writer with a professor? You can't. And without comparatives, no one is "oldest." Old, but not oldest.

Except when asked, I've never felt particularly driven to give advice or play big sister. I must have, but I don't think it's a big part of how I look at us. How could I possibly know anything more than anyone else? I look on my sister and brothers as my best friends, which implies a mutuality of experience and affection, and I've learned more from them than I feel sure they ever learned from me.

So the oldest? I'm not sure it means much in our family. Except for—I'm sure I mentioned this before because they haunt me—the hundreds and hundreds of truly gruesome, revolting baby pictures taken by a young couple who should have saved some film for later.

....

No one cares
who is better
who is worse
who has more
who has less.
Content in our connectedness
we are brothers and sisters
after all.—Adele Faber and Elaine Mazlish

....

Having an Older Sibling
Frank

I would like to write about the effect of having an older sibling. This is much more important than writing about younger siblings. After all, if a person has only one older sibling, then that person should be explored.

I cannot do this, however, because that "older sibling" is the editor, so she would either change everything that I say to make her look better. Or just edit me right out of the whole book. What a shame. I could really spill my guts about her. A happy consolation is that she *is* older than I.

Why We Still Talk
Mary

We talk with each other daily. Among the eight of us, one or more of us calls one or more of us every single day. At the family reunion after Dad died, I asked us why we did that. We threw ideas around but came to no conclusions. It was on a trip back from Fort Dodge that I came up with an answer. I think it is the carpet that binds us together.

At first, I thought it was Dad who, over the years, repeated many times when we fought, "You're blood. You're flesh and blood. How can you fight the same blood that runs through your own veins?"

Then I thought maybe it was Mom saying (when we had acted up in public), "You're Maggios. First and last you are a Maggio, and that's what people will say if you are arrested/go skinny dipping/smoke pot/wear your bangs too long."

Even as a fifty-five-year-old, when I return to Fort Dodge, people say, "You're a Maggio, aren't you." They aren't asking, they're telling.

Put those two ideas together, drill them into your children, and you have outposts in their heads. We were different from everyone else because we were Maggios. We were all the same because we were Maggios.

After their deaths, as I was overseeing the removal of Mom and Dad's furniture to the auction house, I spied a mouse hole that had been hidden for years behind the piano. I poked my giant face down there and tried to look inside, laying my cheek on the rug and peering in with one eye. Unlike on the *Tom and Jerry* cartoons Dad so loved, I could not see in there. But getting up close to the carpet like that gave rise to an epiphany.

No one, certainly no one in Fort Dodge, equally certainly no one in Iowa, and probably no family in the country, had a wool carpet that single-handedly raised eight kids. And even if you could find someone with that carpet, they wouldn't have had it for fifty-six years.

An unusually vibrant Persian pattern of deep teals, golds, and reds, the carpet ran from one end of the house to the other. As children, we were endlessly fascinated by its detailed and intricate pattern, which allowed for roadways and pens and stalls and city streets and moonscapes. It was so versatile, so chameleon-like that over the years Mom was able to use different color schemes as styles and fashions changed.

I once saw the carpet in the hallway of a posh hotel in Chicago. I was stunned at its nobility and regal character. I was also offended that they had our carpet. In Chicago, of all places.

In a visceral sort of algebra, we understood the equation: each of us was related to the carpet—a unique, extraordinary carpet, a carpet that only we would recognize out of a million carpets—and we were thus related to each other in unique, extraordinary ways. That carpet binds us together still.

....

> Siblings. They can be the best of friends, and they can be the worst. No other peer can have as deep and thorough an understanding of our personal histories as can our siblings. If we've emerged from a strong, bonded family, the friendship of our brothers and sisters can be among the most valued relationships of our lifetimes.—Elaine Partnow

....

Telling Stories
Kevin

The first time Mark told a joke, he was in second grade. We were sitting at the dinner table listening to Dad's after-dinner stories. Dad said many of his patients were so afraid of dentists that they often started their appointment by telling a joke. Dad figured it was their way of easing their anxiety but, as a result, he had new jokes for us every night at dinner.

So one evening Mark piped up. "Did you hear about the woman who went to a shoe store to buy a pair of alligator shoes?"

Shocked to hear young Mark toss his hat in the joke-telling ring, we said, "No, what happened?"

"The shoe salesman asked the woman, 'What size shoe does your alligator wear?'"

We laughed our heads off, not so much at the joke but at little Mark's first venture into the world of humor. He was so encouraged, in fact, that he told that joke every day for the next year. We hated to see him coming. What we didn't realize was that this was the beginning of Mark developing a keen sense of humor.

The older kids had participated in a similar cultivation process with P.T.'s humor. At first his taste was pretty childish. But he persisted for years, telling jokes, imitating people's behavior, and adding sound effects of machines and animals as necessary. I remember him telling a joke when he was in sixth grade that took place in a barnyard, so he got to display a full range of sounds and mimicry. His imitation of a pig absolutely did us in, and after that, we considered him not just a Dad wannabe but a funny kid in his own right.

We all told jokes, made wisecracks, and acted out funny scenes—our family culture expected each person to have a sense of humor, both as teller and as listener.

Dad was the most prolific and talented storyteller any of us ever met. And Mom was his best audience. No matter how many times Dad told "The Suit Story" or "The Bombay Bicycle Riders Club" story, Mom laughed at the end as if it were the first time she'd heard it. Since she knew his repertory so well, she could prod him at just the right time, "Tell that one about . . ."

The eight of us have developed our own culture of storytelling. Family reunions overflow with spontaneous and embroidered stories about our childhood, our own families, and our workaday worlds. The storyteller gets our undivided attention along with our smiles, laughter, clapping, cheering, and groaning. Sharing our stories with each other over the years has reinforced the strong bonds among us.

E-mails

From: Matt
Subject: carpet

Dear Family, Ciccio saved the carpet from the dining room where it was least worn. I'm going to have a local carpet store cut and bind 10-sq.-ft. rugs for each of us. Do you want a fringe or tassels on yours? Square or rectangle would be best. No trapezoids please. Let me know how you want yours.

⊠⊠⊠

From: P.T.
Subject: carpet

Dear Matt, I really like the idea of having a piece of that rug. Since you and Laura have such elegant taste I would like you to make me one of whatever you are having.

I have one special request. There should be an area of the carpet under the dining room table that has a large blood stain. That is my blood from when Mary stabbed me. We were under the dining room table and she pulled a 12" hunting knife out of her sock and stabbed me in the hand. For no reason, as hard as she could. I wonder if you could arrange for that piece to be made into a rug for Mary. If she wanted my blood that badly, let her have it!

⊠⊠⊠

From: Mary
Subject: carpet

Everything P.T. says about the stabbing under the dining room table is true except for the size of the knife. It was a 3" penknife. I suppose it was even more dangerous than a butcher knife because it had been used to defoot pheasants, open rocks, cut pie crusts, stab ticks, dig holes, and pound nails. You could not exactly say it had a point. But I believe it broke the skin and, yes, I did it as hard as I could, twice, for no reason, which was the only way you did anything in those days. Love, MMM

⊠⊠⊠

From: P.T.
Subject: carpet

Oh sure, Mary, downplay the whole thing. It wasn't *your* hand that got maimed. Do you think it has been easy doing one-handed dentistry all these years? The more I think about it, the more the repressed memories start to flow. And you are right, it wasn't a butcher knife. It was a chainsaw you stabbed me with.

And you did it three times harder than you could.

✉✉✉

From: Kevin
Subject: carpet

Hello, Yederman. My magic carpet arrived today and it sure is special. One-of-a-kind! When I opened it, I was smiling and admiring it. Then I spread it on the floor and walked on it. I was surprised by a rush of thoughts of all those who had walked on it: all of you, your spouses, your children, Mom and Dad, Grandma and Grandpa, Nonna, aunts, uncles, cousins, childhood friends, neighbors, Fort Dodgers, and on and on. I could feel the energy of the years and years and hundreds and hundreds of footsteps. What an unusual memento! It's just a rug and yet it's something bigger than all of us that I can't quite put into words. I'm so grateful to have this.

Special thanks to Matt for making this happen. Sending my love to all of you, Kevin

✉✉✉

From: P.T.
Subject: carpet

Dear Matt, I wonder if I will be fast enough to beat Pat to the ditto. I liked what Kedin said. It was fun to come home last night and find that mysterious package. I instantly felt a spiritual connection to my carpet. The first image to enter my mind was of us making our human pyramid in the living room. The pad appears to be some pretty high-tech stuff, probably a by-product of the space program and the label on the back is a fantastic touch. So koalas to you for a job well done and thank you ever so much!

Later 'gators. Love to all, P.T.

P.S. Matt, how much are you charging Pat for the rugs?

✉✉✉

From: Mark
Subject: carpet

Matt, You are so good to do this (and many of these kinds of things) for us.

All, I think we should send Matt and Laura either some money or a nice gift from all of us. My rug is beautiful, and since he loves me more than the rest of you, he insisted I take two rugs, which I did. I will build a little hardwood frame for the rear of one of them and make it a wall hanging. If any of you would like such a frame, I can easily make more.

⊠⊠⊠

From: Mary
Subject: carpet

I love every last one of you. You make my day with these e-mails. And, as you know, I have really really high standards.

Of issue to all of us or maybe you just left me out of the loop, are we each sending $200 to Matt for the magic carpet? He won't tell me how much it was and if he doesn't 'fess up, I will send $200 every week until he tells me. Will you join me? Love, MMM

⊠⊠⊠

From: Pat
Subject: carpet

Dear Triple M, We are just going to have to force-feed the pablum down the Baby-'O-Das-Family. He has been hiding in nooks and crannies, in alleys, and in the most unsavory places trying to avoid me. I, for example, just this very morning, wrote again to the lad begging for an answer to the cost of those rugs. I even scratched the bottom of the barrel and threatened to go over his head and directly contact the carpet man to learn the cost. Imagine the rumor mill in Fort Dodge if I were to do that . . .

⊠⊠⊠

From: Matt
Subject: carpet

Glad you all enjoyed the carpet pieces. It's a fun conversation piece—anyone who was ever in the house seems to recognize it immediately.

The carpet store folks (who of course knew Mom and Dad) were amazed at the condition of the carpet after more than 50 years. A friend who has a stitching shop, mainly for athletic jerseys and things, created the labels on the back.

Cost? Roughly $50 per rug. If you just got one and want to send me $50, that's fine. If you got or hope to get more than one, I will not take $ for the extra. There are still two extras. Any takers? Remember this wouldn't have been possible without Ciccio's foresight in saving this part of the carpet. Thanks again, Ciccio.

⊠⊠⊠

From: Matt
Subject: carpet

Everyone has now sent me the $50 for the carpets except six of you. Thanks to all who got their checks to me so quickly! Matt

⊠⊠⊠

From: P.T.
Subject: carpet

What carpet?

⊠⊠⊠⊠⊠⊠⊠⊠⊠⊠⊠⊠⊠

From: Kevin
Subject: photos

Mary, did you really find baby pictures of Matt?

⊠⊠⊠

From: Mary
Subject: photos

Actually, I doctored up a picture of a puppy. I shortened the ears, took a little fur off the face, and, man, it looked just like him. He's none the wiser but he is happier thinking there were photos of him way back when.

⊠⊠⊠⊠⊠⊠⊠⊠⊠⊠⊠⊠⊠⊠

From: P.T.
Subject: the book

Dear Rosalie, When you contacted me and asked me to write a book, I took it to be a very exciting prospect. I dreamt about the glory and accolades to be thrust upon me just before reaping large amounts of cash. I must tell you, I am more than a bit dismayed to learn that you have drug these others into the project. I see no purpose in bartering their drivel and you can expect only the direst results from this association. If you want to toss them a bone, perhaps one or the other could muster a prelude or an introduction, or perhaps you could assuage them by offering them a sequel. I like to fly alone, baby. Yours in humility, P.T.

⊠⊠⊠

From: Kevin
Subject: the book

Hi, P. I hadn't planned to write this piece but I started it last night and couldn't stop. I don't know if the date is correct but I love your advice about not letting the facts get in the way.

This is what you do so well, so I trust your judgment completely except for taking out any of my stuff. Love, M

⊠⊠⊠

From: Pat
Subject: the book

I need to cattle prod (isn't it cool how I turned a noun into a verb?) myself to get working on some contributions to the book.

I'm having trouble thinking of cute childhood stories. I can only think of disagreeable things tonight. What say you?

✉✉✉

From: P.T.
Subject: the book

Mark, nice title suggestions. If we are lucky the publisher will call it something like *The DaVinci Code*. P.T.

✉✉✉

From: Ciccio
Subject: the books

Or if we could relate it to a popular movie, like *Drillbit Taylor and the Missing Tools, Watching the Pink Panther Movie with Dad, The Pineapple Express and a Coin on the Track, Harry Cotter and the Half-Baked Frog, Indiana Jones and the Gympsum Giant?* Just a few thoughts.

✉✉✉

From: Mary
Subject: the book

I still like the first title Punky suggested, "Mary and the Seven Others."

✉✉✉

From: Matt
Subject: the book

Mom often kidded that she and Dad had "two and a half-dozen kids," two girls and a half-dozen boys. Is there a title in that? Matt

✉✉✉

From: Kevin
Subject: the book

I like "Two and a Half Dozen." Thanks, Matt.

✉✉✉

From: P.T.
Subject: the book

Oh, sure, butter him up so maybe he'll send you a nice birthday gift. I think we all saw right through that one.

✉✉✉

From: Mary
Subject: the book

Matt, P.T., me, Kevin, Ciccio, and Punky have written mucho for the booko. Brothers Mark and Pat have not. Can we bombard them with pleas? How about peer pressure? A barrage of phone messages? Postcard reminders? The law?

✉✉✉

From: Ciccio
Subject: the book

Okay, Pat and Mark, your sister is planning a full frontal attack on you as your book contributions lag behind the pace expected of you. You will have to eat at a separate table while in Fort Dodge if this situation doesn't turn around by then. This advisement should be easier on you than a rash of e-mails from all of our combined address books. Nothing personal.

⊠⊠⊠

From: Mary
Subject: the book

Thanks, Ciccio, for taking the wheel by the horns. Cut out the middle and head right to the problems. I like it. Pat, Mark, how about you? Was it effective? You know I love you all! MMM

⊠⊠⊠

From: Pat
Subject: the book

Yes, yes indeed. Very effective.

⊠⊠⊠

From: Punky
Subject: the book

I oppose hounding Pat and Mark. You want them to freeze up entirely? If I need muscle, I know where to find it. In the meantime, leave 'em be! They're just a little shyer than others. But none of us think our writing is very good, except perhaps Ciccio (but don't worry, compound sentences are very difficult for him—he'll never know what I just said). Love, P.

⊠⊠⊠

From: Kevin
Subject: the book

Actually, Punky told me yesterday that Mary hasn't submitted a thing. Punky was worried that Mary might plagiarize something off the Internet and jeopardize our anticipated huge profits. I'm not sure what to do with this information so just keep it to yourselves.

⊠⊠⊠

From: Ciccio
Subject: the book

I thought plagiarizing was okay. I got my material from my cellmate. He is serving life and I don't think he has the brains to sue me. What do u think?

⊠⊠⊠

From: Mark
Subject: the book

Your Viciousnesses:

I had all my stories done on time and, might I add, they were excellent. And then I left them in the barn, where the lambs (the baddest ones) got to the stories and hoofed them and bit and shredded them all up. On top of that, I didn't make a back-up, and my hard drive crashed the next day, so I cannot re-create them. I just sat on my last pencil, which broke in half, and I have no pencil sharpener except a knife, which is too dull to sharpen the pencil because I was using it to butcher meat to give to poor elderly asthmatics.

So could I please have a few days' extension, without any points deducted?

⊠⊠⊠

From: Pat
Subject: the book

This will provide an essential correction to Professor Mark's last message. Let us just say his was a typographical error. He intended to use, in the place of "I" throughout, the pronoun of the first person plural, that is to say "we." Consequently, consider that I hereby associate myself with his comments, especially to the extent that he was speaking for the two of us.

⊠⊠⊠

From: Punky
Subject: book bios

Below is what I have so far for your brief bios at the back of the book. Those who are missing in action, you know what you have to do. Those who've already submitted should see if they have buyer's remorse or second thoughts. (You can change anything right up until I say you can't.)

⊠⊠⊠

From: Pat
Subject: book bios

Punky, Very nice work. Here are my modest suggested changes (in brackets). I only found a need to change P.T.'s bio. Thanks.

Paul Thomas Maggio, aka [El Mismo] Number Six, resides in Waunakee, Wisconsin, where he is a [PM, "Pain Merchant"] general dentist. His undeniably better half is Terry Lee Hay Maggio [if Terry has any more names, insert them here], etc.

⊠⊠⊠

From: Punky
Subject: book bios

oh geez pat it'd serve you right if it went in that way
no, I mean it'd serve peetey right

wait a minute!
p.t., do you have anything to say about pat's bio?
since he hasn't got anything so far
what you have here is called a
tabula rasa

go for it!

p.

⊠⊠⊠

From: Pat
Subject: book bios

Punky, for my bio could I use the one that ran in the newspaper for Dad's obituary? Thanks.

P.S. I have been having trouble with my eyes lately. I just can't see myself in the office this afternoon.

⊠⊠⊠

From: P.T.
Subject: book bios

Dear Rosalie, Thank you so much for inviting me to help with Pat's bio. I guess I am the perfect person to ask since I have done extensive research into the life and times of brudder Pat. I suspect some of what follows may surprise you. It did me, but then life is a series of surprises, isn't it?

Patrick Joseph Maggio was born to Albanian gypsies in 1967. The birth parents decided to put him up for adoption—a tough choice, but they couldn't keep the baby and still feed both ferrets. He was initially adopted by Spaniards and given the name La Oveja Negra de la Familia. The family fell on hard times during the Wool Blight of 1968 and decided they could no longer support little Ovey (nickname). It was at that time that Ovey was adopted as a pagan baby by Sister Generosa's chemistry class. After the class raised 17 cents to save his soul he was sent to this country. Sister Generosa was not deemed a fit mother and the poor homeless little piker was once again put up for the highest bidder. Meanwhile, in Fort Dodge, Iowa, lived a loving and willing couple who had but two live children and felt compassion for this misguided sinner pagan. After months of intense bartering they agreed to take the child, along with a large sum of cash.

The name Ovey was not appropriate for a plain vanilla wrapper town in the mid-plains so they made the decision to change his name. The name Manussus fit him well until they found out that there was another, more handsome boy in the neighborhood by the same name. It was at this time they decided to go mainstrean with Patrick Joseph. Historians believe the name Patrick was chosen because of the connection between St. Patrick and snakes and Joseph, of course, because of Giuseppe the Lip from American Mafia lore. After this, the trail has become cold and the number of articles published is scanty at best. I hope someone can help me bring this bio up to date.

P.S. Ovey was actually born in 1947 according to a more reliable source (*Mad Magazine*) and currently resides in a Colorado town with his three dogs and a woman who refused to be named.

⊠⊠⊠

From: Pat
Subject: book bios

Please don't publish that tripe. I've never told anyone, but as a young Albanian gypsy I ripped off a wagon of baby formula (I was starving) only to learn it belonged to a rival gypsy gang. They have been looking for me ever since. I fear that my future would be cloudy and rainy if this were published and they learned where I live. For those of you seeing this as an opportunity to contribute to my bio, let me say it is complete now.

⊠⊠⊠

From: Mary
Subject: the book

I do feel strongly on all those points and I say unequivocably maybe for sure. Thanks for your thoughtful contributions. MMM

⊠⊠⊠

From: Mark
Subject: the book

Matt, I read your message about the book draft, but I wonder just what you think your posterior has to do with our essays. Are you referencing the stuff Pat wrote?

Just because the great publishing houses in the East have guffawed at our submission does not mean it was because of Pat's essays. I think we should leave your posterior out of this discussion. Let's try to be civil.

⊠⊠⊠

From: Pat
Subject: attributions

Punky, Please correct the ms. so that we have proper attribution. I wrote the following:

Why We Still Talk
Clowns and Wild Gods

And what's this about two of the sibs teaming up to write things? I didn't know anything aboot that possibility. Had I known, I would have been much more prolific. I don't see it as my fault that I didn't write much. I think there is a direct and proximate cause of this fact—that teaming was permitted and I was kept in the dark . . .

Thanks. Love you.

P.S. I wrote a lot of the other titles, too, but I can't remember which ones right now.

⊠⊠⊠

From: Mark
Subject: the book

I've been trying to think of ways to attract a publisher. Could we put on a little family show, like with Mary as our DC? (I was going to say Master of Ceremonies, MC, but I know that is a gendered term. The better term is "Dominatrix of Ceremonies," DC.) P.T. could act out some of his better stories. Matt could do a show-and-tell, with some of Dad's larger leftover giant Pyrex syringes, and so on. We could have it in a tent down by the river. That way, a lot of Ciccio's people would come. Do you think many publishers would show up?

✉✉✉

From: Kevin
Subject: the book

I think you're on to something there, Mark. Publishers would not only come, but they would pay to see us. Pat and Ciccio can dress up as Tall Man, Mary and I can roller-skate backwards, you can show some Yokohamas. Punky needs to figure out a skit, I guess, but it's all doable. July by the river in Fort Dodge?

P.S. Will Mary be wearing leather? Maybe we can put her on the cover of our book.

✉✉✉

From: P.T.
Subject: the book

What book?

✉✉✉✉✉✉✉✉✉✉✉✉✉

From: Pat
Subject: get together

The talk of getting together is a bright spot for me, but I have a 10-day jury trial in Federal Court starting May 26. I've been fighting this since May 17, 2005. It is unlikely to go away. The weeks before that I will be underwater. The afterlife is beginning to look attractive. Sorry to be the fly in the ointment.

✉✉✉

From: Mark
Subject: get together

If we got together in Denver, say about May 26, that would be slick. Pat could host us all at his home, just before the big trial, to help him relax. If his trial "goes," we can all watch from the stately gallery, and urge him on to victory. Like they do on Judge Judy. How many of us have actually witnessed the great barrister in action? If the case settles out ahead of time, we will all be there to celebrate with him and his clients, who I am sure would pick up the tab, like they do on Judge Wapner.

How's that for a plan, Pat?

✉✉✉

From: Kevin
Subject: get together

Mark, we laughed our heads off. Well, I suppose Pat wasn't laughing . . .

✉✉✉

From: Ciccio
Subject: get together

Since you have all laughed your heads off, you will no doubt have difficulty recognizing each other at our get together.

✉✉✉

From: P.T.
Subject: get together

Dear Matt, When discussing a possible Minneapolis venue, you say "Some of us have talked about going to the Mall of America." How far into the bargaining process are you? I am also wondering who "some of us" are and if you are planning to take the big bottle of Benadryl with you.

✉✉✉

From: Ciccio
Subject: get together

California's not a bad idea, but it may not be there by then. Maybe we should consider Mark's place—no fires or earthquakes. Also, there is a decent amount of oxygen at his altitude.

⊠⊠⊠

From: Mark
Subject: get together

Before we discuss Mark's place, I should report that Ciccio has invited us all to Manhattan. He hinted, however, that we shouldn't stay with him for more than two weeks. (I think he was a little peeved about the Ciccio jokes e-mail thread, which was not supposed to include him. But he said he wasn't mad and even claimed the third and the ninth jokes honestly didn't bother him because he has never had "that problem." Oh, right!)

He said he'd take us to the Carnegie Deli for a great big corned beef sandwich Tuesday noon (both weeks). This place is very special to my people. If you are a vegetarian, he said you could get the corned corn sandwich. If you are a vegan, they have nice paper napkins.

⊠⊠⊠

From: Kevin
Subject:get together

Guten Abend, Yederman. I'm a little nervous about visiting the mountain folks in California. I've heard they shoot visitors on sight, men trim their nose hairs with cigarette lighters, women braid the hair under their arms, kids use hand-me-down toothbrushes, and there are only two pall bearers at a funeral (one for each handle on a garbage can). Still debating about going. K

⊠⊠⊠

From: P.T.
Subject: get together

Dear Fellow Orphans, I'm glad we seem to be in unison about the need for a reunion.

Mark, if you make us food could you please leave out the r,sum, part? My daughters like sausage but it doesn't taste so good once they find out it's ground-up "Good Pig Arnold," "Little Pig Little Pig," or some other former pet-like creature.

Can't wait to hug you all. Ciccio, that means y'all.

Love (yes, I admit it), P.T.

⊠⊠⊠

From: Mary
Subject: get together

The gauntlet has been thrown and the challenge is to find a date. Anyone have dates they can't make? List the worst times for you, k? And, Punky, that does not include the whole year.

⊠⊠⊠

From: Mark
Subject: get together

Mary, Sorry your date threw a gauntlet at you.

⊠⊠⊠

From: Pat
Subject: get together

I have not been much help but I appreciate everything that's been said. The only suggestion I have is, and perhaps this will go over like a lead balloon (got that from Mom), is to invite P.T. Love you.

⊠⊠⊠

From: Kevin
Subject: get together

Bonjour, mes amis! Can we make Labor Day work (haha)? Can we reach a meeting of the minds plus Pat? Respondez vous pronto si vous plait! Merci, Kevin

⊠⊠⊠

From: P.T.
Subject: get together

Labor Day is an appealing time to get together, but I bet Dr. Mark will be up to his snot locker in curriculum development.

⊠⊠⊠

From: Ciccio
Subject: get together

Dang! But this democratic process is hard!

⊠⊠⊠

From: Pat
Subject: get together

Now that we are getting closer to an actual face-to-face meeting, I will come right out with it and state my only surviving objections, at this time. I object:

1. to El Mismo, aka The Answer Man, for actually and in point of fact, never, ever, not even once providing me with the correct answer to my question: What is the exact winning number for the next drawing of the Colorado Lottery?

2. to Ciccio.

As for me, I am just going to try to get along with everyone. No more dittoing or other personally destructive carrying-on betwixt now and next week. Looking forward to seeing each of you.

⊠⊠⊠

From: Matt
Subject: get together

Why? What's next week?

✉✉✉

From: Kevin
Subject: get together

Hola, gente. Well, my pointer finger just pushed "enter" and my travel arrangements are a done deal. I'm glad you'll all get to see me. Love, K

✉✉✉

From: P.T.
Subject: get together

I hope things work out okay for you. I always use Mr. King Finger.

✉✉✉

From: Mark
Subject: get together

a la famiglia:

I am amazed that she is willing to have all of us! We can be a pain in the derringer, and on top of that, she has other company, and book-writin' to boot, at the same time, yet! I think it is very generous of you to have us, Punky.

I will "ditto" this message in advance for Pat, and "mimeo" it in advance for P.T., so they won't have to worry about that.

Signed,
* Mark
* Pat
* P.T.

✉✉✉

From: P.T.
Subject: get together

I'm still basking in the afterglow (No, Ciccio, it doesn't always have a sexual connotation) of our time together.

In thinking about hosting a reunion myself, I've tried to come up with interesting activities for us, but I see now that the most important thing is just being together. We seem to make our own fun.

All for now and I love each of you, P.T.

⊠⊠⊠

From: Ciccio
Subject: get together

Hi all, I'd like to say that I really enjoyed seeing all of you (except Pat, and that was okay).

⊠⊠⊠

From: Kevin
Subject: get together

Um, one little negative note. Pat's and my shirts were sabotaged and no one has owned up to it. The buttonholes on Pat's shirt were sewed shut, and elegant gold and pearl buttons were added to the collar of my shirt.

⊠⊠⊠

From: Pat
Subject: get together

Rosalie, Based on the lotus flower and the karma spirit I already know who did it. I become richer by the day, metaphorically speaking, that the culprit refuses to come out of the closet. So I am just awaggin my tail. It is actually a fascinating story as to how I learned who done it. Alababba, all (I mean adios). Love, Pat

⊠⊠⊠

From: Mark
Subject: get together

Punky, I am pretty sure Jason is guilty. If not of this, then probably of something else. He kind of looks guilty. And he's not really one of us. People who are different are usually more guilty than our own kind. I don't like the way he is already calling himself "R. Jason Middleton."

It should be "your jason" anyway not "r jason." He's not r jason. He is new to the family, and would not be here if not for Katie—and he has helped produce only one offspring. He is trying to ingratiate himself with us, as if he is r only jason, and "one of us."

I've been in the family for 50 years and I never refer to myself as "r mark" or "your mark" even. And with Pat, we know he's not r's. So it is just too soon for Jason to think he's r jason. I vote "guilty."

⊠⊠⊠

From: Mary
Subject: get together

What a love-filled gathering. Stories, laughter, singing, playing, and more laughter. Everywhere another group of family to soak up. Thanks to those who fed us, to those who documented the time with photos, to those who allowed us to trample all over her personal space. I miss each and every one of you! Love, MMM

⊠⊠⊠

From: Matt
Subject: get together

And thanks to each of you for including our kids in so many activities—hiking to the waterfall, golfing, swimming, hunting for rattlers. The boys sure enjoyed you letting them drive the curvy mountain roads—Liz's Jaguar might have been a highlight. Kate's time with baby Margot was a special treat for her.

More, more, more, so much more to say. Hope you all traveled well. Love, Matt and Laura

✉✉✉

From: Pat
Subject: get together

Profound change has happened in my life, as a direct and proximate result of the reunion, as I try to move toward absolute harmony with the birds, mountains, and nature. I have thus jettisoned the disrespectful practice of "dittoing" . . . but not just yet.

I rise to ditto everything the Triple M and the one Dr. Matt have said aboot that reunion.

Our few days together were delightful and a good way to cleanse the palate. Thank you for your love and kindness and unselfish attention. I am blessed. Love you all. Pat

✉✉✉

From: Mark
Subject: get together

I loved being with everyone. My little mother-in-law apartment made me want to criticize someone, but once I left the apartment, the feeling would subside.

None of us talked about Dad and Mom much. But they were always there. I felt that Dad was saying, "You kids gave me so much, here's a little treat for you." It was a blessing. If only we could keep that up . . . keep wearing the world like a loose garment as we did during those days in California.

✉✉✉✉✉✉✉✉✉✉✉✉✉

ADDENDA

Who's Who

Rosalie Maggio and David Koskenmaki, Pine Mountain, California, have three children: Liz, Katie (married to Jason, parents of Margot), and Matt (married to Nora, parents of Zoe). Rosalie is the author of twenty-four books and hundreds of stories and articles, some of which have won book and writing awards; one book has sold nearly three million copies. She is devoted to her rose garden and collects inkwells, stamps, coins, mustard pots, demitasse spoons, pottery vases, and anything else she ever had two of. She also reads hundreds of books every year.

Frank M. Maggio and Mary Claire Johnson Maggio, New York City, have three children: Mike, Courtney (married to Rob, parents of Claire, Jack, and Michael), and Anthony (married to Leslie, parents of Katie and Abby). Frank spent a thirty-year career in the securities business, leaving at the age of fifty-five to pursue other business opportunities and to have a little free time.

Patrick J. Maggio practices law in Colorado Springs, is married to Cynthia Casserly Maggio; they are parents of Seery and Cass.

Kevin Michael Maggio went to four colleges, sort of: University of Portland (Oregon); University of Portland Salzburg Extension Program (Austria); University of Iowa (B.A.); and University of Iowa College of Law (J.D.). He studied political science, French, German, and Spanish; practiced state and local government law for twenty years; lived in a one-room log cabin without utilities for a year after quitting law; compiled and published two books of quotations; lived and worked in an intentional community for two and a half years; worked for a Latino nonprofit agency building affordable housing; and currently provides employee benefits counseling. His lifelong avocations are photography and piano. He has a son, David, and six grandchildren, Anastasia, Isaiah, Arianna, Isaac, Edward, and Preston. He would like to receive a sign from God soon about the meaning of it all or at least have a personal encounter with extraterrestrials.

Mary M. Maggio is most like the person who got on her horse and rode off in all directions. She is a freelance writer, a theater director, a kid magnet, an actor, and a friend to new Americans. Mary and her husband, Mike Pliner, have two children.

Paul Thomas Maggio, a.k.a. Number Six, resides in Waunakee, Wisconsin, where he is a general dentist. His undeniably better half is Terry Lee Hay Maggio; and they share the wondrous blessing of three incredible daughters: Kalli, Lauren, and Leah. Paul enjoys spending time with his family, snow skiing, sailing, gardening, traveling, and anything to do with Iowa Hawkeye football and basketball.

Mark E. Maggio farms and teaches in rural Iowa. After many years of big-city life—the Twin Cities; Honolulu; Cairo; New York; Oxford, England; and the Washington, D.C., area—Mark returned to the countryside where he works a small farm and teaches college economics and sociology. He completed the doctoral degree in public policy at George Mason University. His interests include the constitutional and institutional political economy of our unique American experiment in democracy. He continues to be amazed and impressed by his students' dedication and hard work.

Matthew and Laura Jordison Maggio have lived in Fort Dodge, Iowa, since 1986, the year they were married. Sons Sam and Jack are in high school, and daughter Kate is in grade school, all at St. Edmond Catholic School. Sam is honing his wrestling moves while Jack refines his skateboard skills. Kate entertains them with her diligently rehearsed dance routines. Sophie, their beloved golden retriever, is somewhat of a nanny to the family. Laura is not currently working in her chosen field of speech pathology as her focus now is on the home and family. Matt is a general dentist, having taken over his father's practice after years of working together. Friends, family, and community service and involvement fill the remainder of their time.

Essays Arranged by Author

Matt

Death in the Ditches
Radar Woman
The Caste System
The Triple "M" Poultry Farm
Once Was Not Enough
College: Oops!
My Take on Birth Order

Mark

So Many Vines, So Few Watermelons
Desperately Seeking Sugar
Hey, Do You Kids Need Three Hundred Wild Ducks?
God Loves Him Even If He Does Have Bedbugs
The Government Is Here to Help Us
Pieces of Eight
Waiting for Godeer: Not an Absurdist Play
The Redemption of Louie Mortellaro: A Morality Play in Three Acts

Paul

Clowns and Wild Dogs
Finding Your Bliss
Haircuts and Hats
Desperately Seeking Sugar
They Shoot Horses, Don't They?
Feathers and Forks

Mary

How to Make a Rhubarb Pie
Chief Engineer
Hangouts and Lookouts
Saving the Younger Children From Danger
Eating Wasn't Always Fun
My Two Cents' Worth
A Death in the Family
My Perspective
Why We Still Talk

Kevin

Christmas in April
Once Upon a Time There Were Tree Houses
The Untimely Demise of Clark
We Pass On Our Wisdom
Thanksgiving Day 1959
Poor Mrs. Clark
The Exploding Toilet
Wanderlust
Dad's Bread
My Favorite Dad Story
Telling Stories

Pat

Camp Foster
Boris and Natasha
The Black Sheep
The Exploding Toilet
My Catholic Education
Toad's Wild Ride in Sicily

Frank

At Least Two Idiots in the Family
The Development of Moral Thinking
The Innocent and the Guilty
The Exploding Toilet
Smoking Is Bad for Your Teeth
When Asking for Money, Ask the Right Person
Learning to Adapt
The Value of a Dollar
Try, Try Again
My Life With Cars
Reunions
Tight Ship
Large Families
Having an Older Sibling

Rosalie
    The Former Baby of the Family
    For Less Than Twenty-five Dollars
    Miracles and Catechisms
    Small Beginnings
    Passports and Grasshoppers
    The Oldest Child

Get Published, Inc!
Thorofare, NJ 08086
15 March, 2010
BA2010074